THE NATIONAL DEMOCRATIC PARTY

RIGHT RADICALISM IN THE FEDERAL REPUBLIC OF GERMANY

JOHN DAVID NAGLE

With memories of Hitler's Nazi Party and the Third Reich era still very much alive, the recent resurgence of political strength on the extreme right wing in West Germany raises many questions about the future of the German political system. This study examines the National Democratic Party of Germany (NPD), its origins and stages of development, leadership, ideology, voter following, and future potential as a party.

Most previous research and publication dealing with the NPD has been of a polemical nature. Too often the organization is branded as a party of old Nazis who would lead Germany once again to ruin. Such polemics are based on understandable fears, but they have not explained much. Neither a polemic nor an apology, Nagle's study shows that the NPD cannot be dismissed as a resurgence of a uniquely German phenomenon, because right radicalism in other Western countries is also rapidly expanding.

Previous studies of the NPD use analysis of election returns or surveys to bolster their findings about the social structure of the NPD following. Some of these view the NPD as a middle-class movement, thus pinning the "blame" for the NPD success on the sins of the conservative Christian Democrats. Other studies, relying on evidence of working-class voter support for the right radicals, place the responsibility with the moderate left Social Democrats.

Mr. Nagle avoids such static descriptions of the NPD, maintaining that it does not represent so much a class phenomenon as a developmental phenomenon affecting several social classes. Through analysis of survey material, election results, and the propaganda themes of the right radicals, the author develops a dynamic model of the political potential of the NPD.

One conclusion of this model is that among those who possess a basically democratic *Weltanschauung*, even severe crises tend not to destroy their faith in the democratic parties, whereas among those who hold basically authoritarian views, subjectively perceived crises may cause a turn to right radicalism.

Finally, Mr. Nagle explores the means by which the democratic parties may answer the challenge posed by the NPD. A series of much-debated suggestions, ranging from outright suppression to Franz-Josef Strauss' proposal that the Christian Democrats themselves take over the right-wing positions of the NPD, are analyzed and found wanting. An approach to overcoming the problem of right radicalism— which rests on the findings of this study— is offered as an alternative.

The National Democratic Party

THE
NATIONAL
DEMOCRATIC
PARTY

Right Radicalism
in the Federal Republic
of Germany

JOHN DAVID NAGLE

UNIVERSITY OF CALIFORNIA PRESS

BERKELEY, LOS ANGELES, AND LONDON

1970

University of California Press
Berkeley and Los Angeles, California

University of California Press, Ltd.
London, England

Copyright © 1970, by
The Regents of the University of California

Library of Congress Catalog Card Number: 78–101340
International Standard Book Number: 0–520–01649–1
Printed in the United States of America

To Ann

To Ann

Acknowledgments

I give thanks to the several people whose advice and insights were essential to the development of this manuscript, in particular Klaus Liepelt, Dr. Herman Schunck, Dr. Peter Hoschka, and Dieterich Wetzel, of the Institut für angewandte Sozialwissenschaft in Bad Godesberg, and Professor Seymour Martin Lipset of Harvard University. Any misconstruction of their insights is of course my own responsibility. I am also grateful to the Political Science Department of Syracuse University for its support.

Contents

Contents

I

Introduction

One of the wonders of the postwar world has been the economic recovery of the Federal Republic of Germany (*Bundesrepublik*). From its founding, out of the three Western zones of occupation in 1949, it rose from the ruins of Hitler's Third Reich to become once again one of the strongest economic powers in the world. The economic miracle (*Wirtschaftswunder*) of the Bundesrepublik, with Economics Minister Ludwig Erhard as its proclaimed architect, also formed the basis for the construction of a stable democratic system.

Under the leadership of Dr. Konrad Adenauer's Christian Democratic Union (CDU), the Bundesrepublik developed a close alliance with the United States, became the major contributor of ground forces for NATO, and embarked on a road of close economic and political cooperation through the European Common Market. All of these policies were both the cause and the result of the continuing rehabilitation of the German people into the world community. Although the question of reunification and the problem of West Berlin's status remained unsolved, it was commonly accepted that West Germany had been able to overcome its National Socialist past and enter the community of stable democratic societies.

True, there had been several extremist parties in the early years of the republic, which had been able to capitalize on the old resentments of the Nazi era—and some new resentments created by the division of Germany after World War II. It was inevitable that, of the millions of refugees from the Communist-held portions of the former

Third Reich, some would be attracted to the appeals of die-hard nationalists and former Nazis. It was inevitable in the hard years immediately following the collapse of Hitler's Reich that some of the millions of unemployed would turn to extremist parties, both of the left and of the right, as a protest against their suffering. Finally, it was inevitable that some of the most fervent former Nazis would try once again to organize themselves politically, although not openly, as a successor to Hitler's National Socialist German Workers Party (NSDAP).

In the first years after the founding of the republic, the elements of the far right were able to get a sizable percentage of the vote. However, since there were several parties on the far right who warred among themselves as much as with the more moderate and democratic parties of the political spectrum, their strength was fragmented. And as it became clear that the economic situation was improving rapidly under the political leadership of the three major parties—the Christian Democrats, the Socal Democrats, and the Free Democrats—the attraction of the extremist parties faded quickly. The unemployed found work. The war-injured were helped to find a new life. Uprooted Germans from areas now under Communist control were assimilated into the fabric of West German society. Even old Nazi faithfuls found it increasingly more profitable to accept the new system and to share its benefits.

Under these pressures, the original postwar parties of the right began to crumble. The most radical of them, the Socialist Reich Party (SRP), was banned in 1952 as undemocratic, as was the Communist Party of Germany in 1956. The more moderate leaders of the two largest right-wing parties (the German Party, and the League of Refugees and Disfranchised), seeing their cause as lost, switched to the Christian Democrats or the Free Democrats; some even moved to the Social Democrats, where they could more profitably pursue their political careers. The introduction of the 5 percent clause for federal and state elections (which requires that a party must get at least 5 percent of the vote before it can hold any seats under the proportional representation system) further hastened the decline of the rightist parties. By the early 1960s, despite repeated futile attempts by the remnants of the far right to fuse their remaining strength, the rightist movements of the early 1950s had been reduced to meaningless splinter groups, unable to gain any seats in the state and federal parliaments.

As for the major political parties, the trend seemed to be towards a two-party system. The *Sozialdemokratische Partei Deutschlands* (SPD) had decided upon a course of moderation and abandonment of its Marxist doctrine in an attempt to appeal to the middle-class voter. The SPD, under the leadership of Willy Brandt and Herbert Wehner, was trying to overcome the last suspicions of radicalism which were hindering the party from appealing to a much wider voting population. Similarly, the Christian Democrats had learned the electoral advantages to be gained from a more friendly attitude towards the working class and the union movement. The ideological differences between the two major parties were shrinking, and the SPD leadership—with some resistance from the more militant left— began to talk of the possibility of a "Great Coalition," that is, a coalition between the SPD and the CDU. As a part of this trend towards the "end of ideology" in West German politics, it appeared that the future, even for the Free Democrat minority party, was bleak.

Such was the political situation in the early sixties. There seemed little to dispute over the major outlines of governmental policy, of close alliance with the United States, and of cooperation within NATO and the Common Market; the expectations on the economic front continued to be bright. The West German people were living better than at any time in history and the republic was accepted, at least in the non-Communist world, as a responsible member of the world community. In 1963, after fourteen years as Chancellor, Dr. Adenauer reluctantly stepped down to be replaced by Ludwig Erhard, the man who most personified the West German economic miracle. The reins of government had changed, but the government continued with the same policies which had carried the Bundesrepublik so successfully through the period of postwar reconstruction.

Under these conditions, it is not surprising that the founding of a new party in November of 1964 aroused little attention. At its founding, the *Nationaldemokratische Partei Deutschlands* (NPD) had less than five hundred members, little money, and scant reason to expect any political success. The National Democrats were a fusion of the last survivors of the former rightist parties; and their founding represented a last desperate attempt to revive the fortunes of the rightists. At their birth they were written off by political analysts as a party already fated for oblivion. This prediction seemed borne out by the federal election of 1965, in which the new voice of the radical right received only 2 percent of the vote, and of course no seats in the Bundestag.

But the era of postwar reconstruction, along with the viability of the policies which had been appropriate to that era, was drawing to a close. Early in 1966 the West German economy began to experience serious difficulties, and expectations for future growth dropped rapidly. Erhard came under increasing pressure to revise the federal budget in order to end the large deficit which had resulted from governmental overspending. In addition to these mounting difficulties, the close alliance of the Bundesrepublik with the United States and the payment for the stationing of American troops in West Germany also began to be questioned. The Erhard regime reacted sluggishly, and in October the Free Democrats walked out of their coalition with the CDU, bringing on a governmental crisis. While unemployment rose sharply and the parties debated over the formation of a new government, public anxiety and criticism of government inaction grew also. Into this situation of uncertainty stepped the National Democratic Party. Offering no program but plentiful slogans against the United States, NATO, the Common Market, the new "sex wave," the miniskirt, modern art, the mass media, and of course the other parties, the National Democrats came to life. As a sign of their rehabilitation of the Nazi past, National Democratic leaders placed wreaths at the graves of convicted Nazi war criminals. In the state elections in Hessen on November 6, 1966, the NPD pulled a surprising 7.9 percent of the vote and eight seats, thus hurdling the 5 percent clause which had so long blocked rightist parties from the state parliament (Landtag). Two weeks later, with the economic and governmental crises at their height, the NPD garnered 7.4 percent of the vote in the Bavarian state elections and fifteen seats in that Landtag. Even more disturbing was the fact that in Bavaria the National Democrats had overtaken the Free Democrats as the third largest party. Great concern was voiced abroad, both in Communist and non-Communist nations, at the strength of this new right-radical party. A wide array of explanations was offered for the success of the NPD, shedding usually more heat than light on the situation. Dire predictions of the return of the fascists were made, along with statements dismissing the NPD returns as insignificant.

With the formation of the long-discussed Great Coalition between the Christian Democrats and the Social Democrats, the government crisis was solved. A few months later it was clear that the economic crisis also had reached its peak and was receding. In addition, an internal struggle had erupted within the NPD which seemed to threaten to tear the new party apart. It was now assumed that this new extremist party, lacking unity and without the crisis situation of late 1966, would fade again into the background. In fact, the NPD went on in 1967 to win seats in the state elections in Schleswig-Holstein, Rheinland-Pfalz, Niedersachsen, and Bremen, capturing from 6 to 9 percent of the vote in each election. By the end of 1967 the right-radicals held seats in six of the Bundesrepublik's ten states. It appeared that the new party on the right had gained a solid foothold in the West German political system, and that the trend towards a two-party system had been interrupted, if not broken. With the two largest parties now linked in the Great Coalition, only the Free Democrats and the National Democrats were left to provide opposition; and the NPD boasted that it was the only true "national opposition" to the government. Its enrolled membership had grown to over thirty thousand, its finances had increased, and it had spread its local organization to over 75 percent of all counties in the Bundesrepublik. Finally, after a year of electoral successes, it had become a known political party to the West German voting populus.

Between late 1966 and late 1967 a political era ended in West Germany. Dr. Adenauer, the man most responsible for shaping policy in the postwar period, died in April, 1967. Ludwig Erhard, symbol of *Wirtschaftswunder*, had been defeated politically and was forced to retire from the center stage. The economic miracle itself was gone and, though the economy weathered the storms of its first recession, new progress was slow and modest.

The rise of the NPD as a new and virulent voice in the political scene deserves close analysis, because the emergence of this new right-radicalism serves both as a symptom of the transition now taking place in West Germany and as a warning signal to established political parties. The National Democrats represent on the right extreme of the spectrum an alienation from the politics of the reconstruction era, as does the student unrest on the left. The radicalism of the NPD band indicates a growing anxiety and concern over the ways in which the society of the Bundesrepublik is changing. It is a protest which feels that it cannot be expressed through any of the democratic parties— Christian Democrats, Social Democrats, or Free Democrats. This is especially true under conditions of the Great Coalition, in which the two major parties are partners. The SPD, which traditionally played an important role in keeping social protest within the democratic system, has found this role weakened by its partnership with the Christian Democrats. In this period of searching for a new and viable politics which goes beyond the problems of postwar reconstruction, there is a great need for strong opposition which can channel social protest through the democratic process rather than allowing it to become alienated, not only from present policy but from the system itself. Thus the NPD raises serious questions about the effects of the Great Coalition in the future on the course and expression of social discontent and protest in the Bundesrepublik. That there will be a significant rise in discontent following the breakdown of the virtual political consensus of the reconstruction era has already been proven, primarily by the very phenomenon the NPD arising on the far right after more than fifteen years of steady decline and collapse of previous rightist protest movements.

The NPD is also worthy of study apart from its relationship to the present political context of the Bundesrepublik, for the NPD offers an opportunity to examine the social, economic, and political roots of right-wing radicalism as a general phenomenon of modern Western society. The propaganda and voter following of the NPD are closely related to the general evolutionary patterns which characterize all modern Western societies, with some important exceptions arising from the special historical context of political extremism in Germany.

As an example of right-radicalism in a society which is undergoing evolutionary changes—in the modernization of the economy, in the continuation of urbanization, and in the development of new social mores and life styles—the National Democratic Party affords insights into reactions to social change and possible consequences of such reactions for the political system. On this level the analysis of German radicals of the right can be compared cross-culturally to the ideology and following of rightist protest movements such as the Birchites and the Wallace movement in the United States, the Poujadists in France, the Social Credit party in Canada, the neo-Fascist MSI (Movimento Sociale Italiano) in Italy, and many others.

But in addition to NPD's relevance to the present West German political scene and to the cross-cultural phenomenon of right-radicalism, the party also must be seen in the context of right extremism within Germany. What is the relationship of the National

Democrats to Hitler's National Socialists? Are NPD leaders merely old Nazis, or do they represent a new breed of extremist leadership? What correlations exist between voter followings of the NPD and the NSDAP? Then, too, the National Democrats are successors to several earlier right-wing parties in the Bundesrepublik, and should be put into perspective as a continuation of past activity on the far right. Special consideration must be given to the peculiarities of the German situation in any evolution of the impact and future potential of this new right-radical movement. The fact of absolute domination of German society by exponents of the most violent right-extremism for more than a decade during the Third Reich; the particular problem of a German nationalism twice defeated in bitter world wars; the continued division of Germany, and the officially temporary status of the Bundesrepublik; and the continued massive presence of foreign, mostly American, elements within the Federal Republic of Germany all complicate the picture of the NPD and the general phenomenon of right-extremism in Germany.

Finally, the National Democrats are interesting, in and of themselves, as the present most powerful form of radicalism in the West German political arena. Aside from their impact on the total politics of the Federal Republic, their general identification as a normal sign of backlash against change in modern Western societies, and their role as successor to the family tree of German right-radicalism, they have a character and a history which is their own and which tells something about the peculiarities of the party, its leaders, its propaganda themes, and its adherents. The National Democrats are neither the sum nor essence of movements of their general type; the NPD has added new elements to the appeals of the right wing, and has done considerable manipulation with the necessary symbolism of their protest against the present social trend. These additions (and deletions) in the vocabulary of the right-radicals are important as indications of changes which have taken place in the Bundesrepublik social setting, since the Weimar Republic and since the Third Reich. Similarly, the carry-over of other symbols from the National Socialist era into the NPD ideology indicate the limits of social change, or lack of change, between the two periods in certain areas.

The next two chapters of this study consider the NPD as a historical reality. Chapter II views the NPD first as a successor to several earlier rightist movements in the Bundesrepublik. It is impor-

tant to outline the history of the main strands of earlier far-right political parties in order to understand the preconditions for the original
emergence of the National Democrats and to examine previous records
of the present NPD leadership in their many attempts to organize
scattered elements of the extreme right into a coherent, viable political
force. It is necessary also to understand that the NPD is not the first
right-radical party to appear since the founding of the Bundesrepublik;
nor, in terms of electoral strength, is the NPD as yet the strongest of
these right-radical parties. But it is now the only real voice of the
extreme right, and it appeared after all previous parties at that end of
the political spectrum had withered or died.

Chapter III relates the electoral history of the NPD from its
founding in November of 1964 through its first campaign for the federal election of 1965; its breakthrough in the state elections in Hessen
and Bavaria in November of 1966; the struggle within the NPD in
early 1967; and its showings in the various state elections to the present.

Here the general situational factors which played a part in the
original founding of the NPD and its subsequent stages of development are discussed. The established parties, the Christian Democratic
Union/Christian Socialist Union (CDU/CSU), the Social Democratic Party (SPD), and the Free Democratic Party (FDP) figured crit-
ically in the situation favoring the birth of a movement such as the
NPD. The trend of the SPD towards the middle of the political spectrum and towards a coalition (the Great Coalition) with the CDU/
CSU, and the breakdown of the ruling Christian Democrat-Free
Democrat coalition under Chancellor Ludwig Erhard are intertwined
with the fortunes of the NPD. It was the governmental crisis which
came with the fall of the Erhard regime that helped create the crisis
atmosphere in which the National Democrats produced their original
electoral victories.

The fall of the Erhard government, however, was only the
superficial climax of a series of basic troubles which preceded its final
collapse and which lived after it. These must be examined to understand the resentment and anxiety which opened doors so long closed
to the right-radical in the Bundesrepublik.

The underlying problems which led to the governmental crisis
in late 1966 included an uneasiness over the state of the Bundesrepublik's relationship with the United States; the stagnation of foreign-

policy initiative; the breakdown of Erhard's economic policy; and several scandals concerning the military policy of the government, particularly the Starfighter issue and the HS-30 tank contract.

Most important of these was the growing economic difficulty which in 1966 would bring an end to the economic miracle (*Wirtschaftswunder*) of the Bundesrepublik. The signs of slowdown which had long been apparent within certain sectors of the economy, particularly the long-suffering coal industry, now spread to previously expanding sectors such as the automobile industry. With the end of the *Wirtschaftswunder* came the political demise of its chief architect, Ludwig Erhard. For the first time since the early 1950s the Bundesrepublik's future looked something other than rosy, and the voices of discontent —not only against the Erhard government, but against the democratic system itself—were listened to. The NPD in particular was able to attract large numbers of people to vote for a party about which they knew little except that it stood in basic opposition to the establishment, the present political system of the republic. Despite reports that the NPD was a party of old Nazis who wanted to resurrect the past, many people were drawn to the NPD's side. After its victories in the state elections in Hessen and Bavaria there was a deluge of predictions of even greater successes for this new extremist party—successes which would, it was said, endanger the very structure of democracy. Then, within a few months, the NPD underwent an internal struggle which threatened to destroy the party. Now analysts predicted not victories for the NPD, but political oblivion of the sort which had overtaken all previous parties of the far right in the Bundesrepublik. In fact, however, the NPD survived its intraparty conflicts and went on to win seats in all state legislatures for which elections were held in 1967. The victories were of the same order as their original breakthrough in Hssen and Bavaria. The party had stabilized its strength at about 6 to 9 percent of the electorate.

Just as it is important to describe the historical sequence of events which led up to the founding of the NPD and the episodes in its development, it is necessary also to examine the NPD's ideology and rationale. In Chapter IV I present the propaganda themes of the National Democrats as a part of an ideological structure; only after a rather comprehensive study of these themes as an integral whole can one understand the goals and tactics of the party. What are the relationships between the xenophobic appeals of the NPD and its total ideology? Why does it seek to inflame old resentment against minority groups and foreign influences? What is the driving force which impels the NPD to denounce such diverse elements of West German society as miniskirts, long hair styles for men, the Communists, the Bonn government, Americans, television, radio, the film industry, and modern writers and artists? In short, what is the NPD view of the Bundesrepublik and of the world? Many analysts dismiss the slogans and themes of the right-radicals as simple demagogery reminiscent of the National Socialists, but not worth the effort to analyze their content. Yet it is basic to an understanding of the National Democrats to piece together the various propaganda themes in order to perceive that they do in fact comprise an ideology, and that this ideology is rooted in a specific view of the development of modern Western society. This same chapter examines the popular support for various elements of this NPD ideology in order to gauge the potential listening audience for the party's propaganda. The potential numbers of sympathetic or like-minded citizens on each basic theme are analyzed according to demographic breakdowns—namely religion, occupation, party preference, age, and education. These demographic breakdowns of the potential listening audience for NPD propaganda are intended to show that the slogans of the NPD ideology are not limited to any one sector or any few sectors of society, but rather are widely distributed over all major segments of West German society, with some differences, which may be significant and which are noted. The analysis of voter response to the whole gamut of NPD appeals also clearly indicates that to date the National Democrats have not been able to mobilize into ballot strength the total potential of voters who, in their underlying attitudes, agree with the emotional pitch of the party. It is clear that more people agree with the slogans of the right-radicals than are willing to vote on the basis of these attitudes. There must be other factors, or combinations of factors, which impel certain voters to support a party which as its basic appeal denounces wholesale the present social and political establishment of the republic.

Since apparently there is no congruence between the size of the voter audience sympathetic to the NPD propaganda and the size of the actual NPD voter following, it is necessary to examine the social structure of this NPD votership in relation to the total voter population of the Bundesrepublik. Hopefully this will tell us whether the National Democratic Party depends not upon the above-mentioned attitudinal structure but rather upon some definable social class for its votes. Who are the NPD voters? Do they come predominantly from some particular income, age, occupation, residence, education, regional, religious, or other isolatable groups? Or is the NPD, as it claims, a people's party (*Volkspartei*) which draws its support from all levels of society, in approximate proportion to the representation of each level in the whole society? What is the relationship of certain attitudes or expectation structures to NPD voting?

Just as it was clear in the previous chapter on NPD propaganda and its resonance in the voter population that there was no simple explanation for the NPD success on the basis of its ideology, it becomes clear too that no one-faceted socioeconomic thesis can adequately describe the facts of the NPD voter following. Again it must be accepted that the National Democratic Party does not have a strictly isolatable votership, although there are certain relative strong points in that votership. And, while there is some correlation between economic anxiety and the tendency to vote NPD, this single factor alone does not explain NPD success in a convincing manner. Likewise the attempt to connect NPD voting to the holding of basic antidemocratic or authoritarian attitudes leaves much to be desired.

However, one combination of factors does seem to clarify a major part of the recruitment process of the right-radicals. It can be shown that the combination of underlying antidemocratic attitudes with economic frustration does produce a very noticeable increase in the probability of voting NPD. This probability drops sharply when the person's economic expectations are favorable, even if his basic orientation is antidemocratic. The probability of an NPD vote reaches its low point when the basic attitude orientation is not antidemocratic. Here the voter, even if beset with economic worries and expectations of hard times, tends to remain within the established democratic system rather than to threaten that system with a vote for the NPD.

It would seem from the evidence presented that right-radicals can recruit votes primarily among those who are predisposed against democratic processes, but that even here they need a sense of personal crisis—in particular, a threatening economic outlook—to act as a catalyst. The action of this catalyst upon the original attitude structure tends to raise qualitatively the probability that the voter will seek out a protest party which renounces attempts to work within the system. On the other hand, people who have formed democratic attitudes, at least in some basic matters, tend even under stress to stay within the framework of the established party system and to seek redress through established parties. The long-term factor in the NPD potential thus lies in the basic attitude structure of the citizenry. As long as the attitudes and prejudices which form the NPD ideology are held by large numbers of people, there will be the danger that such attitudes, in time of personally felt crisis can be mobilized for political action by a movement such as the NPD.

What, then, is the proper solution to the challenge of right-radicalism? This depends primarily upon understanding the meaning and impact of the NPD within the Bundesrepublik. The final chapter of this study discusses the problems which the Bundesrepublik faces in its transition from a society undergoing reconstruction to a society evolving under a new dynamic. The NPD is a sign that policies which may have been appropriate to the previous period are not adequate to meet the demands of a new era. Continuing urbanization in the Bundesrepublik and the drive for modernization and concentration of industry are creating problems to which the established parties have as yet not fully addressed themselves. The growing discontent on the left (among students) as well as on the far right are signs that increasing numbers of citizens no longer feel that the SPD, CDU/CSU, or FDP are addressing themselves to the frustrations which they feel. The result is alienation from the political system, as evidenced on the left by criticism of all parties and disorganized protests and demonstrations, on the right by growing support for an antiparty, the NPD. The potential of this "party to end all politics" depends to a great extent on the ability of the present system to open a dialogue with those who can interpret the real roots of the discontent and to keep them within the system. The problems of the small businessman, the small farmer, and the unskilled laborer, among others, in an age of increasing concentration of industry; increasing urbanization, and destruction of rural and small-town life styles; demands for higher skill levels, must be recognized and the transition eased by rational explanation and problem-solving approaches. The frustrations and tensions involved in this social evolution must be seen in their original nature, not in caricatured form as presented by such movements as the National Democratic Party. To respond only to the caricature is to fail to recognize the existence of legitimate anxiety. Yet most of the suggested solutions to meet the NPD fail in just this way. In my final analysis I examine the dangers and shortcomings of such solutions. It is necessary to see why a simple ban on the NPD does not in the long run solve any but the most superficial problem, and why a reform of the election laws which would in practice have the same effect, at least at the national level, would be similarly inappropriate for purposes of ridding the Bundesrepublik of the NPD. These proposals involve only technical changes which alone cannot answer the basic causes of the NPD phenomenon.

Another proposed solution, namely that of scandalizing the National Democrats and making supporters of that party social outcasts, would only harden feelings of alienation from society and resentments against it. The NPD voter feels already that he is outside, or on the margin of, society and his marginality, his sense of insecurity, is a basic factor in his support for the National Democrats. To solidify this impression of exclusion from established society only aids the NPD and its own view of the world.

A fourth proposal involves a take-over of certain nationalistic propaganda slogans of the NPD by one of the major parties. This view is perhaps the most dangerous because it calls for competing with the National Democrats on their own grounds.

A fifth view of the NPD suggests that the party will mellow with age and thus become less radical, less menacing. It assumes that, as the party leadership gains some of the status and recognition which it seeks, it will become more cautious lest it lose the positions it had gained. This outlook fails to consider the underlying social pressures which gave the NPD its electoral successes, and which the party must stir up to maintain a hold on its following. If anything, the NPD grew more strident as it grew in size and gained seats in the state parliaments. NPD slogans are not meant to nullify the social conflicts which are at the root of the NPD vote; rather, they seek to exacerbate such tensions and to propose fantasy explanations and solutions.

To meet the challenge of the NPD requires an appraisal, not only of the National Democratic Party, but also of the basic resentments which lead citizens to leave the established political arena. Such resentments are real; the society of the Bundesrepublik is evolving in ways which many people do not understand and in ways which seem to and, indeed, do threaten, the life style they once found appropriate and proper. Some of these conflicts are the inevitable product of such basic processes as urbanization and expansion of the world market.

Given these personally felt conflict situations, aggravated in times of economic recession, it is readily understandable that citizens who already hold antidemocratic attitudes become easy targets for recruitment by extremist movements. The final section of this study looks at the general requirements for dealing with this problem, both in the long and the short run. It suggests ways in which the anxieties which many voters feel can be kept within the parliamentary system of democratic parties. It suggests, finally, that the real problem is not how to handle the NPD—for the NPD is a superficial warning signal —but how, politically, to cope with the tensions of transition which individuals must undergo in a developing society.

II

Earlier Rightist Parties
in the Bundesrepublik

The National Democratic Party of Germany is by no means the first right-radical party to appear in the Bundesrepublik. The NPD has its roots in several earlier right-wing parties which arose in the Bundesrepublik after its founding in 1949. Even before then it was clear that there were substantial groups in the three Western occupation zones of Germany who could provide a voter base for right-wing parties with nationalist and revanchist appeals. According to an estimate by Helmut Schelsky, there were in the Bundesrepublik approximately nine million refugees, expellees, and emigrants from the Communist-controlled sectors of the old Reich; about two million discharged former Reich officials, National Socialist (NSDAP) party function-aries, and professional soldiers; two-and-a-half million war widows and orphans; one-and-a-half million people severely crippled by the war; two million late returnees; four to six million other civilian war injured; plus, in the year 1950, one-and-a-half million other unemployed. There is, of course, substantial overlap between these groups, but it is readily understandable that a sizable potential following for radical political appeals existed.[1]

Even before the founding of the Bundesrepublik there had been beginnings of new right-wing political movements. During the first four years of occupation the Allied authorities in each zone had the power to license only those political parties which they deemed

---

1. Helmut Schelsky, *Wandlungen der deutschen Familie in der Gegenwart*, (Stuttgart: Enke Verlag, 1955), p. 47.

appropriate. The four parties which were originally licensed in all zones as "democratic" parties were the Christian Democrats/Christian Socialists (CDU/CSU), the Social Democrats (SPD), the Liberal Democrats (LDP), who later became the Free Democrats (FDP), and the Communists (KPD). In right-wing circles these four parties, later reduced to three by the banning of the KPD in 1956, became known as the "licensed parties" (*Lizenzparteien*) because they had been granted permission to organize by the Allies. In their view this meant that these parties were founded as agents of alien conquerors, and that they did not represent the interests of the German people, but those of the United States, Britain, and France.

As for parties which were outspoken right-wing movements, the Allies in each zone adopted separate policies. The British, in the Protestant North (a traditional stronghold for rightist activity), were the first to permit right-wing groups to organize for political activity. In Niedersachsen arch-conservative groups still loyal to the Guelph monarchy formed the Niedersachsen Land Party (NLP). The NLP was a sort of states-rights party within the framework of a larger Germany. Soon, however, the NLP expanded its organization beyond Niedersachsen to the other northern states of Hamburg and Bremen and, in June, 1947, changed its name to the German Party (*Deutsche Partei*—DP). The DP, in its expansion beyond the state of Niedersachsen, attracted new adherents whose character was more closely connected with the German nationalist or National Socialist tradition rather than the states-rights or monarchist strain. For this reason the DP always had a certain split between its monarchist wing and its German nationalist wing. The style of its appeals and rallies was patterned more after the National Socialists than the traditional Guelph monarchists.

Along with the DP the British authorities also licensed the formation of several other right-wing groups, several of which in June of 1946 formed the German Party of the Right-Conservative Union (*Deutsche Rechts-Partei-Konservative Vereinigung*); later this party became simply the German Party of the Right (*Deutsche Rechtspartei* —DRP) and still later, in 1949, the German Party of the Right/ German Conservative Party; finally it was renamed the German Reich Party (*Deutsche Reichs-Partei*—DRP), which name it kept until its self-dissolution in December of 1965. One of the earliest and most active organizers within the DRP was Adolph von Thadden, young

178|03

(born in 1921) and ambitious son of a Pomeranian nobleman. Von
Thadden had been an artillery officer during the war and had been a
member of the NSDAP. After the war he had been arrested by the
Polish authorities and reportedly had been forced to do some work
for the Polish secret police. He fled into the British zone of occupation, where for a time he worked as an employee of the British Property Control in Göttingen. Von Thadden had been denounced by his
enemies in rightist circles for his associations with the Polish and
British authorities, and yet it had been a mark of his talents that he had
retained a central influence in the evolution of right-radical politics in
the Bundesrepublik. In 1949 the German Party of the Right formed
an alliance with the National Democratic Party (NDP), a right-wing
party which the Americans reluctantly had licensed in the state of
Hessen. Like the early German Party of the Right, the Hessian National Democratic Party, under the leadership of Dr. Leuchtgens, had
rather pronounced monarchist leanings, which only later were gradually dissolved and replaced by more nationalist and National Socialist
orientations.

In the French zone nationally oriented groups formed the Ger-
man Union, which was modeled somewhat after the Gaullist RPF.
Later the German Union broke apart, with part forming the German
Community (*Deutsche Gemeinschaft*—DG) in 1949 with August
Haussleiter at its head. Haussleiter had originally worked within the
Christian Social Union in Bavaria, but broke with that party on the
issue of the founding of the Bundesrepublik, which he opposed as
separatism.

The activities of right-wing activists were still constricted before the Bundesrepublik, and many rightist leaders took refuge in the
major democratic parties, the CDU/CSU, SPD, and FDP. Some local
organizations of the major parties, particularly the FDP, leaned very
far to the right, forming a right wing of the party. After the founding
of the republic and the end of licensing by the Allied powers, however,
many of these right-wing elements, which had never really been integrated into the major parties, felt free to set out on their own. The
years of the first *Bundestag* (Federal Parliament) from 1949 to 1953,
witnessed a new burst of activity in the far right of the political spectrum.

It was clear to many rightists that, as soon as the creation of
the Bundesrepublik became a certainty, it would be to their benefit

to form a coalition or front to combine into one stream the several threads of political activity on the far right.

In June of 1949, therefore, a conference of leaders of the DP, DRP, and the Hessian National Democratic Party (NDP) was held in Hanover. A tentative agreement seemed to have been reached for a fusion of the DP, NDP and DRP, the three main centers of rightist activity at that time. According to notes taken by von Thadden, the conference concluded that a fusion must be undertaken, but only after the federal elections. It was feared that if such a merger were completed before the elections, it could be interpreted by occupation authorities as the founding of a completely new party, and that occupation authorities might delay licensing the new party until after the federal elections. These fears were voiced primarily by the more moderate leaders of the DP, Hellwege, Seebohm, and von Merkatz, while the more radical leaders in the DRP had pressed for action on a merger before the federal elections which would confront the Allied authorities with a fait accompli. The risk of this was too great for the DP leadership, however, and so the DP, DRP, and NDP entered the 1949 elections separately. However, some local organizations of the DRP went over to the DP, and the DP seemed convinced that its decision to maintain its own separate identity had been profitable.

In the first federal elections the DP gained twenty-five seats and became a member of the government coalition, holding two ministerial posts. This event signaled the beginning of the absorption of the more moderate DP elements into Christian Democratic circles. After years as a member of the coalition government led by the CDU, and after years of fighting the extremist elements within the schizophrenic DP, such leaders as von Merkatz and Seebohm eventually became members of the CDU.

The DRP was far less successful in its first national electoral showing, yet it managed to enter the Bundestag with six seats. Its main voting support came from the state of Niedersachsen, where it gathered 8.1 percent of the vote, more than the FDP. In several districts, especially where economic conditions were very depressed, the DRP made major breakthroughs, with 31.5 percent of the vote in Wilhelmshaven, 30.7 percent in Gifhorn, 26.3 percent in Emden, 30.7 percent in Hammeln, and 23.6 percent in Salzgitter.[2] In these areas the DRP

2. Manfred Jenke, *Verschwörung von Rechts?* (Berlin: Colloquium Verlag, 1961), p. 66.

worked particularly hard to mobilize economically anxious and fearful voters behind their increasingly more radical appeals. The DRP, which had originally had a more conservative and monarchist orientation, had clearly swung much farther to the right. A sign of this transformation came soon after the federal elections, when on August 29 Dr. Franz Richter was elected head of the DRP in Niedersachsen, the stronghold of the party. Richter had been dismissed from his teaching position after the war for neonazi tendencies, and now the DRP had voted him to the top post of their strongest state organization. Richter, however, had no record of being a former Nazi. Only in 1952 was it discovered that Richter's real identity was Fritz Rössler, whose long career in the NSDAP began in 1930. At the end of the war Rössler had been able to obtain false papers identifying him as one Dr. Franz Richter, who had never been a Nazi party member. On May 4, 1952, Richter (Rössler) was sentenced to eighteen months in jail for use of false identity and for activities contrary to the election laws.

This swing to the right by the DRP resulted in a splitting of the party, with the most radical leaders, primarily Dr. Fritz Dorls, Dr. Gerhard Krüger, and Otto Remer, leaving the old DRP and forming the Socialist Reich Party (SRP) in October of 1949. Many members, and later whole local organizations of the old DRP, converted to the SRP; the remaining leadership of the DRP decided to rename the party as the *Deutsche Reichs-Partei* (DRP) in January, 1950.

From its founding the SRP had an erratic but often surprisingly successful career. This matched in kind the careers of its leaders. Dorls had joined the NSDAP as a nineteen-year old student, but he also offered resistance to the Third Reich, which had gotten him into trouble more than once. Yet he had remained a teacher at the National-Socialist school of Erwitten. Krüger had joined the NSDAP in 1928, had been chairman of the Nazi student organization from 1931 to 1933, and had made a career within the NSDAP. He served as the unofficial party theoretician of the SRP. Otto Remer, not a member of the NSDAP, had instead made a military career for himself during the Third Reich. His claim to fame within the SRP was his role in putting down the attempt to overthrow Hitler in July of 1944. Among right-wing circles, the July 20 assassination attempt on Hitler is regarded as the worst sort of treason, and Remer was hailed within such groups as one who had blocked the "Betrayal of the 20th of July."

The SRP's ideology rested upon the claim that the Third Reich

had not gone under, that Admiral Dönitz, sitting in Spandau, was still
its Führer. The Bundesrepublik was seen as illegitimate. The "Führer
principle" of the NSDAP was also used by the SRP as its organization
principle, and SRP meetings and campaign tactics were patterned after
the NSDAP format. Through its far more explicit use of Nazi trap-
pings and its strident denunciation of the Bonn republic the SRP was
able to attract many former DRP, DP, and NDP members, including
the above-mentioned Dr. Richter (Rössler).

In the first real electoral test of the SRP, the state election in
Niedersachsen on May 6, 1951, the SRP garnered 11 percent of the
vote and fifteen seats in the Landtag as compared with only two seats
for the new DRP. The SRP voter following was heaviest in agricultural
districts, and was disproportionately low in predominantly Catholic
districts. In addition the SRP, like the DRP, showed its greatest successes in areas of high unemployment. Kurt Tauber has noted that the
SRP voter not infrequently had suffered a loss of status of some sort
following the collapse of the Third Reich, and blamed this deprivation
on the new republic and the new social establishment.[3] In certain electoral districts, the SRP had simply cut into past voter followings of
the DRP, but in many areas the Socialist Reich Party had been able
to mobilize previously untapped rightist potentials. (See Table II.1.)[4]
Again in October, 1951, the SRP made a strong showing in the state
elections in Bremen, gaining eight seats in the Burgerschaft. However,
the SRP had actually reached its high-water mark in the Niedersachsen
election, and was experiencing increasing difficulties, both internally
and with the authorities, which were eventually to lead to the banning
of the party as a successor organization to the NSDAP. The road to
final banning of the party was marked by an ever increasing radicalism
in the propaganda of the SRP, by the trial on various charges of individual SRP leaders, and the partial prohibition of certain SRP activities and groupings. The trial of the SRP before the federal courts
was drawn out through the summer of 1952, before the final verdict
on October 23, which dissolved and banned the SRP. A portion of the
SRP membership returned to the DRP, but nowhere did the SRP
attempt to reform as a new party.

At the same time that the Socialist Reich Party was making its

3. Kurt Tauber, *Beyond Eagle and Swastika*, (Middletown, Conn: Wesleyan University Press, 1967), Vol. I, pp. 703–704.
4. Jenke, *Verschwörung*, pp. 91–92.

TABLE II.1

COMPARISON OF THE DRP AND SRP VOTE IN NIEDERSACHSEN,
1949 AND 1951
(in percent)

Area*	1949	1951	
	DRP	DRP	SRP
Gifhorn	30.7	4.5	9.6
Wilhelmshaven	31.5	6.2	18.6
Helmstedt	20.8	2.7	12.2
Salzgitter	23.6	5.2	7.3
Hameln	25.3	6.7	6.7
Hildesheim	17.3	4.1	4.9
Area†			
Celle-Stadt	10.0	2.1	21.5
Aurich	8.2	3.5	27.1
Holzminden	5.2	2.0	16.2
Rotenburg	5.2	3.7	27.6
Lüneburg	5.1	2.3	28.3
Verden	3.8	2.7	23.9
Diepholz	3.2	1.1	32.9
Bremervoerde	3.1	2.5	28.0
Oldenburg-Land	1.4	2.9	17.9
Area‡			
Emden	26.3	7.0	18.8
Soltau	19.1	5.7	17.0
Celle-Land	13.2	3.8	21.0

* Areas in which the SRP and the DRP did not split the radical vote, where the DRP had done extremely well in 1949.
† Areas in which the SRP tapped new radical vote-potentials in 1951, not reached by the DRP in 1949.
‡ Areas in which the SRP made great inroads into the previously tapped DRP voter potential.
SOURCE: Manfred Jenke, *Verschwörung von Rechts?* (Berlin: Colloquium Verlag, 1961), pp. 91–92.

presence felt, another major attempt at political organization was in progress on the right. Out of August Haussleiter's original German Community (DG) came the founding of the Federation of Expellees and Disfranchised (*Bund der Heimatvertriebenen und Entrechteten—* BHE) in January of 1950. The BHE appealed mainly to emigrants and refugees from Communist-held parts of the old Reich, war-injured, and to those "disfranchised" after the war. The "disfranchised" refers mainly to Nazi party functionaries and Third Reich officials removed from positions of influence during the denazification period. In the

political history of the Bundesrepublik the BHE is noted as the interest party for these groups. This, as Jenke notes, is only partly accurate,
since large numbers of refugees, emigrants, and war injured, as well as
"disfranchised" former Nazis were absorbed by the major Bonn parties
as well as by other right-wing groups.[5] Perhaps it is more accurate to
say that the BHE represented those expellees and "disfranchised" who
had not been assimilated into the new society of the Bundesrepublik.

The BHE's appeal to the uprooted masses of Germans who had
not yet been assimilated found a quick and powerful response. In the
state of Schleswig-Holstein, where the proportion of recently uprooted
Germans was very high (in some communities over 40 percent), the
BHE received 23.4 percent of the vote in the state elections in July
of 1950, becoming the second largest party in the Landtag after the
CDU. Following its success in Schleswig-Holstein, the BHE rapidly
expanded its organization to other states, combining with the German
Community to garner 14.7 percent of the vote in the Baden-Württemberg state elections and 12.3 percent in the Bavarian state elections.
In Bavaria the BHE was accepted by the SPD and CSU into the government coalition and received two ministerial posts. In Niedersachsen,
where the SRP and DRP had already been agitating among potential
right-oriented voters, the BHE nevertheless was able to collect 14.9
percent of the vote in early 1951, as opposed to 11 percent for the SRP.
In Niedersachsen the BHE, as the third-strongest party in the state,
accepted a coalition bid from the SPD to form the state government.

The BHE from its outset showed that, in contrast to most
right-wing parties in the Bundesrepublik (with the exception of the
DP), it was quite ready to go into coalition with the Bonn parties, to
abandon its general orientation as an opposition party, and take up
the responsibility of a government partner. Yet already in its earliest
years the BHE showed symptoms of the same sort of schizophrenia
which affected several other right-wing parties. From its founding, the
BHE explicitly appealed for the vote of the "disfranchised," for Nazis
who had suffered some penalty for the National Socialist activities.
BHE leadership from the outset was heavily laden with former high-
level, unreconstructed National Socialists, such as Dr. Wilhelm Stuck-
art, second in command in the BHE, Dr. Karl Ott, who received a

5. *Ibid.*, p. 201. In this regard the BHE in particular affords a rough index,
during the 1950s, to the ability of the Bundesrepublik in reassimilating the great
masses of war-uprooted Germans.

cabinet post in the SPD/BHE coalition in Niedersachsen, and Hans Schepmann, who was elected deputy mayor in the city of Gifhorn. All had had long and successful careers in the NSDAP.

On the other hand, the BHE also encompassed more conservative leaders and activists who were not willing to extinguish their successful political careers and lose their newly won government posts by following too radical a course. Thus, as with the DP, there was a rather steady conflict between the conservative leaders (often referred to as the "ministerial wing" of the party) and the more radical ones. In general both wings of the BHE were led by former National Socialists, and the party vigorously defended those leaders with long NSDAP careers—a special characteristic of parties of the far right.

To summarize, the period of the first Bundestag from 1949 to 1953 saw the formation and growth of the main strands of right-wing activity which were to mark the postwar era of the Bundesrepublik. By 1953, the BHE, DP, and DRP were the chief electoral vehicles on the right. The SRP had for a short time seized the initiative on the extreme right, had made some spectacular demonstrations of strength, but had quickly run afoul of the courts and had finally been banned. Of the three main rightist parties, two, the BHE and DP, had taken part in the building of governing coalitions, either on the state or federal level. In these two parties there were already signs of conflict between the more conservative leaders—often those holding government posts—and the more radical membership.

However, it was already clear by the time of the second federal elections in 1953 that these right-wing parties had reached and passed their high water mark.

For the second federal elections to the Bundestag the election laws had been changed to exclude proportional representation for parties which did not get at least 5 percent of the total vote. However, each voter was given two votes. With the second vote the distribution of the total number of seats for the individual party lists was determined, but there was also the possibility with the first vote of directly electing a candidate from a particular district regardless of whether his party got 5 percent of the nationwide vote or not. Thus an individual candidate could be elected by getting a plurality in his district even if his party did not get 5 percent of the vote.

For the DP, which was a coalition partner of the Adenauer government, assurances had been given that in several districts, in which certain DP leaders were candidates, among them Hellwege, Dr. von Merkatz, Dr. Seebohm, and Dr. Elbrechter, the CDU would not put up opposing candidates and instead would campaign for these DP leaders. This would insure the reelection of these leaders, whether the DP received 5 percent of the vote or not. In fact, the DP won only 3.3 percent of the vote as compared with 4.0 percent in the 1949 elections. In addition to the above-mentioned "guaranteed" seats, two additional DP candidates received pluralities in their districts with first votes and were therefore elected from those districts. While the DP had maintained some representation in the Bundestag, its vote had decreased markedly in its former strongholds, dropping from 13.8 percent to 5.9 percent in Hamburg; from 12.1 percent to 4.0 percent in Schleswig-Holstein, and from 17.8 percent to 11.9 percent in Niedersachsen. Only in Bremen did the DP maintain its strength at 17.0 percent as opposed to 18.0 percent in 1949.

The BHE, after its rather impressive beginnings, garnered only 5.6 percent of the 1953 vote, thus dampening its hopes of becoming a government coalition partner. However, the Adenauer government, as part of its continuing tactics to win over prominent leaders of the right, offered the BHE several special ministerial posts. This led to an even wider split between the conservatives and the radicals who wanted to carry the party into opposition against the Bonn government. In the summer of 1955 the "ministerial wing" of the BHE, led by the party chairman Kraft and Minister Oberländer, joined the ranks of the Christian Democrats. This process eventually deprived the BHE of its most respected and able leaders and hastened the already apparent decline of the party.

The DRP, third and least powerful of the three main threads of right-wing political activity, also fared poorly in the 1953 federal elections, slipping from 1.8 percent of the vote in 1949 to only 1.1 percent. Even in the right-wing stronghold of Niedersachsen, the German Reich Party lost heavily, coming out with only 3.5 percent of the vote (8.1 percent in 1949).

The years of the second and third Bundestag periods (1953 to 1961) were marked by the steady decline, splintering, futile attempts at fusion, and often final demise of parties on the far right.

The DP, under the chairmanship of Heinrich Hellwege, continued to be split between the more moderate monarchist conservatives and the Reich-oriented radicals. Hellwege had already in 1950 expelled whole groups of DP organizations which supported the pro-fascist statements of the DP Bundestag member Wolfgang Hedler; Hedler and his supporters then went over to the more radical DRP. In February of 1953 Hellwege, though always in a precarious position as leader of the DP, boldly announced that the whole DP organization for the state of North Rhine-Westphalia had been sabotaged and was therefore declared dissolved. Actually, the DP in North Rhine-Westphalia had been negotiating with Nazi-oriented elements of the Free Democratic Party, and Hellwege feared a further rise in the influence of the radicals within the DP. The dissolved state organization constituted itself as the "Independent German Party" but, after a complete failure in the state elections, splintered into small groups which went over to the FDP, the BHE, or the DRP. The last notable success of the DP came in the 1955 state elections in Niedersachsen, where the DP was able to get a healthy 12.4 percent of the vote in the "anti-Marxist" coalition which the DP had formed with the CDU. The DP not only became a partner in the CDU/BHE/DP/FDP coalition, but its chairman, Hellwege, became Minister-president. This extremely unstable four-party coalition lasted only until September, 1957, when the BHE and FDP walked out, at which point Hellwege declared the government coalition dissolved.

Meanwhile the DP was suffering the same sort of attrition which the BHE experienced. In 1958 Theodor Sonnenmann, an old founder of the DP, declared his conversion to the CDU. Two DP members of the Bundestag, Otto Eisenmann and Dr. Alexander Elbrechter, converted to the FDP and the CDU respectively. This process continued until on July 1, 1960, nine DP Bundestag members simultaneously announced their conversion to the CDU. Among these were two top leaders of the party, Dr. Seebohm and Dr. von Merkatz.

At this point it was clear that the DP was in imminent danger of going under. In the fall of 1960, therefore, Hellwege made one last attempt to create a viable "third force" in the form of a fusion of the BHE, FDP, and DP. In the end, however, only the DP and the BHE combined to form the All-German Party (*Gesamtdeutsche Partei*—GDP). Hellwege, dismayed and weary after years of struggle, resigned his political offices soon afterwards. In 1961 the DP ceased to exist as a national party, and only a few scattered local organizations, which had refused to support the GDP experiment, continued to operate. The one significant exception was the still active DP in Bremen,

which decided to go its own way. The GDP fusion of the remnants
of the old DP and BHE proved ineffective in reversing or even slowing
the downward spiral of the rightists. In various regions the rumps of
the old party organizations continued a hopeless struggle, and thus
the GDP was never a complete fusion of the two former parties.

The DRP is to be counted among the three main right-wing
parties of the postwar reconstruction period, but not because of its
success as a vote-gathering vehicle. In this respect the DRP fell far
behind the showings of the BHE and DP. Jenke, writing in 1961, lists
the DRP as one of the many parties "on the political periphery."[6] The
DRP's electoral showings after 1949 were poor, although in 1955 the
party achieved 3.8 percent of the vote and six seats in the Landtag in
Niedersachsen, which at that time still had no 5 percent cutoff clause.
In 1959, after the introduction of the 5 percent clause, the DRP lost
its seats with a return of 3.6 of the vote. In 1959, only in the state of
Rheinland-Pfalz was the DRP able to go over the 5 percent mark,
gaining 5.1 percent of the vote and one seat in the Landtag. This latter
success in Rheinland-Pflaz was quickly negated by acts of anti-Semitic
vandalism in Cologne committed by two DRP members. Although
the two offenders were promptly expelled from the party, and in addition the whole Cologne DRP organization was dissolved for anti-
Semitic tendencies, the press took this opportunity to heavily criticize
the DRP. The DRP began to run into the same sort of conflict with
the authorities which the SRP had experienced before its banning.
In fact, in January of 1960 the state administration in Rheinland-
Pfalz decided to bring the DRP to court as a successor organization
to the forbidden SRP. The DRP was forced to rebuild its state organization in fast order to avoid a complete ban, but after a few months
the DRP could once again take part in the local elections.

The real importance of the DRP is that, despite its relatively
small voter following, it was able to build up an able and well distributed cadre of activists and to establish several stable party publications, *Reichsruf* (*Clarion of the Reich*) and *Deutsche Wochen-Zeit-
ung* (*German Weekly Newspaper*), which formed a sound if limited
financial basis for the party's activities. The real director of the party

6. *Ibid.*, Chapter 4. Jenke relegates the DRP to a lower political category
primarily because of its consistently poor electoral showings; but, at the same time
he takes into account the rather impressive apparatus which the DRP, despite its
poverty at the polls, was able to maintain.

cadre and publications was Adolf von Thadden, nominally second in command behind the respected chairman Wilhelm Meinberg. Although an old National Socialist, Meinberg was rather widely respected and was regarded as the fatherly, nominal head of the DRP, while the real direction and handling of party affairs was left to von Thadden's apparatus.

The DRP's general orientation underwent several shifts from its founding in 1950 through the periods of the second and third Bundestag. Having largely abandoned the original monarchist-conservative leanings of the German Party of the Right by the first federal election campaign in 1949, the new DRP was seriously weakened by continuing defection to the splinter SRP, and was for some time at a loss for a real political course to advocate. This period of uncertainty was somewhat eased by the banning of the SRP in late 1952, and soon thereafter the DRP set out to attract the former members and voter following of the Socialist Reich Party. This phase of the DRP's development also met with no success, and after the extremely poor showing of the DRP (1.1 percent) in the 1953 Bundestag elections the party began a shift to a national-neutralist position which lasted into the early 1960s. During this period, certain DRP party members maintained contacts with nationalist front organization in East Germany. One of the DRP members of the Niedersachsen Landtag, Johannes Herte, reportedly received financial support from the *Nation*, a newspaper funded from the DDR. The DRP denied that it was politically or financially dependent upon East German sources, but its adventure with such contacts further contributed to the bad publicity which the party had always received, and to the isolation of the DRP even from other parties on the far right. The DRP's national-neutralist cause, which strongly opposed the NATO ties and pro-Western course of the Adenauer government, found some response among the Paul's Church Movement which opposed the NATO Treaties of 1955. The one notable electoral success of the DRP, the 5.2 percent vote which the party achieved in Rheinland-Pfalz in 1959, may be partially explained by adverse popular reaction to the taking of land in that state for NATO airfields and the fear of the stockpiling of atomic weapons in the state.

These gains were, as mentioned before, largely canceled by the role of DRP members in vandalism against a synagogue and other Jewish memorials in Cologne soon after the election.

The DRP continued with its national-neutralist course until

the returns were in from the 1961 Bundestag election. The DRP in these elections suffered still further declines, receiving less than 1 percent of the vote. At this point a new split arose in the party between the strict national-neutralist leaders, including the new chairman of the party, Dr. Heinrich Kunstmann, and the apparatus led by von Thadden. At the party conference in December, 1961, Dr. Kunstmann was outvoted by von Thadden's cohorts and left the party, followed by many other strong advocates of the national-neutralist policy. Kunstmann then founded the German Freedom Party, which in 1965 merged with the German Community to form the Action Community of Independent Germans (*Aktionsgemeinschaft unabhängiger Deutscher*— AUD). To this date this party has remained a meaningless political sect, with miniscule voter following.

As a result of the internal struggle, the DRP began to modify its party line to make the party more acceptable as a possible coalition partner for other nationalist parties, which did not share DRP neutralist views. Slowly the DRP adopted a more or less "Gaullist" view of the NATO alliance and gave reluctant agreement to a generally pro-Western policy. This came at a time when the other right-wing parties, the DP and BHE, were both showing symptoms of final collapse, and were negotiating for the formation of the All-German Party. The DRP did not participate in this venture, but decided instead to try its hand one more time. The party did not put up candidates for the 1962 round of state elections; it saved its resources for the two state elections in Niedersachsen and Rhineland-Pfalz, which would be coming up in 1963. These were the two states in which the DRP had made its strongest showing, and it may have hoped to benefit from the splintering of the DP and BHE to attract more votes. But when the DRP vote declined even further in these two elections, the leadership of the party determined to give up its independent efforts and to seek some sort of fusion with remnants of the other rightist parties.

What I have outlined here shows the continuing decline of the main sources of opposition to the Bonn government from the right. I have left out any account of the myriad of smaller parties, often better designated as political sects, which made their appearance during this period. The stories of these small splinter groups and their leaders are often fascinating; for the interested reader, I recommend the more lengthy and detailed accounts of these groups given in Manfred Jenke's *Verschwörung von Rechts* and Kurt Tauber's *Beyond Eagle and*

Swastika. These groups, however, were often limited to a few locali-
ties in their impact and did not have much bearing on the main
course of events for the far right. Indeed, the great majority of these
groups were the creation of a few active and often embittered individuals. Jenke cites the example of Erwin Schonborn who, aside from his
limited activities within the DRP, was the founder of no less than ten
right-radical movements, each of which lasted for only a few years and
whose membership was limited to close associates of Schonborn.
Obviously the political effects of these ten movements is not to be
overestimated. On the other hand, the case of Erwin Schonborn is
illustrative of the kind of political adventurer who practiced his trade
on the margin of the larger right-wing organizations.[7] For a general
understanding of the history of the far right in the Bundesrepublik
prior to the founding of the National Democratic Party of Germany
in November of 1964, however, a close examination of these smaller
groupings is not necessary.

The records of the DP, BHE, and DRP through the Adenauer
era in the Bundesrepublik showed the difficulty of the rightists in
holding their originally impressive voter followings in the face of the
growing prosperity under the economic miracle (*Wirtschaftswunder*)
and the steady assimilation of the millions of war-uprooted Germans
into the social structure.

Under these conditions, the more opportunist elements in the
right-wing leadership, including some with lengthy Nazi records, who
had held cabinet posts and shared governmental responsibilities in
coalitions with the CDU or SPD, converted to the major parties as it
became clear that the great numbers of early voters of the DP and
BHE were being attracted to those more viable political vehicles.

With the loss of their most respected and more moderate leaders, the DP and BHE went by default into the hands of more radical
nationalist leaders who had from the start challenged the "ministerial
wings" of these parties for control. The case of the DRP was basically
different. It had always been somewhat isolated on the far right, as it
was from the start a more radical organization than either the DP or
BHE. In addition, it had always been in the opposition and had never
taken part in a government coalition, although this possibility had
once been discussed in Niedersachsen. For much of the 1950s the DRP
had followed its own course of national-neutralism, which had alien-

7. See especially Jenke, *Verschwörung*, pp. 279–284.

ated it from the right-wing parties which had willingly formed coalitions with the major parties pursuing a pro-Western policy of close political and military alliance with the United States.

The DRP, as an isolated party through much of its history, was able to hold its organization together and did not develop the same splits between the more moderate leaders who held government posts and the more radical elements. The splits which did plague the German Reich Party were more ideological in nature and did not affect the stability of the party organization. With its relatively sound financial basis and its core of loyal activists the DRP survived beyond both DP and BHE as a coherent party structure despite its generally miserable showing at the polls.

From the first federal elections almost all major leaders of the right had given lip service to the desirability, even the necessity, of merging their efforts. Yet despite continuing attempts at partal cooperative efforts, limited either to specific regions or to certain elections, no lasting fusion of the three main right-wing parties was accomplished. It would seem that as long as some hope, even an ill-found one, remained each party could still go it alone, none were willing to merge their own party hierarchies into a single fusion party organization. Thus, whenever even limited cooperative efforts were made, the inevitable frictions and disagreements which arose would end the common venture and a period of cooling off was required before further coordination of activity could be attempted.

By the end of 1963 it seemed apparent that the downward spiral on the far right would result in the final elimination of all but the smallest right-wing sects in the course of the next few years. Even a last attempt by the rightists to form a new fusion party did not arouse any fears of a resurgence of their electoral fortunes. The *Wirtschaftswunder* was still in high gear, and its proclaimed chief architect, Ludwig Erhard, had replaced Dr. Adenauer as leader of the CDU/FDP coalition government. All signs indicated that the extremist movements had been relegated to the past.

III

History of the National
Democratic Party of Germany

In the previous chapter I have outlined the decline and disintegration of the various right-wing political parties in the Bundesrepublik
prior to the founding of the National Democratic Party of Germany
(NPD). By the early sixties it was clear that the main strands of the
far right, the *Deutsche Partei* (DP), the *Deutsche Reichspartei*
(DRP), and the *Bund der Heimatsvertriebenen und Entrechteten*
(BHE) were already fated for political oblivion. It was eminently
clear that there was, in fact, no voice for the far right which could
make itself heard nationally. None of the parties of the far right had
even a national organization worth the name. In short, the first round
of postwar right extremism was at an end.

In an important sense, the final collapse of the original postwar
parties of the far right was a prerequisite for the founding of the NPD,
for as long as these parties lingered on as essentially meaningless
political splinter groups, no real "national opposition," that elusive
goal of the rightist leaders, could be formed. Each splinter power structure resisted attempts at amalgamation until finally the situation was
hopeless. Only when they hit bottom could the rightists be convinced
to submit to a single, unified party structure. Even then the danger
remained that, if and when the NPD got off the ground, the old divisions would reappear, which to some extent they did. But by early
1964 this problem was completely subordinate to the task of revitaliz-
ing the political structure of the far right. The petty baronies of the

early and middle fifties lay in ashes, and the only choice remaining was a realistic attempt at unity under one party label.

There were other factors which favored a new attempt to establish a "national opposition" to oppose the Bonn parties, the CDU/CSU, the SPD, and the FDP. Chief among them was the decision of the Social Democrats at their Bad Godesberg Conference in 1961 to renounce their claims as a Marxist party. A majority of the SPD leadership felt that the party should abandon even its theoretical ties to Marxism in an attempt to attract votes from the middle class and to strengthen its image of loyalty to the Bundesrepublik. By divesting itself of its ties to Marxist theory and by offering up its affiliated *Sozialistische Deutsche Studentenbund* (SDS) as a sacrificial lamb, the SPD hoped to lose any lingering traces of radicalism which were still hindering the party from going beyond the working class as a voter base. Although by most standards the SPD had long since lost its "radical" traits or leanings, the Bad Godesberg Conference was the official presentation of the SPD as a party for all people, as opposed to a class party.

As the SPD moved towards an image of greater respectability among the West German middle class, it also gradually lost its reputation for social opposition and came still more to be seen as an integral fixture of the establishment of the Bundesrepublik. This was marked by the proposal of a Great Coalition government between the CDU/CSU and the SPD as an alternative to the CDU/CSU coalition with the FDP which then prevailed. The Great Coalition idea, pushed principally by Herbert Wehner within the SPD, was a further step to provide the SPD with the trust and confidence necessary, in Wehner's view, to achieve the status of a majority party in the Bundesrepublik.

With the diminishing of the SPD's role of social opposition, the political arena became increasingly open to a movement which would claim to offer "real" opposition to the government. The NPD, if it could successfully promote itself as a national opposition, could fill this role.

This trend became more evident as signs of discontent with the regime of Ludwig Erhard multiplied. As the mistakes and general lack of confidence in the Erhard government increased, there was a growing need for some party to voice opposition. As the crisis of the government grew and remained unsolved, the opportunity presented itself for opposition not only to the government, but to all three parties then represented in the Bundestag. For some the opposition to continuance of the Erhard government presented by the SPD and the FDP was not strong enough nor decisive enough.

The founding of the NPD was also favored by signs that the postwar economic miracle (*Wirtschaftswunder*) of West Germany was drawing to a close. Some of these difficulties, such as in the long-suffering coal industry, were in fact produced by the remarkable success in the modernization of West German industry, which found itself ever less dependent on coal as a basic fuel. Others, such as the growing distress of the West German farmer, could be laid in part to increased competition from abroad, especially from other Common Market countries. These trouble signals were still slight in late 1964, but they would steadily mount in 1965 and 1966 and aid the NPD in its search for a voter base.

During 1964 there were several attempts made on the far right to breathe new life into meaningless fragments of that end of the political spectrum. Not all elements of the far right participated in the founding of the NPD. The *Deutsche Gemeinschaft* (DG), for example, according to an account by Fred Richards,[1] was not even invited to the preparatory talks for the NPD founding. Rather, the neutralist-minded elements of the DG joined with the DFP (*Deutsche Freiheitspartei*) and other scattered rightists to form the *Aktionsge-meinschaft unabhängigen Deutschen* (Action Community of Independent Germans—AUD), which to date has had no electoral success.

The main elements which formed the original basis of the National Democratic Party were Adolf von Thadden's DRP party apparatus and rump elements of the old DP and BHE, all described in the previous chapter. The NPD came into being in Hanover on November 28, 1964, with a membership of 473. Titular leadership of the new party was bestowed upon Fritz Thielen, a leader of the DP from Bremen. Real control, however, rested in the hands of Adolf von Thadden, who held the loyalty of the party apparatus. As had been von Thadden's practice with the DRP, he preferred to hold the post of vice-chairman while putting forward another figure as a front man for the party. At the founding of the NPD, members were permitted to hold double membership with other parties as well; by 1966, when it was apparent that the NPD was the only viable vehicle for the

1. Fred Richards, *Die NPD*, (Munich: Günter Olzog Verlag, 1967), pp. 41–42.

rightists, several of the previous far-right parties were dissolved, either formally, as with the DRP in December of 1965, or informally through simple neglect.

There has been much publicity given to the charge that the NPD is a party of *Ehemalige* ("formers," meaning former Nazis). The NPD always replied that it was a party of the young, and that most of its members were too young to have been members of the NSDAP. While it will be shown later that the NPD is not really a youth party, it is true that former Nazis do not statistically predominate in total NPD membership. However, it is not the average member who actually runs the party; at the highest levels of the NPD party structure former NSDAP members are much more in evidence and in control. It is true that Thielen was not a member, nor was von Thadden an activist member of the NSDAP. However, of the 18 national committee members, 8 were former members of the NSDAP, and of the 218 county committee members in the state of North Rhine-Westphalia, 86 were former members of the National socialist party.[2]

The NPD is quick to point out that many former Nazis are now active in the CDU, SPD, and FDP, and that their past records are neither questioned nor denounced. As Fritz Thielen stated at a press conference in March, 1966:

> For a member of the NPD, a previous membership in the NS-DAP is a fatal sin. Herr Ahrens' former party comradship [with the NSDAP], his golden party symbol, his activity as county leader and state commissar, is forgiven, because he is connected with the SPD. Were he with us, he would be headline material.
>
> I can take my own case. I was among the founding members of the CDU in Bremen, represented the party [CDU] twelve years in the Bremen legislature and belonged to the state committee. Apparently I was at that time a positive element in our democratic system. As a member of the German Party (DP), as its state chairman and representative in the Bremen legislature, nothing bad was reported about me. Like a thunderbolt however this condition changed with my election as chairman of the NPD. The reason is undiscoverable.[3]

This is undoubtedly true in the sense that former NSDAP members now working within established parties are not berated for past asso-

2. Figures from a *Spiegel* study, Number 15/1966, pp. 30–44.
3. Fritz Thielen at a press conference in Bonn on March 31, 1966.

ciations as would be true were they NPD members. However, the present parties represented in the Bundestag are not proud of past NSDAP associations, nor do they allow the "rehabilitation" of the National Socialist past within their ranks as is true for the NPD. Nor do members with records of past NSDAP activity occupy most of the key positions within the CDU, SPD, or FDP as they do within the NPD. The notable exception of no less than Chancellor Kiesinger, who was a member of the NSDAP, does not alter the validity of this statement. Furthermore, Kiesinger's past record in the NSDAP is not looked upon with pride by the other party leaders, as it is for those within the NPD leadership.

At its birth the NPD inherited the news organs which had served the DRP and, as such, were under the control of Adolf von Thadden's clique. The old *Reichsruf* (*Clarion of the Reich*), weekly party newspaper of the DRP, was renamed *Deutsche Nachrichten* (*German Reports*), and has increased its circulation from twelve thousand to approximately forty-five thousand as of late 1966.

Another weekly newspaper which is in fact if not in form an organ of the NPD is the *Deutsche-Wochenzeitung* (*German Weekly Newspaper*). The personnel of the *DWZ* is essentially identical with that of *Deutsche Nachrichten* (*DN*), although there are some differences in the line taken by the two papers. The advantage which is gained by the *DWZ* is, as Fred Richards suggests, that as a supposedly independent paper, it can polemicize with greater freedom than the *DN*. *DN*, as an organ of a party which avows its loyalty to the democracy, must take greater care not to say anything which could bring the NPD before the courts on charges of advocating the overthrow of the republic. The publisher of the *DWZ* is Waldemar Schütz, who is also in charge of the printing and publication of the *DN*. Schütz, also a member of the NPD national committee, is an integral part of von Thadden's old DRP apparatus which is still intact and which constitutes the basic power structure of the National Democratic Party. Schütz, as mentioned above, an old National Socialist and member of the Waffen-SS, is also a partner in *Nation Europa*, monthly publication of the European neofascist movement. The articles for the *DWZ* are written primarily by old NSDAP functionaries—Heinrich Härtle, Enrich Kernmayr, and Dr. Peter Kleist—all of whom are also members of the von Thadden inner circle in the DRP and now the NPD.

The finances of the NPD for the year 1965, the first and least successful year for the party, consisted of an income of DM 332,000.[4] Of this income 40 percent was provided by the sale of official party publications, chiefly *Deutsche Nachrichten*. A further 33 percent of the party's revenues came from donations, and 24 percent from membership dues.

The finances of the NPD, as the party itself says, are "in order." The National Democrats are not a wealthy party, but they have been able to establish a relatively sound financial basis for their activities, unlike most other parties of the far right. The NPD, like the DRP, which forms its core, is able to call on its members to contribute generously to the party's cause.

That the party's income has increased greatly since 1965 is demonstrated by the fact that the NPD raised DM 200,000 for the printing and distribution of campaign material in the November, 1966, state election in Bavaria alone. In addition, the party gathered approximately DM 150,000 to be used for the construction of new offices for the party headquarters in Hanover.

The NPD, as a new and radical party, has also attracted larger audiences to its local meetings than have some older established parties. Usually an entrance fee of one or two marks was collected; thus such gatherings have been another lucrative source of income for the party.

From time to time rumors are heard to the effect that the NPD is being secretly financed from abroad. One such rumor has it that the party received financial aid from the John Birch Society. Another, going to the other end of the political spectrum, claims that the National Democrats are financed from East Germany through the "National Front" in East Berlin. This rumor is traceable to contacts which the DRP had with the East German "National Democratic Party of Germany," a puppet party constructed as a national-oriented front for the East German regime. Considering the difficulties which the DRP experienced because of such contacts, it is extremely doubtful that the NPD (West German) would risk entanglement with the like-named East German party.

More credible are stories that tell of NPD functionaries gathering funds for the party from former National Socialists in South America.

4. Richards, *Die NPD*, pp. 57–61.

However, all such rumors are to date unsubstantiated and should not detract attention from the main sources of NPD revenue which are within the Bundesrepublik, and which provide the National Democrats with the basis for their propaganda and organizational activities.

At its founding little publicity was given to the NPD by the German press. The news magazine *Spiegel* ran a short article describing the different factions which had combined to form the NPD, and the National Socialist backgrounds of some of its leaders.[5] The article intimated that while von Thadden was nominally only second-in-command and while he had said "not one word" at the founding, he was in fact the real power within the new party.

The *Spiegel* coverage, however, did present some of the general slogans which the NPD would use in the federal election campaign of 1965:

Instead of nihilistic destruction [we want] a healthy order, instead of national lack of esteem, once again the esteem.[6]

We want Germany not to remain on one hand a Russian province, on the other, an American satellite.[7]

Most of the German press, however, saw the NPD as just another in the long series of attempted mergers designed to revitalize the extreme right wing of West German politics. As such, no greater results were to be expected from this latest effort than from previous tries.

The NPD's first major electoral appearance came in the federal elections of September, 1965. Once again the West German press pointedly ignored the NPD except on one occasion a few weeks before the election. At that time the NPD leadership in one of its attempts to dramatize its stand, visited the graves of the German war criminals who were hanged and buried in Landsberg. They laid flowers at the graveside and a prepared statement was read to the press by the head of the NPD in Bavaria, Franz-Florian Winter: "We commemorate here all those who innocently lost their lives arbitrarily through force and the lust for power. While the whole world remembers such victims of Dachau and Bergen-Belsen, no one visits the graves here. . . . We

5. *Spiegel*, Number 50/1964, p. 67.
6. Fritz Thielen, then NPD chairman, cited in *Spiegel*, Number 50/1964, p. 67.
7. Emil Maier-Dorn, NPD national committeeman, cited in *Spiegel*, Number 50/1964, p. 67.

are doing that."[8] This story was covered in most of the West German press, and in even more detail and at greater length by much of the foreign press. Again *Spiegel* ran by far the most extensive West German account of the event, along with the past Nazi record of NPD leaders.

Most nonparty press coverage given to the NPD campaign, therefore, attacked the NPD as a neonazi party. Even this coverage was so minimal that after the elections only a small fraction of the voting populus could correctly identify the NPD as the new party of the far right.

Fritz Thielen, at one point in the campaign, said "We're figuring on getting 15 percent."[9] If this was so then the National Democrats were certainly disappointed by the election results of September 19, 1965. The NPD got only 2 percent of all votes cast, which represented an even greater decline in the electoral strength of the far right from 1961. The press reaction is perhaps best summarized by the *Allgemeine Zeitung* (Frankfurt) article:

> All parties regret the weight that was attached to the NPD in the foreign press during this election campaign. They pointed out that in all federal elections there have been such right-radical groups. If their amalgamation into a coalition party had now resulted in a higher percentage, still, basically not much would have been changed. As opposed to other countries this election again demonstrates the democratic stability of the Bundesrepublik.[10]

Most references to the NPD were short and tended to dismiss the new party as an already proven failure. *Spiegel* commented that the 1965 election had two basic features: first, the continued approach of the two major parties (SPD and CDU/CSU) to each other in program and slogan; second, the continued trend, evident since 1953, towards a two-party system.[11] There was no specific mention made of the NPD.

In summary, the first year of the NPD's existence seemed to confirm the original expectations of its eventual failure and collapse, as had been the pattern for all earlier right-radical parties in West

8. *Spiegel*, Number 37/1965, p. 51.

9. *Ibid.*, p. 46.

10. Editorial in *Allgemeine Zeitung* (Frankfurt), September 20, 1965, p. 1. Comment on the NPD's showing in the 1965 elections was similar in other national newspapers, *Die Welt, Frankfurter Rundschau,* and *Süddeutsche Zeitung.*

11. *Spiegel*, Number 39/1965, p. 21.

Germany. At the end of 1965 the NPD had still not even established itself as the name of a political party for most voters.

Yet, by that time the NPD had achieved one goal: it had been recognized within rightist ranks as the only hope for a viable electoral vehicle in the Bundesrepublik on the far right. In December of 1965 von Thadden staged the funeral of his DRP, and sounded the NPD's challenge for 1966. The first goal for 1966 was to gain at least some representation on local councils in community elections to be held in Bavaria, Schleswig-Holstein, and Hamburg early in the year. Also von Thadden pointed hopefully to what were already noticeable signs of the coming economic crisis as a basis for optimism: "Just read the opinion about the economic situation which the government has delivered. In that stands our whole propaganda."[12] The campaign of the NPD in Hamburg and Bavaria during the local elections in early 1966 did not arouse much national attention. Yet the results of the NPD campaign, especially in Hamburg, could not be ignored. In the election for the Hamburg parliament the NPD gained 3.9 percent of the vote, as opposed to the 1.8 percent which they had received in Hamburg in the federal elections of September, 1965. (See Table III.1.)

TABLE III.1

HAMBURG ELECTION RESULTS
(in percent)

Party	State: 1957–1966			Federal: 1965
	3/27/66	11/12/61	11/10/57	9/19/65
SPD	59.0	57.4	53.9	48.3
CDU	30.9	29.1	32.2	37.6
FDP	6.8	9.6	8.6	9.4
DFU	— *	2.9	—	2.7
NPD	3.9	—	—	1.8
DRP	—	0.9	0.4	—

* The dash means "not applicable to this category," i.e., that party did not enter this election.
SOURCE: Allgemeine Zeitung (Frankfurt), March 29, 1966, p. 3.

Even though the NPD was still not able to jump the 5 percent mark to gain seats in the Hamburg parliament, it had been able to more than double its share of the vote in only six months. Most concerned about

12. Adolf von Thadden, then vice-chairman of the NPD, cited in Spiegel, Number 51/1965, p. 66.

the NPD's showing were the Free Democrats, who declined from 9.6 percent of the vote (1961 elections) to 6.8 percent in 1966.

Still, the general reaction of the major parties was one of caution rather than concern: "The state chairman of the CDU, Blumenfeld, expressed dissatisfaction over the relatively small vote and seat gains of his party. The increase of the NPD should not, according to Blumenfeld's statement, be overestimated as a sign of danger, but it would be worthwhile to be watchful."[13] The showing for the NPD in Hamburg was even more surprising since that city has long been a stronghold of the left side of the political spectrum. Thus the Hamburg election got more notice than the equally illuminating local elections in Bavaria, where in early 1966 the National Democrats achieved vote turnouts which enabled them to gain representation in several local councils. In the important traditional right-wing stronghold of Mittelfranken, one of the seven administrative districts of Bavaria, the NPD got 6.4 percent of the vote. Many of these votes, as in Hamburg, came at the expense of the FDP. Since in Bavaria a party must get at least 10 percent of the vote in at least one of these seven administrative districts to gain seats in the state legislature (*Landtag*), and since Mittelfranken was the only district in which the Free Democrats previously had gained the necessary 10 percent, this was again an ominous sign that the NPD would make it difficult for the FDP to gain seats in the November state elections in Bavaria. In several Bavarian cities the NPD made even better showings, with 8.9 percent in Erlangen, 7.3 percent in Nürnberg, 8.4 percent in Bayreuth, 7.4 percent in Passau, and 8.9 percent in Kaufbeuren.[14]

The stage now was set for the November state elections in Hessen and Bavaria. During the summer of 1966 the signs of economic difficulties increased; the number of unemployed rose from 105,743 in August to 145,804 in October, with the expectations of still greater rises in unemployment for the coming months. (See Table III.2.) Concern over the imbalance in spending in the federal budget grew also as the Erhard regime began first to stumble and then fall in its efforts to save the situation. In the last week in October the Free Democrats broke their coalition with the Christian Democrats in the Bundestag and precipitated the governmental crisis. Erhard no longer

13. *Allgemeine Zeitung* (Frankfurt), March 29, 1966, p. 3.
14. Institut für angewandte Sozialwissenschaft (INFAS), *Rechtsstimmen unter der Lupe* (Bad Godesberg: April, 1966), p. 7.

TABLE III.2

INDICES OF THE ECONOMIC CRISIS IN THE BUNDESREPUBLIK

Unemployed		Workers on short time		Foreign workers	
Date	Number	Date	Number	Date	Number
1964*	169070				
1965*	147352	1965*	1105	1962*	629022
Aug. 1966	105743			1963*	773164
Oct. 1966	145804	Oct. 1966	18844	1964*	902459
Dec. 1966	371623	Dec. 1966	90383	1965*	1118616
Jan. 1967	621156	Jan. 1967	240160	June, 1966	1314031
Feb. 1967	673572	Feb. 1967	343718	Jan. 1967	1068025
Mar. 1967	576047				

* Taken on a sample day for each year.
SOURCE: *Statistisches Jahrbuch für die Bundesrepublik Deutschland*, 1967.

had a majority in the Bundestag, but no new majority had been formed. According to the Basic Law of the Bundesrepublik, a new majority must be formed before the old government can be voted out and replaced.

The Erhard government was clearly on its way out, but its successor had not yet appeared, and there were several possibilities. The government could call for new elections, or it could continue to rule as a minority government; it could be replaced by an SPD/FDP coalition government, or it could try to reconcile the FDP back into the old coalition; finally, the CDU could form a Great Coalition with the SPD. In addition, a new candidate for chancellor would have to be chosen for the CDU/CSU. The sorting out of these different possibilities would take time, and meanwhile the public's concern would grow as the economic crisis loomed. Unemployment would rise to 371,632 by December and then to 621,156 by January of 1967. Resentment against the more than 1.25 million foreign workers (*Gastarbeiter*) would rise as more German laborers found themselves actually out of work or threatened by unemployment. The longer the Bonn parties hesitated, the longer no government was formed to take strong action to meet the rising crisis, and the more the NPD would be able to attract voters with its slogans of protest against the *Gastarbeiter* and the *Bonner Parteien*.

It was in such an atmosphere that the last two weeks of the state election campaign in Hessen took place. The national press again largely ignored the NPD, except to publicize attacks on it. For example, the resignation of the Bavarian head of the NPD, Franz-Florian

Winter, from the party was given publicity, along with his statement
that he had resigned so that he would not be responsible if Germany
"was once again ruled by godless fanatics and thrown into misfortune."[15] Thielen had reportedly tried to convince Winter that he,
Thielen, could maintain control over the more radical elements in the
party, but Winter apparently saw the writing on the wall. He perceived that von Thadden's more radical DRP clique was slowly
strengthening its hold over the party and either converting or replacing those with relatively more moderate views. Winters' defection,
and denunciation of extremist control of the NPD, was heralded as
proof of the NPD's National Socialist tendencies.

The returns from the November 6 elections in Hessen gave the
NPD 7.9 percent of the vote and eight seats in the new Landtag. The
other right-wing entry, the GDP/BHE, got only 4.3 percent and thus
lost the six seats which it had held in the previous Landtag. The SPD
gained one seat for a total of fifty-two, the CDU lost two for a total
of twenty-six, and the FDP lost one for a total of ten. (See Table III.3.)

TABLE III.3

HESSEN ELECTION RESULTS

| | State: 1962 and 1966 | | | | Federal: 1965 |
| | November 6, 1966 | | November 11, 1962 | | September 19,1965 |
Party	percent	Seats	percent	Seats	percent
SPD	51.0	52	50.8	51	45.7
CDU	26.4	26	28.8	28	37.8
FDP	10.4	10	11.5	11	12.0
BHE	4.3	0	6.3	6	—
NPD	7.9	8			

SOURCE: *Allgemeine Zeitung* (Frankfurt), November 7, 1966, p. 1.

The press response to this first NPD reaction was a flood of
articles and statements giving several different analyses of the NPD
success. It was generally surmised that the NPD had drawn votes away
from the BHE, FDP, and CDU. It was noted that with its losses in
Hessen, the BHE no longer held seats in any state legislature. Bundes-
minister Heck (CDU) stated that the NPD was a sign that for the
younger generation not all expectations had been fulfilled. Herbert
Wehner (SPD) called the "symptoms of crisis in the democracy" the

15. *Allgemeine Zeitung* (Frankfurt), November 2, 1966, p. 1.

main reason for the success of the National Democrats. SPD chairman Willy Brandt labeled the NPD an "opportunist of the Bonn crisis." Most concern seemed to be directed at the bad image which the election results would produce abroad. The *Allgemeine Zeitung* editorialized: "The National Democrats have provided an unpleasant surprise with a vote percentage surpassing expectations. Their entrance into the Wiesbaden Landtag causes still more repercussions and damage in public opinion abroad than is justified by the facts."[16] The expectation of heavy foreign coverage of NPD success was justified. From every major capital of the world came statements of concern at this new appearance of right-radical strength in West Germany. In the November 8, 1966, issue of the *Allgemeine Zeitung* were reports of NPD election victory from London, Washington, Paris, Moscow, Zurich, and Rome. From the Hessen election on November 6 to the Bavarian election on November 20, the German press was filled with reports and analyses of the NPD, its leaders, the speculated causes of its success, and predictions of its future. Many German reports emphasized that the NPD was not something new, that there had always been right-radical parties in the Bundesrepublik. One such article, again in the *Allgemeine Zeitung,* stood next to a report on the decline in the number of open jobs from 1965 to 1966 and the climb of unemployment from a low of 33,000 in 1965 to more than 145,000 by October, 1966.

Most of these articles noted the NPD's relative weakness among Catholics and their reported strength among refugees from the eastern regions now held by Poland, the Soviet Union, and Czechoslovakia. The National Democrats were seen as drawing most of their votes from former BHE and FDP supporters, and it was thought that the FDP's position in particular was endangered in Bavaria.

News coverage of the Bavarian election campaign gave heavy play to its possible role in determining the formation of a new government in Bonn. The CDU/CSU was still in the process of choosing its new party candidate for Chancellor, with Barzel, Gerstenmaier, Kiesinger, and Schröder as the possible choices. The Protestant wing of the party, of whom Erhard had been the head, now supported Schröder. When the CSU faction under Franz-Josef Strauss announced its backing of Kurt Georg Kiesinger, the Catholic *Minister-präsident* of Baden-Württemberg, Gerstenmaier, who had been a

16. *Allgemeine Zeitung* (Frankfurt), November 7, 1966, p. 3.

leading contender, bowed out of the race. Rainer Barzel, another Catholic candidate, still remained in the running, but it became clear now that Kiesinger was confirmed in that role on the third ballot of the party leadership on November 10, 1966.

As the Bavarian elections neared, it became clear that the CDU/CSU could not continue as a minority government. With the position of the FDP becoming weaker at every election, chances for a new CDU/FDP coalition also were fading. The possibility remained for new federal elections to be called, but the dangers in such a move clearly outweighed the gains for the Christian Democrats. The most likely outcome would be a substantial gain for the SPD and, perhaps just as likely, the entrance of the NPD into the Bundestag. Whether the expected SPD gains would be great enough to form an SPD-led government was also in doubt; new elections thus might not solve the problem of finding a new government, but instead tighten the dead-lock. Chances for an SPD/FDP coalition were still being discussed, but such a coalition would have a majority of only a few votes and would have to face the great problems of the economic crisis without a really dependable majority in the Bundestag. This left the possi-bility of a Great Coalition between the CDU and SPD with the FDP as the opposition in the Bundestag. Such a coalition would provide the vote strength in the Bundestag needed to carry through strong measures to meet the problems of stabilizing the economy, although also it would leave the role of opposition to a relatively weak FDP. Still, while the Great Coalition appeared more and more to be the final solution which would eventually be reached, there would be pro-longed debates between the CDU and SPD to work out the problems of chancellorship, cabinet posts, and a common program for the new government.

From November 6 to November 20 the German press was oc-cupied with three major themes: the search for a new government, the growing economic anxieties, and the NPD.

The NPD was denounced by the Bavarian CSU and the trade union organization (DGB) in Bavaria. Both warned young voters especially not to vote NPD in the coming elections.[17]

An analysis of the National Democrats by Helmut Hercles doubted the ability of the NPD to resist the internal strains between the more moderate elements and the radicals. Hercles suggested that

17. *Allgemeine Zeitung* (Frankfurt), November 14, 1966, p. 1.

the NPD might then break up into meaningless fragments, following the example of previous strong rightist groups.[18]

Other reports emphasized the campaign of the NPD in Bavaria, especially in Mittelfranken. Otto Hess—an old NSDAP member, and propaganda chief of the NPD—was reported as replying to a question as to what the program of the NPD was: "We refuse to present a program. It is necessary only to have the will to make something out of the present situation."[19] Several NPD slogans denouncing the Common Market for "oppression" of the German farmer and denouncing NATO were cited. NPD chairman Fritz Thielen was quoted as stating: "The party stands resolutely behind the German soldier of the past and the present. . . . We are deeply unhappy that the federal army (*Bundeswehr*) does not stand under German command."[20]

Voting returns from November 20 confirmed the strength of the new party on the right. The National Democrats got 7.4 percent of the vote in all of Bavaria, and 12.2 percent of the vote in the district of Mittelfranken. The party, thus, by surpassing the Bavarian 10-percent clause, qualified for entrance into the 204 member Bavarian *Landtag* with 15 seats. The Free Democrats received 5.1 percent of the vote, a decline of only 0.8 percent from their showing in the previous state elections in 1962, but in the key district of Mittelfranken, which had been their stronghold, they lost votes heavily to the NPD, getting only 9 percent of the vote there and thus failing to gain at least 10 percent of the vote in any district. In addition, the Bavarian Party (BP), which had held 8 seats in the old Landtag, failed to get the necessary 10 percent in their strong district of Lower Bavaria, and so lost their seats too. For the most part the SPD and CSU representation remained stable, with the CSU gaining two seats for a total of 110 and the SPD retaining its former strength of 79 seats. (See Table III.4.)

Since neither CSU nor SPD had received any notable gains or losses, most of the postelection interest was focused again on the NPD and the elimination of the FDP (and the BP) from the Landtag.

The German press now realized that the NPD was not a regional phenomenon: "After last Sunday the conclusion is near that

18. Helmut Hercles in *Allgemeine Zeitung* (Frankfurt), November 10, 1966, p. 2.

19. Otto Hess, in *Allgemeine Zeitung* (Frankfurt), November 16–17, 1966, p. 2.

20. Fritz Thielen, in *Spiegel*, Number 37/1965, p. 51.

TABLE III.4

BAVARIAN ELECTION RESULTS

| | State: 1962 and 1966 | | | | Federal: 1965 |
| | November 20, 1966 | | November 25, 1962 | | September 19, 1966 |
Party	percent	Seats	percent	Seats	percent
CSU	48.2	110	47.5	108	55.6
SPD	35.8	79	35.3	79	33.1
FDP	5.1	0	5.9	9	7.3
BP	3.4	0	4.8	8	—
NDP	7.4	15	—	—	2.7
GDP/BHE	0.1	0	5.1	0	—

SOURCE: *Allgemeine Zeitung* (Frankfurt), November 22, 1966, p. 4.

in the Bundesrepublik about seven percent of the voters lean to the right extremist party."[21]

The other parties, especially the CDU/CSU and SPD, were called upon to explain in stronger terms the harmfulness of the NPD. It was felt now that not only the FDP and other right-wing splinter parties were losing votes to the new party of the right, but that even the CDU/CSU and SPD voters were not immune to NPD appeals.

Once again, heavy emphasis was laid upon the foreign reaction to the latest NPD triumph. The November 22 issue of the *Allgemeine Zeitung* carried reports of reactions to the Bavarian elections and the NPD from Zurich, Madrid, Rome, Tokyo, London, Paris, Brussels, and Washington. Most of these foreign reactions sounded a note of alarm not only at the fact of the NPD success but also at its timing. The turning of many voters to the NPD at a time of economic crisis prompted some foreign observers to speculate that many West Germans still held little faith in the democracy, and during this crisis period were turning to antidemocratic movements.

The Bavarian election results sparked a series of predictions for NPD successes in state elections to be held in 1967 in Schleswig-Holstein, Rheinland-Pfalz, Niedersachsen, and the city of Bremen. Having first ignored the National Democrats only to be surprised at their victories in Hessen and Bavaria, many analysts now went to the other extreme and predicted enormous gains for the NPD in the 1967 round of elections. Some predictions and warnings of future triumphs were extended even farther than 1967. Some pointed to the fact that

21. Editorial in *Allgemeine Zeitung* (Frankfurt), November 22, 1966, p. 1.

in 1928, only five years before the Nazi seizure of power in the Weimar Republic, the NSDAP had received only 2 percent of the vote in the whole Reich. Dr. Kuhnl of the Institute for Political Science in Marburg, looking ahead five years from 1967, warned of a similar fate for the Bonn Republic.

> Dr. Kuhnl accused the German public of an "enormous ignorance" in not wanting to admit the true causes of the rise of the National Democratic Party. The government, and government parties, should not be surprised when their dubious and undemocratic motives in altering an election law lead to an even stronger growth of this party. If the economic recession continues, it is possible that the NPD could win an absolute majority in the 1972 federal elections.[22]

Most speculation, however, centered around more immediate election possibilities. Of particular interest was the election to be held on April 23 in Schleswig-Holstein. Here many factors seemed to indicate a large NPD turnout. First and foremost, Schleswig-Holstein had been one of the strongest Nazi bastions. It was the first province in the Reich to give the NSDAP an absolute majority, Schleswig-Holstein is an almost completely Protestant state, with a large farming population. The state has one of the lowest income levels in West Germany, and the economic crisis was creating much discontent among farm groups and unskilled workers, especially dike workers along the western coast. Discontent among farmers had been growing for years as a result of increasing competitive pressures from other Common Market countries under agreements with the Market. For the first time since the depression year the black flag, with white plow and red sword symbolizing the farmer rebellion, was seen at protest marches in Schleswig-Holstein. Edmund Rehwinkel, leader of the major farmers' association (*Deutscher Bauernverband*) threatened to break his traditional alliance with the Christian Democrats and said that he wouldn't mind if a "few hundred thousand farmers voted NPD." Rehwinkel obviously was attempting to use the NPD as a threat to get more subsidies for the farmers, but his announcement that the NPD was an acceptable party for farmers to vote was almost certain to increase the NPD's attraction for the rural population, regardless of the final disposition of the question of subsidies. The farmers were generally looking for a way to symbolize their protest, and the head of their own farm organization had pointed the way.

22. *Allgemeine Zeitung* (Giessen), January 19, 1967, p. 10.

The situation among coastal dike workers was also seen as a potential gold mine for the NPD. Here, expected cutbacks in federal spending would sharply reduce the number of unskilled workers hired for these public works projects. The NPD had already been at work campaigning among these workers, and it was expected that this would pay off handsomely in the April elections.

Another advantage for the NPD was seen in the large numbers of refugees and emigrants from Communist-held areas who had settled in Schleswig-Holstein. In some districts up to 40 percent of the population was composed of such people, and the NPD had shown great strength among emigrant and refugee settlements in the local Bavarian elections in early 1966.

In terms of the Landtag calculus, the SPD held twenty-nine seats, the CDU thirty-four, the FDP five and the Danish minority party (SSW) one seat. For fifteen years the state had been governed by a CDU/FDP coalition. If now the FDP were to fall below the 5 percent level and thus lose all its seats, with the NPD taking the FDP place as it had done in Bavaria, the only possible solution for a government in all likelihood would be another Great Coalition between the CDU and SPD. Since neither CDU nor SPD would form a coalition with the National Democrats, a Great Coalition solution would be forced upon the Landtag. However, the dynamic young leader of the Schleswig-Holstein SPD, Joachim Steffen, was a bitter enemy of CDU leader Lemke. As Helmut Aht, political correspondent for *Die Welt* concluded in this prognosis for the election: "CDU and FDP, as well as the SPD, have declared that never would they form a coalition with the NPD. The SPD is pressing upwards. A Great Coalition would be the lesser evil. A Great Coalition, however, would be a Lemke-Steffen government. He who knows both men knows that that is hardly imaginable."[23] In view of these factors, many observers looked to Schleswig-Holstein for the first NPD opportunity to get over 10 percent of the vote. Fred Richards, in his analysis of future NPD electoral victories, wrote: "Even opponents of the NPD give them at least 15, if not 20, percent of the vote, locally even 30 percent."[24]

Another state election would be held on April 23 (on the same day as the Schleswig-Holstein election) in the state of Rheinland-Pfalz. Certain sections of Rheinland-Pfalz had been early Nazi strong-

23. Helmut Aht in *Die Welt*, February 14, 1967, p. 6.
24. Richards, *Die NPD*, p. 20.

holds and were also DRP strongholds, with a loyal voter base among wine growers and farmers. Like Schleswig-Holstein, Rheinland-Pfalz is one of the poorest states in the Bundesrepublik.

Again in Rheinland-Pfalz the possibility arose that the NPD might drive the FDP from the Landtag. If this occurred and the SPD and CDU strength in seats remained close, as it had been in the previous Landtag, the only political solution would again be a Great Coalition in the state between the CDU and SPD. This would give the NPD the opportunity to play the role of sole opposition to the government in the legislature, a role which it had already claimed for itself while still outside the Landtag.

Here the prophets were somewhat more conservative than in Schleswig-Holstein, but all were certain that the NPD would be represented in the next Landtag. Estimates of political observers in Bonn ranged as high as 20 percent.[25]

A major test and opportunity for the NPD in 1967 was considered to lie in the June 4 elections in Niedersachsen. The state of Niedersachsen is predominantly Protestant with a considerable farming sector as well as heavy industry. In the early 1950s this state had had a strong right extremist *Sozialistische Reichspartei* (SRP) voter following before that party was banned as undemocratic. As late as 1959 rightist parties in Niedersachsen were still able to earn nearly one fourth of the vote (20.7 percent for the GDP and 3.6 percent for the DRP). The NPD leadership announced that it was figuring on a vote percentage of at least 15 percent in June, and at the end of 1966 this did not seem unreasonable to many observers.

As for the October elections in Bremen, there was speculation that the NPD would be able to combine old DP voter bases with the DRP strength, which as late as 1959 gained over 20 percent of the total vote (16.4 percent for the GDP and 3.8 percent for the DRP).

Several factors were to combine in the first months of 1967 to change the prospects of the National Democrats from the above predictions of great triumphs to hopes that the NPD was about to destroy itself.

The first was the rising popularity of the Great Coalition and the Kiesinger-Brandt leadership. After much negotiation and development of a common program of action the Great Coalition of the black

25. *Ibid.*, p. 21.

(CDU/CSU) and the red (SPD) was initiated on December 1, 1966, with Kurt Georg Kiesinger as *Bundeskanzler*. This act alone served to ease some fears of continued inaction in regard to the economic crisis. A new cabinet had been formed, with Karl Schiller (SPD) as Economic Minister and Franz-Josef Strauss (CSU) as Finance Minister, to attack the problems of putting the federal budget in order and renewing the badly shaken business confidence in the basic soundness of the economy.

Unemployment, which had climbed at an alarming rate from just over 105,000 in August of 1966 to 371,623 in December and to 673,572 by February of 1967, had been expected to go over the 1,000,-000-mark in the spring of 1967. Instead, it had dropped to 576,067 by March. By March 16, the press could report that unemployment had reached its high-water mark and was receding, that the rate of unemployment had dropped from 3.1 percent to 2.9 percent in less than a month.[26] By the beginning of April, unemployment had dropped by 100,000 from its February high and the number of workers forced to work short hours had fallen from 343,718 in February to 251,700. It could be announced that the number of available jobs had risen by some 27,000 to over 300,000.[27]

This progress, coming in the first hundred days of the Great Coalition, gave a great impetus to popular confidence in the government's ability to deal with the problems facing the country.

In addition to its successes in reestablishing a measure of economic confidence, the Great Coalition also launched a new policy towards the countries of Eastern Europe, a new *Ostpolitik*. This policy, led by Vice Chancellor and Foreign Minister Willy Brandt, aimed at a normalization of diplomatic relations with the nations of Eastern Europe, with the exception of the East German regime. This was a reversal of the former Hallstein doctrine that the Bundesrepublik could not maintain normal relations with any nation which recognized the *Deutsche Demokratische Republik* (DDR). A corollary was now added, that nations which were Communist and therefore had recognized the Ulbricht government, would be treated as exceptions to the Hallstein formula. The first success of the new Ostpolitik initiative came quickly with the establishment of normal diplomatic relations between Bonn and the Bucharest regime. On the heels of the exchange

26. *Allgemeine Zeitung* (Frankfurt), March 16, 1967, p. 1.
27. *Allgemeine Zeitung* (Frankfurt), April 6, 1967, p. 1.

of ambassadors between the Bundesrepublik and Rumania came signs and speculation that there were also chances for similar success with Yugoslavia, Czechoslovakia, and Hungary.

The foreign policy of the Bundesrepublik, which had so long seemed listless and defensive, had suddenly taken the initiative and made some quick advances. Only the Polish and East German Communist regimes steadfastly denounced the new Ostpolitik as an aggressive attempt to split the Eastern bloc. In fact this new approach to relations with Eastern Europe had caught the East German and Polish regimes by surprise and had caused them to overreact out of fear that they would be isolated from the other Communist nations of Eastern Europe by the attractive offer of normal diplomatic, and especially trade, relationships with the Bundesrepublik.

These two major successes of the Kiesinger-Brandt government in their first few months in office redounded to the credit of the new coalition, and especially to the popularity of Chancellor Kiesinger.

In addition, it appeared that, despite Rehwinkel's threats of supporting the NPD, the president of the *Deutscher Bauernverband* would still remain basically with the Christian Democrats. Rehwinkel earlier had seemed ready to become the first major establishment leader openly to back the National Democrats. Rehwinkel's mere mention of the NPD as a possible protest vote undoubtedly brought many farmers into the voter following of the right-radicals, but his solid endorsement of the NPD would have given the NPD its first major breakthrough in the established social organizations of the Bundesrepublik.

At the farm organization's convention in Dortmund in early March, however, Rehwinkel turned back attempts by the NPD to transform the meeting into an endorsement of the National Democratic Party. Rehwinkel had repeated his threat that if the farmers' demands were not met, the Christian Democrats could expect to lose farmers votes. At this point, several NPD members unrolled party banners from the balconies of the hall. They were met, however, with boos and angry gestures, and several scuffles broke out. After some time, order was restored, and Rehwinkel admonished NPD members against such propaganda tactics at the convention. The farm leader then continued to castigate the old Erhard government, but he left the new Great Coalition relatively unscathed. Apparently Rehwinkel saw greater advantage in giving the Great Coalition a chance to satisfy farmer discontent than in leading the farmers into a radical opposition against the government.

With this to its credit, the Great Coalition could be expected at least to hold the line against the NPD in the coming state elections. Then, in March, the first signs of a deep split within the National Democratic Party appeared to threaten the very existence of that party. Since NPD beginnings in November, 1964, some analysts had predicted that sooner or later the DRP clique under Adolf von Thadden would clash with the DP faction led by Fritz Thielen. These analysts assumed that when this final showdown occurred, the NPD would be split into its original components, with neither splinter party remaining of any political consequence. However, the DRP apparatus had been working slowly but surely to win old DP functionaries over to von Thadden's side and, by early 1967, von Thadden felt sure enough of his hegemony to begin directly squeezing out the remaining top figures still loyal to Thielen or, better defined, not yet loyal to von Thadden. On February 5 von Thadden was elected chairman of the NPD organization in the important state of Niedersachsen. The ousted chairman, Dr. Lothar Kühne, belonged to the more conservative Thielen group. In an attempt to regain Kühne's position as chairman, another leader of the Thielen group, Winkelmann, brought suit against von Thadden's election as a violation of party bylaws.

On March 7, 1967, it was reported that the NPD national committee had voted 16 to 2 to back von Thadden's position, and they called upon Winkelmann to drop his suit in the interests of the party.[28] Thielen's associates, however, refused to drop the suit, giving rise to hopes in the press that the NPD was about to enter a self-destructive internal struggle. News of the impending NPD intraparty struggle came just as the Kiesinger-Brandt regime was being generally praised for the achievements of the Great Coalition in its first hundred-day honeymoon period. Also it happened at a time when the NPD was coming under press attack in the Schleswig-Holstein and Rheinland-Pfalz election campaigns. In Rheinland-Pfalz, the press in particular attacked the National Democrats' campaign brochures which charged that each citizen of Rheinland-Pfalz was being taxed in the amount of DM 114.40 (about $28.50) for reparations dating back to the Third Reich. Official figures were cited giving the actual cost per citizen for

28. *Allgemeine Zeitung* (Frankfurt), March 7, 1967, p. 5.

reparations as DM 13.92, with an extra DM 3.63 for administrative costs and 2 to 3 marks for court costs.[29] At most reparations costs could not be construed as more than approximately DM 20. Under threat of court suit for such falsification of war reparation costs, always a prime propaganda target for the NPD, the party eventually was forced to rip the offensive pages out of its leaflets before they could be distributed.

On March 8, the Eighth Civil Chamber of the Bremen State Court ruled that von Thadden's election as chairman of the NPD in Niedersachsen had violated the party bylaws and was therefore void. The previous chairman, Kühne, was confirmed as chairman of the NPD in that state.

The Bremen court decision seemed a clear victory for the Thielen group within the party in the face of growing signs of their isolation. Perhaps emboldened by the court ruling, Thielen took to the offensive and announced on March 10 that he had thrown von Thadden, Otto Hess, Maier-Dorn and five other members of the Niedersachsen state committee out of the NPD for "actions damaging to the party."[30] Thielen announced that he had taken this action to prevent the party from the possibility of being banned as undemocratic. If von Thadden's right-radical clique were to triumph, said Thielen, the NPD would stand in danger of such a ban.

Simultaneously it was reported that party state committees loyal to von Thadden had called an extraordinary conference of the NPD national committee to meet in Frankfurt to deal with the question of expulsions. The reinstated NPD chairman in Niedersachsen, however, charged that such a meeting would be illegal and that neither he nor Thielen would attend.[31]

The conference in Frankfurt on March 11, 1967 resulted in the decision to reinstate von Thadden and his associates. Further, it was announced that Thielen had been thrown out of the party by his own Bremen state organization, and that his associates Kühne and Fritz Winkelmann had been suspended from their party offices. Von Thadden and Otto Hess directed the performance from a nearby hotel, as the conference voted to have the NPD chairman in Baden-

29. *Allgemeine Zeitung* (Frankfurt), March 9, 1967, p. 3.
30. Fritz Thielen, then NPD chairman, cited from in *Allgemeine Zeitung* (Frankfurt), March 11, 1967, p. 3.
31. *Ibid.*

Württemberg, Wilhelm Gutmann, assume the role of acting national chairman.

Thielen and his associates did show up for about twenty minutes at the sitting, primarily to announce their intention to challenge the proceedings with another court suit. As Thielen was about to leave, the Hamburg NPD chief, Schweimer, called out, "A traitor [*Volksschädling*] goes." The word *Volksschädling* belongs to the vocabulary of the National Socialist era and has specific connotations within the Nazi ideology. Thielen threatened that he might bring a libel suit against Schweimer for that remark.[32]

Later, von Thadden and Hess arrived at the sitting to celebrate their victory. Von Thadden told an English reporter, in English, "Thielen is out."

The West German press hailed these developments as "Chaos in the NPD": "The conflict now unfolding in the NPD, was unavoidable. Heterogeneous forces, moderates to the right of the middle, radicals of the far right, were attached to this conglomeration of rightists."[33] Along with reports of the Thielen-von Thadden struggle in the party and in the courts were reports of resignations from the NPD of members who were dismayed or disillusioned by this course of events. For example, it was widely reported that the NPD chairman in Berlin, Klaus Ehlers, had resigned his office and had walked out of the party as a result of the internal struggles.

Ehlers announced that he had not been able to contend with his deputy chairman, Gerhard Borris, who was, in Ehlers' words, one of the "unreformable ex-Nazis." After the apparent victory of von Thadden's more radical group, Ehlers gave up the cause of trying to keep the party on a more moderate course.

Stories of party resignations and formation of meaningless, rightist splinter groups were to become common in the next few months, giving the impression that the NPD was indeed fading. On March 14, it was reported that Joachim Kotzias, a former NPD deputy county chairman who had been expelled by the von Thadden wing of the NPD in December of 1966, now planned to form a *National-*

32. *Die Welt*, March 13, 1967. The word *Volksschädling* means much more than just "traitor"; in the language of the right-radicals, it connotes one who has betrayed his cultural heritage, who has become an antisocial parasite. There is no real English equivalent.

33. *Ibid.*

Liberale Volkspartei or a *Liberal-Nationale Volkspartei* as an alternative to the NPD. On March 23 the press reported that the former
county chairman of the NPD in Beche/Unterweser, Reims, had
called for the founding of an "independent NPD."[34]

Then on April 3 Franz-Florian Winter, who had left his position as NPD chairman in Bavaria over similar concerns in November
of 1966, announced that he was ready to form a new party together
with Fritz Thielen. The combined impression of these reports was
that the NPD was coming apart at the hinges and that its strength was
being diminished piece by piece through defection and the inception
of new rightist parties. The fact that none of these newly founded
parties would ever get off the ground was not yet clear. Nor was it
seen that while a few individuals defected from the National Democrats, the party structure remained completely intact.

Still, it was true that the internal party struggle complicated
NPD election campaigns in Schleswig-Holstein and Rhineland-Pfalz.
Although von Thadden had been able to hold the party organization
firmly behind him, it was not yet clear whether Thielen could regain
his post as chairman through court action. It was also not certain that
von Thadden could safely assume the NPD chairmanship in Niedersachsen. To act on the presumption that Thielen and associates were
legally out of office might be dangerous, since it would involve the
possibility of a total ban on the party for undemocratic practices.
Therefore, von Thadden and Hess directed party campaigns by tele-
phone without actually taking over the party central headquarters.
This did not mean, however, that Lothar Kühne and Fritz Winkelmann were allowed to preside over the party apparatus either. Associates of von Thadden notified Kühne that his election as chairman
in Niedersachsen in April of 1966 had not been legal, and that he
therefore could not use the party headquarters facilities to continue
the intraparty struggle.

In any event, estimates of electoral outcomes for the NPD in
the coming elections were now produced on the basis of the new party
split. Whereas earlier the NPD had been seen as getting about 15
percent in Rheinland-Pfalz, it was now expected to net only 7.5 to 8.5
percent, still enough, however, to gain seats in the Landtag.[35]

34. *Allgemeine Zeitung* (Frankfurt), March 23, 1967, p. 3.
35. *Allgemeine Zeitung* (Frankfurt), March 14, 1967, p. 2.

Von Thadden tried to keep up the appearance of optimism for the April elections. Informed of a survey by Elisabeth Noelle-Neumann's Allensbach Institute, in which the NPD vote percentage for Schleswig-Holstein was reckoned at 8 percent, von Thadden replied: "If Frau Noelle-Neumann has calculated only 8 percent for us in the North [Schleswig-Holstein] then we'll get twice that much for sure. That's just how it was in Hessen and Bavaria. She miscalculated there too."[36]

While Thielen's suit to regain chairmanship of the party was still pending, von Thadden launched a further attack on the former chairman. Von Thadden explained Thielen's attempt to expel the DRP clique in conspiratorial terms: "I know for sure that Thielen is in contact with the security police. They have told him: Throw Thadden out, and then you won't have to worry about a ban on your party."[37] This charge of collusion between the authorities and Thielen was immediately denied by Thielen, who threatened another libel suit against von Thadden.

On March 22, the Bremen court again supported Thielen's claims and upheld his position as the legally elected chairman of the NPD.[38] Yet by this time it was already becoming clear that, court decision or no, Thielen was in fact powerless within the party. At this point, the Bundesrepublik was treated to the ludicrous sight of a party chairman in search of a party. Thielen and von Thadden engaged in a series of petty encounters which took on the atmosphere of a low farce. Thielen, as chairman, decided to impound all party records and even the furniture at NPD headquarters. When he arrived there with moving vans and police, however, he found the offices empty. Von Thadden and friends had moved everything out for safekeeping. For the next several weeks, NPD leaders hid keys, envelopes, stamps, and other official party facilities from the party's own chairman. This is illustrated in a letter written by Thielen to all NPD members sometime in April, 1967, but released on May 2:

This is the text of a letter which should have reached you three weeks ago. Those who fear the truth hindered this by violating legal order and by behaving as robbers. It is superfluous to say that Herr

36. Adolf von Thadden, in *Die Zeit*, March 17, 1967, p. 3.
37. Adolf von Thadden, in *Allgemeine Zeitung* (Frankfurt), March 23, 1967, p. 3.
38. *Ibid.*

von Thadden, in accordance with the decision of March 28, not only declared himself ready to place the addressed envelopes at my disposal, and then broke his word to me, but also broke his word to Herr Dr. Kühne that he would leave the cabinet key at my disposal so that I could address the envelopes myself to party friends.

Experience seems to prove it natural for Herr von Thadden to break his word, and to lie and betray those with whom he works; this can be proved by many examples. That is his policy and his lack of political character. It would be sad for the German people if such people were to win political influence.[39]

Thielen lists the charges against von Thadden and Otto Hess which led him to throw them out of the party. In addition Thielen implies that von Thadden had misused party funds. He closes with an appeal to overthrow the "Thadden-Hess clique" and to save the party. Thielen of course knew by May 2 that there was not the slightest hope of his triumph with the NPD. On April 16, in a party state-committee sitting in Bad Gandersheim, Harbord Grone-Endebrock, loyal to von Thadden, had been elected the new state chairman in Niedersachsen over Hans-Joachim Richard by a vote of 105 to 74, replacing Dr. Kühne, who had now quit the party. More likely Thielen, in his last act as chairman, was preparing the ground for the formation of his own new rightist party: "I am convinced that nationally oriented patriots will find a way to free themselves from these destructive forces and their henchmen, in order to promote the breakthrough of a true national self-consciousness. Only a trustworthy national party will have a place in the future and speak successfully to a great voter class."[40]

Such was the state of the National Democratic Party a week before the April 23 elections in Schleswig-Holstein and Rheinland-Pfalz. The party was not split, but was in disarray; the press had given extensive coverage to the Thielen-Thadden fiasco, remarking pointedly about the state of order within the party of "law and order."

The Great Coalition, on the other hand, was still enjoying the fruits of its first successes from its new Ostpolitik and the restoration of business confidence. Then, on April 19, only four days before the elections, Dr. Konrad Adenauer, *der Alte*, the grand old man of the CDU/CSU and first Chancellor of the Bundesrepublik, passed away.

39. Excerpts from a letter: Fritz Thielen to all NPD members, dated May 2, 1967.
40. *Ibid.*

The effect of his death so close to election time cannot be exactly determined, but it is safe to say that some voters who might have strayed from the CDU to the NPD voted their traditional party as a final mark of respect for Dr. Adenauer. It is fairly clear too, especially in Rheinland-Pfalz which has a large Catholic population, that many Catholics who would have voted SPD voted for the party of their faith and the party of Dr. Adenauer, a devout Catholic.

The results of the elections of April 23 were disappointing for the NPD. In Schleswig-Holstein the National Democrats got only 5.8 percent of the vote, though it had widely been forecast that in this former Nazi stronghold the new right-radicals would certainly get over 10 percent. Instead, this was their worst showing of all the state elections they had entered since November of 1966. They captured only four seats in the 73 member Landtag. The CDU maintained its former total of 34 seats, the SPD gained one for a total of 30, and the FDP lost one for a total of four. The Danish minority party, SSW, retained its single seat. (See Table III.5.) None of the complications

TABLE III.5

SCHLESWIG-HOLSTEIN STATE ELECTION RESULTS: 1962 AND 1967

Party	April 23, 1967		September 23, 1962	
	percent	Seats	percent	Seats
CDU	46.0	34	45.0	34
SPD	39.4	30	39.2	29
FDP	5.9	4	7.9	5
SSW	1.9	1	2.3	1
DFU	0.9	0	1.2	0
NPD	5.8	4	—	—

SOURCE: *Allgemeine Zeitung* (Frankfurt), April 24, 1967, p. 3.

which had been foreseen as the result of a large NPD vote materialized. The FDP vote declined from 7.9 to 5.9 percent of the total, but the Free Democrats remained in the Landtag, and the old CDU/FDP coalition was retained in power. The SPD, which had waged a vigorous campaign under Joachim Steffen, the rising angry young man of the SPD, was somewhat disappointed by its meager gains, but in comparison to SPD losses in Rheinland-Pfalz the SPD could consider its northern campaign a success. The effects of Adenauer's death had been too much to overcome and the sympathy for the CDU undoubtedly reduced SPD gains. However, Steffen's outspoken opposition to the CDU/FDP coalition had also turned many dissatisfied and frustrated voters away from the NPD to the Social Democrats as the voice of the opposition. Especially among job-threatened dike workers on the coast and textile workers in cities like Neumünster, Steffen's defense of the anxious and his demands for action in their behalf kept these working-class groups within the SPD and accordingly diminished the vote of the NPD. In district after district where surveys had indicated large NPD returns there were instead gains for the Social Democrats. The Schleswig-Holstein SPD had shown the ability of the Social Democrats to retain at least some of their former reputation as the party of social opposition, and had demonstrated that when a viable social opposition is offered, the NPD's potential is reduced.

In Rheinland-Pfalz the National Democrats did somewhat better (6.9 percent of the vote), although through the electoral system of the state they still received only four seats in the hundred-member Landtag. (See Table III.6.) In Rheinland-Pfalz the effects of Ade-

TABLE III.6
RHEINLAND-PFALZ STATE ELECTION RESULTS: 1963 AND 1967

Party	April 23, 1967		March 31, 1963	
	percent	Seats	percent	Seats
CDU	46.7	49	44.4	46
SPD	36.8	39	40.7	43
FDP	8.3	8	10.1	11
NPD	6.9	4	—	—
DFU	1.2	0	1.3	0

SOURCE: *Allgemeine Zeitung* (Frankfurt), April 24, 1967, p. 3.

nauer's death and the popularity of the new Catholic Chancellor, Kiesinger, were more apparent than in the Protestant North. The SPD lost four of its former forty-three seats while the CDU gained three for a total of forty-nine. The Free Democrats kept eight of their eleven seats, and remained the coalition partner of the CDU in the state government. Once again, the election had not changed the basic complexion of the Landtag, with one exception, that the National Democrats were now represented with four seats. The old coalition which had governed for years continued in power, with the SPD as the loyal opposition. The FDP had lost some of its seats, but with 8.3 percent of the vote it remained comfortably above the 5 percent cutoff point.

The National Democrats candidly expressed disappointment at

the return. To some analysts the NPD appeared to have been stopped in its rise, but had reached a relatively stable plateau of from 6 to 8 percent of the electorate throughout the Bundesrepublik.

With the election returns in, the NPD continued its internal struggle to restore order in time for the June 4 election in Niedersachsen. The party announced that a full party conference would be held in Nürnberg in the first week of May to elect a new chairman. Thielen, rather than appear to be voted out, chose this time to quit the NPD, and to announce in Bremen the formation of a new party, the *Nationale Volkspartei* (NVP—National Peoples' Party). Thielen admitted that "at the moment the NPD cannot be cleansed by us," and predicted that the NPD would now "sink into complete meaninglessness."[41] Furthermore, Thielen claimed that about five thousand members of the NPD, including whole county organizations, would switch to his NVP immediately.

Thielen, in his final exit from the NPD, did not omit a little extra name-calling—in the true tradition of the far right:

> Thielen: I had very great doubts from the first about accepting von Thadden and his group [in the NPD]. There were at that time a lot of letters, in which it was said: For God's sake don't accept von Thadden. He will be the gravedigger of your party, he destroys every national emotion, and one never knows whether it is out of a sick need for esteem—out of an inferiority complex—or whether it concerns an order.
>
> Spiegel: You mean from the security police?
>
> Thielen: It concerns not only the security police, but also his earlier activity as an agent of the Polish GPU [secret police]. He himself said that in a survey, when it was still very attractive.[42]

The final exit of Thielen from the NPD was somewhat premature, for the planned national conference of the NPD in Nürnberg never took place. The National Democrats ran into the familiar problem of being shut out of rented meeting halls by the leading citizenry of the city; this had happened several times before. The NPD usually rented a meeting hall far in advance. Later, when the local city fathers learned that the hall had been rented by the socially unacceptable NPD, they would bring pressure to bear on the hall owner, forcing him

41. Interview with Fritz Thielen in *Spiegel*, Number 21/1967, pp. 36–41.
42. *Ibid.*

to break his contract with the National Democrats. Usually courts upheld the NPD's right to use the hall, or awarded damages for their loss
of time and money if they did not get to use the hall. All in all, such
displays of social pressure and denial of civil rights to the National
Democrats by the self-appointed, supposed defenders of the democracy
brought only sympathy for the NPD. This pattern, of meeting intolerance with intolerance, had been established at the Karlsruhe NPD
party conference at which the city fathers attempted to shut the NPD
out of the "Black Forest Hall" which the party had already rented.
Then, in Stuttgart at the beginning of 1967, the city administration
had refused to allow the party to use the "Gustav Siegle House." In
February, 1967, the courts again had to help the NPD against the city
magistrates of Flensburg to free the "German House" for the party's
gathering. The NPD also won a similar case in Munich, where a contract for a meeting hall had been canceled.

For this latest conference von Thadden had originally planned
to rent the "Rhein-Main Hall" in Wiesbaden. Von Thadden had expected five thousand of the thirty thousand NPD members for this
conference, at which Thielen was finally to be ousted, and the date
had been set for the tenth of May. But then, as had happened so often
before, the city government canceled the contract, and this time the
court appeal remained unsuccessful. After some searching, on May 5
von Thadden finally contracted for the use of the exhibit hall for May
10 at a price of DM 1700, and the NPD membership was rerouted to
Nürnberg. The city of Nürnberg had a reputation as a stronghold of
the rightists—a reputation which certain of its upstanding luminaries,
led by its mayor, Dr. Andreas Urschlechter (SPD) were trying to
erase. Through the mayor's pressure on the firm which rented the hall,
and in which the city held a 75 percent interest, the business manager
was persuaded to break the contract. The NPD was informed that the
contract had been broken on account of assassination threats, threat
of damage to the hall, repercussion in the world press, and finally, the
danger of bad publicity for the coming Nürnberg International Toy
Exhibit.

The NPD immediately took their case to court, but it soon became clear that the hall owners were prepared to pay a fine of DM
4,000 to the NPD as damages rather than open the hall to the party
conference. The final act in reshuffling the party hierarchy was put off
until after the coming elections in Niedersachsen. Now that Thielen

and his associates had left the party, there was no longer any pressing need for a national conference. Indeed, as *Spiegel* pointed out, there were still some members within the NPD who mistrusted von Thadden, and it would be far better not to antagonize them with an overwhelming display of power.[43] Rather, it would be better to allow feelings to cool within the party ranks and to proceed with the business of the state campaigns in Niedersachsen and Bremen.

By all accounts the state campaign in Niedersachsen was for the CDU and SPD a lifeless affair; they already had formed a Great Coalition in that state several years ago with the SPD as the stronger party, and there was little doubt that the same governing coalition would rule after the June balloting. The only question was whether the CDU, which had profited quite handsomely in the April elections, would be able to overtake the SPD to become the strongest party in the state. By the rules of the coalition, if this happened, the present Minister-President, Diederichs of the SPD, would step down to be replaced by the CDU leader, Langeheine. Paradoxically, the Christian Democrats did not want this to happen, for it would have endangered the stability of the national Great Coalition. The April elections had convinced many Social Democrats that the Great Coalition was working to their detriment, and too great a defeat in Niedersachsen might have precipitated a new evaluation of the Great Coalition by the SPD. Therefore, the CDU did not campaign hard in Niedersachsen, for fear of winning too many voters from the SPD, and the SPD reciprocated. Only the NPD and FDP battled each other in the rural areas and small towns where each had its greatest support.

The results of the election were hardly surprising. The SPD again lost some of its seats, but remained the strongest party in the state, with 66 seats in the 149 seat Landtag. The CDU took 63 seats and continued their coalition with the Social Democrats. The National Democrats, receiving 7.0 percent of the votes, entered the Landtag with 10 members. The NPD was now represented in 6 of the 10 state parliaments of the Bundesrepublik. The Free Democrats lost 4 seats, but with 6.9 percent of the vote kept 10 seats in the Landtag. (See Table III.7.)

The Bremen elections in October followed much the same pattern, with the dominant SPD losing heavily but remaining the strongest party in Bremen. Again the old coalition of Social Democrats

43. *Ibid.*, pp. 40–41.

TABLE III.7

NIEDERSACHSEN STATE ELECTION RESULTS: 1963 AND 1967

Party	1967		1963	
	percent	Seats	percent	Seats
SPD	43.1	66	44.9	73
CDU	41.7	63	37.7	62
FDP	6.9	10	8.8	14
DFU	0.8	0	0.6	0
NPD	7.0	10	—	—
DRP	—	—	1.5	0
GDP/BHE	—	—	3.7	0
DP	—	—	2.7	0

SOURCE: *Allgemeine Zeitung* (Frankfurt) June 5, 1967, p. 3.

and Free Democrats was continued in office. The CDU made rather insignificant gains. The NPD, with 8.8 percent of the vote, made a strong showing and captured 8 seats in the hundred-member *Bürger-schaft*, Bremen equivalent of a Landtag. The National Democrats also shut out Thielen's new NVP, which got only 0.9 percent of the vote and disappeared into the shadows. (See Table III.8.)

TABLE III.8

BREMEN STATE ELECTION RESULTS: 1963 AND 1967

Party	1967		1963	
	percent	Seats	percent	Seats
SPD	46.0	50	54.7	57
CDU	29.5	32	28.9	31
FDP	10.5	10	8.3	8
DP (NVP)	0.9	0	5.2	4
DFU	4.2	0	2.7	0
NPD	8.8	8	—	—

SOURCE: *Die Welt*, October 4, 1967, p. 1.

But there were new aspects to the Bremen election. First, the FDP, rather than losing votes had, for the first time since November of 1966, gained votes and reversed its downward trend. The Free Democrats gained two seats for a total of ten in the new legislature. It would appear that the Free Democrats for the first time were able to attract some votes as an opposition party, despite their coalition with the SPD in the Bremen government.

Second, the German Peace Union (*Deutsche Friedensunion—*

DFU), which had been to date a meaningless opposition party of the far left, suddenly jumped to 4.2 percent of the vote. This was, to be sure, not quite enough to gain seats in the Bürgerschaft, but it showed that the opposition of the left, as well as of the right, was benefiting from continued general discontent in the Bundesrepublik.

With the 1967 round of state elections finished, and the next important election, state elections in Baden-Württemberg, still six months away, von Thadden could return to demonstrating and solidifying his hold on the NPD. The Third National Convention of the National Democratic Party of Germany was held in November in Hanover, spiritual capital of the NPD, and Adolf von Thadden was elected national party chairman by the fourteen hundred delegates present. The slogans of unity for the coming state election were put forward, along with longer-range plans for the federal election campaign of 1969.[44] Von Thadden's election (by 93 percent of all delegates voting) left no doubt as to the course which the NPD would take in the approach to the federal elections of 1969. Anti-American slogans; demands for withdrawal from NATO; attacks on intellectuals, leftist students, the mass media, and the *Bonner Parteien* were even more shrill than before.

By the end of 1967 the NPD had stabilized its voter following at a plateau of from 6 to 9 percent of the nationwide vote. It had undergone the severest internal struggle of the sort which had shattered many previous attempts at rightist coalition parties; the party had remained inact and its organization throughout the Bundesrepublik had continued to grow. The state elections of 1966 and 1967 had given the NPD seats in six of the ten state parliaments, and had presented a steady picture of the NPD electoral performance. In all of these elections the National Democrats had been able to enter the parliament. Except in Bavaria, which has a special 10 percent clause, the Free Democrats had been able to remain in parliament, although generally suffering some losses. Not once had the NPD's entrance limited the number of possible governmental coalitions to a single choice, as had been feared after the elections in Hessen and Bavaria. Established coalitions had remained in power; the SPD generally had suffered some losses; and the CDU had made some minor gains. All in all, the relative balance of power had remained the same despite the presence of the new radical-right party at the state level of government. In

44. *Spiegel*, Number 48/1967, pp. 41–42.

short, neither predictions of destructive interference with the parliamentary democracy nor later prognostications of imminent doom for the NPD had proved correct by the end of 1967.

As the April, 1968, state elections in Baden-Württemberg approached, there were several reasons for the established parties to hope that the NPD vote could be reduced. First, the economic recession of 1966–1967 had largely been overcome, and it was this economic crisis which had given the NPD much of its early impetus. Now, with the economy again flourishing, it could be reasonably assumed that some potential protest voters would return to their traditional party affiliations. Second, Baden-Württemberg has a large Catholic population, and it had been widely accepted that the NPD drew its support overproportionately from Protestants. Thus it might be expected that the NPD would have a more difficult time attracting voters in those areas of Baden-Württemberg which are predominantly Catholic. Thirdly, Baden-Württemberg has no past history of special support for right-radical causes. Minister-President Filbinger, who succeeded Kiesinger as head of the Baden-Württemberg government when Kiesinger became Chancellor, could claim with some assurance in 1967 that the NPD would be stopped in his state.

However, the events of April in the Bundesrepublik intervened to upset these optimistic predictions. First, there was the attempted assassination of New Left student leader Rudi Dutschke by a young man with rightist political views. As Dutschke lay in a West Berlin hospital in critical condition, students throughout the Bundesrepublik reacted with violent demonstrations against those elements of West German society, in particular publisher Axel Springer, whom they held responsible for the antistudent climate of suspicion and hostility typified by Dutschke's would-be assassin. These student rebellions, lasting through the Easter holidays, in turn touched off a new wave of backlash sentiment against the student movement, and it was feared that some of this backlash would be captured by the NPD, which had shown itself most intolerant of, and most inimical to, the student left.

During the actual election campaign, Chancellor Kiesinger advocated a united front (*Einheitsfront*) of CDU, SPD, and FDP against both the extreme left—represented partly by the newly formed Democratic Left (DL)—and the extreme right, the National Democrats. The campaign again, by most accounts, was a dull affair in terms of CDU, SPD, and FDP efforts, while the NPD leaders railed long and loud against recent student unrest, and in some areas militant students conducted heckling campaigns against candidates of established parties.

Voting results seemed to confirm the worst predictions of the backlash effect. (See Table III.9.) The NPD came through with 9.8

TABLE III.9

BADEN-WÜRTTEMBERG STATE ELECTION RESULTS: 1964 AND 1968

	1968		1964	
Party	percent	Seats	percent	Seats
SPD	29.1	37	37.3	47
CDU	44.1	60	46.2	59
FDP	14.4	18	13.1	14
NPD	9.8	12	—	—
DL	2.3	0	—	—

SOURCE: *Süddeutsche Zeitung*, April 30, 1968, p. 1.

percent of the vote, its highest vote yet, and entered the Baden-Württemberg parliament; the SPD and the CDU each declined in their proportion of the vote; and the opposition FDP gained slightly. The Democratic Left (DL) received a mere 2.3 percent of the vote, thus failing to gain any seats in the Landtag. Most disturbed at the results was the SPD which sank from 37.3 percent of the vote and forty-seven seats in 1964 to only 29.1 percent and thirty-seven seats in 1968. This severe setback, climaxing a series of electoral losses following the formation of the Great Coalition with the CDU, once more embroiled the party leadership in vehement debate over the future course of the party. To a large and growing number of Social Democrats, it now seemed clear that the days of the Great Coalition were numbered.

In various analyses, both in the Federal Republic and abroad, most commentators laid responsibility for the NPD's success at the feet of students. It had been widely assumed that the Easter unrest would unleash a right-wing backlash, directed against those parties which had, in the view of some citizens, coddled or been too permissive with the militant students. Now the NPD's dramatic gains, in a state where many factors had seemed unfavorable to von Thadden's cohorts, appeared to bear out this cause-and-effect hypothesis.[45]

45. *Süddeutsche Zeitung*, April 30, p. 1, May 1–2, pp. 1–2.

However, it was noted also that surveys taken before the student riots at Easter already indicated strong gains for National Democrats (and losses for SPD). It may be that, even without the violence of April and the hypothesized reaction to it, the NPD would have made its strong showing in Baden-Württemberg. This of course does not deny the effect of the strong antistudent theme of the NPD, and that many voters chose the NPD as a protest against student militancy. NPD slogans against the students on the one hand, and the growing militance of the student Left on the other, had been developing for some time; thus, the hypothesized backlash may have actually developed well in advance of the Easter riots.

One of the more alarming aspects in the latest electoral turnout for the right-radicals was the disillusioning realization that the end of the economic recession would not alone deflate the NPD's voter potential. While there were still areas of economic distress in Baden-Württemberg, primarily among small farmers, and while the National Democrats had indeed done best in those areas where economic crisis might be expected to produce protest votes, this could not explain their widespread gains among all sectors of society. Now it began to be perceived that the National Democratic Party was perhaps based on longer-range issues and had established a voter following which would not drift so quickly or easily back to the establishment parties.

Finally, it became clear after the state election in Baden-Württemberg that the NPD was costing the Great Coalition more than a few seats in the state parliaments as well as an embarrassing reaction in the foreign press. One of the prime goals of the Great Coalition, and particularly of SPD leaders—namely the new Ostpolitik—was being endangered by the continued presence of the National Democrats. Brandt's Ostpolitik, a long-envisioned reform and improvement of the Bundesrepublik's relationship to Eastern Europe, had begun on an optimistic note with the establishment of diplomatic relations with independent-minded Rumania and, later, resumption of normal relations with Yugoslavia. It was widely assumed that the reformist Czech government and Kadar's Hungary would soon also be attracted by the offer of normal diplomatic and economic relationships with the Bundesrepublik. Only Ulbricht's DDR and Gomulka's Poland, along with the Soviet Union, continually denounced the new Ostpolitik as a trick to lure Eastern European states out of their Soviet orbits and to replace Soviet ties with a Bundesrepublik sphere of economic influence. Indeed, the Soviets found it very difficult to counter the attractiveness of the new Ostpolitik. But at every possible occasion they could (and did) point to the NPD as proof of the rebirth of revanchism and aggressive nationalism in the Federal Republic. The Soviets could use the National Democratic Party as a straw man to justify their charge that the Federal Republic still held territorial claims in Eastern Europe and that no Communist regime should therefore fall into the clutches of this still menacing power. One notices in the Soviet Union, both in the press and in street posters, that polemics portray the NPD not as a minority opposition party but as the leading political force in the Federal Republic. After the Baden-Württemberg election, the Soviet press linked the NPD's success to "Bonn's dangerous policy of revanchism and war preparations," Soviet terminology for the new Ostpolitik.[46] Chancellor Kiesinger's own comments on the election recognized the difficulties which the NPD vote would cause for this new Eastern Policy of the Great Coalition.[47]

As the round of state elections preceding the September 1969 federal elections came to a close, the NPD could claim representation in seven of the nation's ten states, a rather steady if not spectacular rise in electoral strength, upped by showings of 8.8 percent in Bremen in October of 1967 and 9.8 percent the following April, both elections occurring after the potentially fatal intraparty power struggle of early 1967, and at the end of the economic recession period in which the NPD had first come to the fore. Adolf von Thadden's right-radicals now looked with confidence to the *Bundestagswahl* of 1969 in the expectation of being established finally at the federal level as a viable political force.

46. *Ibid.*
47. The Soviet-led invasion of Czechoslovakia has made clear Soviet determination to prevent development of close ties between the states of Eastern Europe and the Bundesrepublik without Soviet permission. The NPD is still used by Soviet and particularly East German propaganda as proof of revanchist tendencies in the Bundesrepublik, justifying the kind of "fraternal assistance" given to Czechoslovakia.

IV

Propaganda and Ideology of the National Democratic Party

I have traced the electoral and intraparty history of the NPD and its forerunners on the extreme right wing of West German politics. I have followed the founding of this new party on the right and its rise in the Federal Republic. Now I must turn to some explanations for the success of the National Democrats. This chapter will discuss propaganda appeals of the NPD and their impact upon the electorate.

To do this I must, however, distinguish between propaganda themes of the National Democrats, and their consequences for the democratic and social structure of the Bundesrepublik if transformed from themes to a policy program. The NPD itself has been reluctant to make this distinction, to spell out the actual changes which they would try to bring about if they were to attain power. So far they have had no need to do this, since they have had impressive, indeed disturbing, successes relying upon the strength of their propaganda themes.

What are these propaganda themes? What topics do they relate to, and what impression do they seek to give of present West German society? We can divide these themes into several broad areas in order to discuss them with some coherent pattern in mind, and also to see more clearly what response these themes evoke in the electorate.

Many NPD themes relate to a judgment of nationalism and the National Socialist past. The NPD presents itself as upholder of the rights of the German people to territories lost when the Third

Reich collapsed and Germany was divided into occupation zones by the allied powers. "The German Reich has not gone under, the victors have merely divided it up into occupation areas. Therefore the minimum demand is: Germany with the boundaries of 1937 [the boundaries of Versailles] including the Sudetenland, which became German territory through a treaty valid under popular sovereignty."[1]

This minimal demand of the NPD thus includes territories now firmly under Polish, Soviet, and Czechoslovakian control. By including the Sudetenland, the NPD also lays claim for Germany to territories gained by the Third Reich before World War II. If this is to be seen as the minimal demand, perhaps we can get a better idea of the maximum demands from Section XI of the manifesto of the NPD: "Germany has a right to those regions in which the German people has lived for centuries. We are not contesting the native territory of any people, but we stand with equal determination for the right to our land. Any willingness to renounce [these rights] destroys our legal position in the representation of the life rights of the German people."[2]

This statement extends claims of German sovereignty not only to territories encompassed by the boundaries of 1937 (including the Sudetenland), but would include also areas lost after World War I to Poland and France, to the Baltic areas settled by Germans, to the Bessarabian regions settled by Germans, and even to areas settled, until World War II, by the Volga Germans.

Who is to blame for the continued division of the German people and for the fact that these lost territories, which rightfully belong to the German people, have not been regained? In the first instance, it is of course the foreign powers which occupy these lost territories. "Our people live under two conflicting systems. While many West Germans thoughtlessly forget the national need, the right of self-determination is being denied to the Middle Germans. Foreign powers are silencing the peoples of Europe and together maintain the division of Germany and of Europe for their own political goals."[3]

The "foreign powers" meant here are the United States and Soviet Russia, both of whom have a common interest in keeping Ger-

1. NPD State Committee of North Rhine-Westphalia, "Einheitliche NPD Aussage" ("Standard NPD Replies"), 1966 (mimeograph).
2. NPD National Committee "Manifest der Nationaldemokratischen Partei Deutschlands" (NPD) NPD Section XI, 1965 (mimeograph).
3. Preamble to the "Manifest."

many and Europe divided. No mention is made of the reasons why Germany came to be divided, or whether the aggression of the National Socialist dictatorship was to blame for this situation. The aggressors here are those foreign powers who somehow find themselves occupying territories rightfully belonging to Germany and maintaining a divided Germany. Also chastised are those "thoughtless" West Germans who forget the plight of the Middle Germans (inhabitants of East Germany—viewed as Middle Germany if one has in mind another "East Germany" consisting of territories which are part of Poland, the Soviet Union, and Czechoslovakia).

The crime of continued division of the German people is seen as that of the Allied powers, but these Allied powers have had help from internal collaborators, namely, the three major parties of the Bundesrepublik: SPD, CDU/CSU, and FDP. These three parties, the *Bonner Parteien* or *Lizenparteien* (licensed parties), are denounced as collaborators with the Allies, as betrayers of the nationalist interests of the German people, and as helpers in the continued division of Germany.

Twenty years after the unconditional capitulation, extorted illegally and contrary to all rights of war from the three armed forces and not from the Reich, we testify with pride to the greatness of our German people and to the German nation. We see already that we have accomplished revitalization of the national consciousness.

From our pledge arise new tasks for us:

1. The rehabilitation of the proper representatives of national thought.

2. The reestablishment of the rightful condition for our fatherland.

3. The application of a righteous justice for all Germans.

In order to fulfill these tasks we as a party have taken the initiative in this federal election campaign. The three Bonn parties, CDU, SPD, and FDP live according to a different law. Their law reads: No initiative without a license.[4]

The three Bonn parties, originally licensed as political parties by the Allied powers, are condemned as tools of these powers. They are responsible for suppressing all feelings of nationalism in the Federal Republic; they, as collaborators, will undertake nothing to do with reunification without permission of the three western allies. The NPD,

4. From the NPD official party newspaper, *Deutsche Nachrichten*, Special Issue, Number III/1965.

on the other hand, with much breast-beating, avows its will to achieve German reunification: "In the question of the unity of our people we National Democrats allow no one in the world to give us permission. We will strive with . . . all our strength to realize this unity and in this we will be surpassed by no one."[5] The NPD supports the rebirth of a vigorous nationalism which it claims is being suppressed by a conspiracy of the Bonn parties and the mass media, saying that while the nationalism of others is being praised, the German people are being deprived of their right to nationalistic pronouncements. In one of the standard speeches prepared to be given by party speakers, this theme is mixed with a generous helping of other prejudices:

> It is an obvious contradiction when . . . the race and national consciousness of other peoples is admired and promoted on German television and radio. The chauvinism of the Poles who, against all people's rights, have robbed us of a third of the Reich, is valued as an idol by this sort of publicist. Long broadcasts are given to the freedom of the young Negro states in Africa, although those colored people have no national, but at most tribal, consciousness and generally use their freedom only to kill each other. For the Negroes of the Congo the right of self-determination is demanded in heart-rending terms, but for the East German refugees it is denied through scorn, mockery, and falsification of historical truth. Nationalist policy finds the highest recognition when practised in France or Israel or when it serves the Italian NATO comrades in order to oppress the Germans in South Tyrol. In Germany the word national is a sign of a worse crime than sexual murder of children.[6]

What level of agreement does this sort of strident nationalism meet in the West German public? Has the NPD struck a theme which finds a sympathetic response within the voting public and, if so, within which sections of that public?

A national survey of 1503 persons done by INFAS during the spring of 1967 shows that indeed there does exist a high agreement-level with this type of theme. The statement, "The claims to our eastern territories are indisputable. The winning back of this German soil must be worth every sacrifice to us," received approval from fully 42 percent of those interviewed, and disapproval from 45 percent, with 13 percent undecided or unwilling to give an opinion. Further, this

5. *Ibid.*
6. From "Musterrede D" ("Standard Speech D") for NPD speakers, given out by the NPD national committee.

42 percent approval can not be isolated along usual demographic lines. This propaganda theme has considerable support within all major sectors of West German society, with differences to be sure, but always with 35 to 50 percent agreement. There is no evidence that the younger generation, or the more highly educated, or the adherents of any group do not present, in approximately the same proportions, similarly predisposed listeners to this major NPD appeal.

Another NPD propaganda goal is to rehabilitate National Socialism. This is attempted along several lines: "The NSDAP was founded to lead Germany out of the national crisis, which was brought about by the Versailles Treaty and the anti-German red November revolution. The NSDAP was supported by the best German elements. It had the goal of giving Germany the place which belonged to her."[7]

Such positive pronouncements about National Socialism as the above by Peter Stöckicht, NPD speaker, are not usually found in the widely circulated publications of the National Democrats. They are much more likely to be heard at small local NPD gatherings where one can be sure of being among like-minded people.

The usual NPD approach to rehabilitating National Socialism is more indirect. It involves finding scapegoats to blame for the crimes of the Nazi regime, or answering Nazi brutality by charging other groups with equal, if not greater, crimes. This tactic seeks not to deny Nazi atrocities, but to direct discussion away from them and to thrust another group, usually a foreign power or a social minority, into the spotlight as the true criminal.

This is especially true in the question of guilt for the outbreak of the Second World War. Section X of the NPD manifesto states quite clearly: "Germany needs for its future a true picture of history. We oppose the celebration of treason and the accusation that Germany is to blame for all misfortune in the world. This leads to the moral self-destruction of our nation. We demand therefore: Away with the lie of sole German guilt with which our people are continually blackmailed for billions."[8]

This section of the basic declaration of purpose of the National Democrats raises several questions, one of which is: If Nazi Germany was not to blame for World War II, who was? This question

7. Excerpt from a speech by NPD speaker Peter Stöckicht in Munich on July 16, 1965.
8. Section X, NPD "Manifest."

is given several answers in standard NPD propaganda, all of which revolve about a conspiracy of World Judaism to destroy Germany. As NPD speaker Stöckicht explains: "The war against the internal enemy and international Judaism was lost, whose goal was to destroy Germany as an independent nation."[9]

The first tactic in denying the National Socialist dictatorship's responsibility for the war is the tactic of hyperbole. The NPD denies that Germans (but not the National Socialist regime and its henchmen) are to blame for all the troubles of the world (but not World War II and the brutalities of the Third Reich). This, of course, was never in question; the NPD simply uses exaggeration to set up a straw man to be knocked down.

The next tactic, as seen above, is to claim that the real aggressor in the war was international Judaism, purportedly trying to destroy Germany. (The reasons for this Jewish conspiracy are not mentioned.) Last, the blame for extermination of the Jews is shifted to the Jews themselves. The official party newspaper, *Deutsche Nachrichten*, reports: "Unconditional hate led Jewish officials at the change of power in 1933, in 1939, and 1941 to clumsy and . . . even criminal declarations of war on Germany. The right-radicalism of the Zionists carries perhaps more conscious guilt for the crimes of the Hitler-era than the whole German people."[10] In other words, the NPD claims nothing less than that the Jews themselves were guilty of their own extermination. They, in a plot to destroy Germany, had supposedly declared war against Germany as early as 1933.

But the Jews, according to the NPD, had help in their conspiracy against Germany. During the campaign for the federal elections of 1965 the official NPD news organ published the "Great Inquiry" of the NPD on the Federal Government, which reads:

> The National Democratic delegation in the Fifth German Bundestag directs the following "Great Inquiry on the Question of War Guilt" to the government: Members of the government have often declared that Germany undoubtedly is alone to blame for the Second World War. We ask: Does the government know that a similar claim was used before as the basis of a radically unjust peace treaty?
> Does the government know that the accusation of guilt in Article 231 of the Versailles Treaty of 1919 has long since been contra-

9. Peter Stöckicht, NPD speaker, Munich, July 16, 1965.
10. *Deutsche Nachrichten*, Number 52/1965.

dicted? The First World War was not Kaiser Wilhelm's war: that is known today to every historian.

Events leading to the Second World War also are no secret now. Is the government for example aware:

1) That the American President Roosevelt as early as 1937—that is, before the annexation of Austria—called on the world to rise against Germany?

2) That the English government took the Munich Conference as an excuse for war preparations?

3) That the German suggestions to Poland in 1938 and 1939 were reasonable and just?

4) That hostilities were begun by the Polish general mobilization on August 30, 1939?

5) That a cease-fire suggestion on September 2, 1939, failed because of English opposition?

6) That England did nothing when the Soviet Union marched into Poland on September 17, 1939—that is, that the "guarantee" for Poland was not meant seriously?—and many other historical facts. . . . [11]

Another person seen by the NPD as particularly responsible for the war was Winston Churchill, because his government blocked Hitler's noble plans for destroying world communism. In an interview of NPD party chief von Thadden by Churchill's grandson, the following explanation was given by von Thadden:

Churchill: Your newspaper [*Deutsche Nachrichten*] has called my grandfather a war criminal. Do you share this opinion?

von Thadden: I know nothing about that. I think it is said that he shared responsibility for the war.

Churchill: That's not true. Your newspaper named my grandfather a war criminal. Do you find that a fair representation?

von Thadden: Perhaps not, but in spite of it he shared responsibility for the war.

Churchill: You mean, because he didn't give in to Hitler?
von Thadden: Now let's just say that Hitler didn't want a war with England.

Churchill: Naturally not; he wanted to get everything without war.

von Thadden: Yes, but his motives were misunderstood. He wanted

11. *Deutsche Nachrichten*, Special Issue, Number VI/1965.

to put an end to communism. But before he could make war against Russia, he had to finish with Czechoslovakia and Poland.[12]

According to this line, Hitler was simply a crusader against communism who was "misunderstood." Therefore, the real responsibility for the war lies with those who "misunderstood" him, not with the National Socialist dictatorship itself.

It is clear from the above discussion that anyone—be it the Jews, Roosevelt, or Churchill, but not National Socialist Germany—was guilty of precipitating World War II. What support does this prime NPD propaganda line have among the voting public? Surveys taken by the Allensbach Institute from 1951 to 1959 showed that the percentage of West Germans who accepted National-Socialist Germany's sole responsibility for the war steadily increased, from 32 percent in 1951 to 43 percent in 1955, 47 percent in 1956, and 50 percent in 1959.[13]

At the same time the percentage of those blaming only others for the war dropped from 35 percent in 1951 to 22 percent in 1959. Had this trend continued uninterrupted, one would have expected by the later sixties that a healthy majority of West Germans would have accepted the idea that indeed Nazi Germany had been guilty of starting the World War II.

Unfortunately there was an apparent reversal of this trend. National surveys by the Institut für angewandte Sozialwissenschaft (INFAS) in the spring of 1967 show that 43 percent of all interviewed agree with the proposition: "It is high time to get rid of the claim that Germany was to blame for the outbreak of the World War II." Only 38 percent disagreed with this NPD propaganda theme, while 19 percent were unwilling or unable to make a decision. Once again, this NPD position received support in approximately the same proportions from all major sectors of West German society. To be sure, only 25 percent of those with university degrees and only 19 percent of the admitted FDP followers agreed with this theme, but these are small groups comprising only 3 percent and 4 percent of the total population.

How does the NPD handle the problem of the crimes against

12. *Spiegel* interview with Adolf von Thadden, Number 3/1967, p. 37.
13. Elisabeth Noelle and Erich Peter Neumann, *Jahrbuch der öffentlichen Meinung* (Allensbach am Bodensee: Allensbach Institut), 1947–1955 volume, p. 137; 1957 volume, p. 142; 1958–1964 volume, p. 233.

humanity committed during the Third Reich—the huge machinery of extermination which the National-Socialist state operated until its collapse?

Occasionally, again usually at local NPD gatherings, where the NPD can be sure of sympathetic ears and no press coverage, it denies entirely that the Nazi state committed any crimes. For example, the local chairman of the NPD in Munich, Josef Truxa, at an NPD meeting on June 18, 1965, declared: "There were never any crimes in National Socialist Germany. These slanders are only propaganda of international Judaism and the Jewish press."[14]

This is, however, the exception, not the rule. The more usual tactic is to confuse the issue by accusing others of equal crimes against the German people by minimizing the extent of Nazi crimes, or by shoving all knowledge and responsibility for the mass annihilation onto a tiny group of fanatics who have long since been dealt with.

According to the NPD, the millions of Germans killed during the war make it impossible to condemn German war criminals without also condemning the allies for their actions. "Those two-and-a-half million Germans who fell victim to the Allied bombing terror were in no way more humanely killed than the Jews."[15] In war people simply are killed, according to the NPD view. That the Jews involved were unarmed civilians killed in cold blood, many even before the war broke out, is not mentioned. The call is an emotional cry to brand the allied powers as murderers at least as brutal as the National-Socialist state was convicted of having been: "Murders occurred on both sides and a one-sided judgement is not Christian but paganistic."[16] And from Article IX of the NPD manifesto: "We demand twenty years after the war's end: away with the one-sided trials for repenting the past, while in other countries millions of war crimes against German men, women, and children remain unatoned."[17] On the other hand, millions of war crimes against the German people go unpunished, and the allies and the government of the Bundesrepublik "paganistically" go on looking for Nazi war criminals; at the same time the NPD claims this, it minimizes the extent, and tries to conceal the true nature, of National-Socialist crimes against humanity. "One should

14. From a speech by NPD speaker Josef Truxa in Munich on June 18, 1965.

15. NPD speaker Erich Kern, in *Spiegel*, Number 15/1966, p. 40.

16. *Ibid.*

17. Section IX, NPD "Manifest."

not forget the educational effect of the 'Kzs' [Concentration camps: 'Konzentrationslager'] which made good Germans out of many Reds and Marxists."[18]

The NPD, beside its list of standard speeches lettered from A to H, also has a list of standard answers to expected questions for its speakers. For example, the National Democrats have the following answer to the question of the Kz, the concentration camps: (The abbreviation Kz, never the entire word "concentration camp," is always used by NPD speakers and writers. This abbreviation helps to turn attention away from the purposes of the concentration camps.) "How does the NPD stand towards the Kz? The NPD did not set up the Kz of the Third Reich, nor does it represent them. The NPD regrets that political opponents of the Third Reich were locked up with criminals. Damage to health and fortune has been made good through reparations within the framework of the possible."[19] In other words, all inhabitants of the concentrations camps were criminals and political opponents of the state. Again no mention is made of the systematic persecution of Jews whether political opponents of the state or not, nor is the true fate of these inmates mentioned. Only the inconvenience of being thrown together with criminals, and loss of property or health (the word "death" is not used) are regretted. Those losses have already been taken care of through reparations, so any further discussion of the persecution during the Third Reich is unjustified, and meant only to oppress the German people. Another standard answer for NPD speakers includes this passage:

> Are there figures for the deaths in the Kz?—Unfortunately there are no correct figures or else correct figures are not being given out.... For a moral judgement it is all the same, whether 100,000, a million, or six million people were killed because of their belief or their race. When, however, widely exaggerated figures are given, it is with the intent of exercizing psychological pressures on Germany all over the world.[20]

Besides, adds the NPD, since the German people knew nothing of any crimes during the Third Reich they cannot be held responsible. "Every German knows that the crimes in the Third Reich were

18. Peter Stöckicht, NPD speaker, Munich, July 16, 1965.
19. "Einheitliche NPD Aussage," 1966.
20. Ibid.

committed by a tiny handful, while the mass of our people had no knowledge of them."[21]

The variety of tactics is great, and not necessarily consistent. There were no crimes during the Third Reich. All talk of Nazi crimes against humanity is aimed at blackmailing the German people. The Allies committed many more crimes against Germans than were committed by Germans. Alleged German war crimes have already been made good, but thousands of war crimes against Germans go unpunished. The German people knew nothing of the atrocities which took place in the Third Reich.

Again, the question is, how many people in West Germany are predisposed to listen to such irrational, emotion-laden themes? An indication can be found in the level of support given in nationwide surveys to the following propositions:

1) "The Allies committed far more crimes during the war against the Germans than ever were committed in the concentration camps."
2) "As long as the number of Jews actually killed in the war is not established, one should not speak constantly of the supposed cruelties."
3) "The Jews have no rights to reparations. It would have been better if Germany had not given the Jews a penny."
(INFAS surveys in the Bundesrepublik, April-May, 1967, 1503 persons.)

The last statement is so strongly worded that one would hardly expect an accurate picture of emotional predisposition towards reparations to the Jews. For this reason, I shall also examine the response given in a survey in Niedersachsen to the less strongly formulated statement: "Germany has already paid much too much money to the Jews as reparations. We should end the payments to Israel." (INFAS survey in Niedersachsen, February-March, 1967, 633 persons.)

The first statement, which encompasses the NPD tactic of accusing the Allies of being the real war criminals, received support from 34 percent of the population, and denial from 45 percent, with 21 percent giving no opinion. Here, as in previously discussed questions, the level of support is surprisingly similar in almost all major sectors of society. One exception here, perhaps, is white-collar em-

21. In "Musterrede B" for NPD speakers.

ployees who make up over one-fourth of the population, and whose support for this NPD theme is noticeably lower at 22 percent than the level of support of other occupational groupings.

The second statement, implying that uncertainty over exact numbers of Nazi victims puts the whole question of German responsibility in doubt, received the support of 42 percent of the West German votership, with 39 percent opposed to this theme and 19 percent giving no opinion. Especially discouraging here is that within the younger generation this proposition receives just as much support as in the older generations who lived as adults during the persecutions of the Jews. This, and similar results on other statements concerning condemnation of past actions of a German government and crimes of individual Germans, indicate that a large proportion of the younger generation feels that those condemnations are directed also against them, and they react against those who would continue to discuss crimes of the Third Reich. This segment of West German youth feels that it had no part in the crimes of the Third Reich, and that now the past should be forgotten and buried so as not to embarrass the young of today and to brand them as the same sort of people who committed such crimes. The NPD knows this feeling well and exploits it with zeal. For example, this passage from a *Spiegel* interview with an NPD representative in the Bavarian parliament, Wolfgang Ross, a thirty two-year-old captain in the Bundeswehr:

Spiegel: Your party demands that the trials of war criminals be ended. Why?

Ross: We have allowed ourselves to be forced by outsiders into extending the limitation date for murders in the Third Reich. There was for example, as I read in *Der Spiegel*, a Jewish veteran's organization in New York which proclaimed: If this law does not pass in the Bundesrepublik, they will act as they did before with an economic blockade against Germany.

Spiegel: Don't you have any understanding of this sort of moral pressure?

Ross: I think we shouldn't let ourselves be blackmailed from any side. I didn't kill any Jews.

Spiegel: Don't you think that a people has the moral obligation to judge the horrors of its most recent history?

Ross: Don't you think there are other ways?

Spiegel: What way do you see?

Ross: The exemplary life of our people. We have proved for twenty years, that we are decent people. And if a war criminal has not yet been caught by the law, he just had luck.[22]

The third statement, which says that Jews had no rights to any reparations, tests the really hard-core feelings of anti-Semitism. This extreme proposition nevertheless received the support of 17 percent of those surveyed nationwide, with 65 percent opposed and 18 percent giving no opinion. The two most noticeable deviations from this pattern come from the youngest age group (18–20 years of age) surveyed, with only 8 percent supporting the proposition and fully 81 percent opposing it, and from the university-educated, again with only 8 percent in agreement with this antisemitic formulation and 80 percent opposed. These were, however, small segments of the total surveys. In terms of major social groupings, white-collar employees were the least antisemitic with only 12 percent in favor of the statement and 74 percent opposed to it.

Since this third statement was so strongly formulated, I have included a somewhat watered-down version of this same NPD theme which comes closer to the actual NPD propaganda line as it is expressed in public, whereas the first, and harsher, theme is more likely to be heard in private conversations or in small groups of NPD followers. Here the thrust is that Germany has been blackmailed for reparations far in excess of any supposed war crimes against the Jews, and that these reparations should be stopped. This formulation received support from fully 67 percent of all surveyed in the state of Niedersachsen, with 16 percent disagreeing and 15 percent giving no opinion.

In other words, with this weaker attack on the extent of National-Socialist crimes against humanity, as opposed to a complete denial of any Nazi atrocities, the percentages in favor and opposed are reversed, and this weaker NPD theme seems to have a rather impressive majority of the people behind it.

If, as NPD propaganda would have it, the Third Reich is not to be condemned for its suppression of freedom, its program of mass annihilation, and its military aggression then once again it becomes a legitimate political entity which can rightfully demand the loyalty of its citizens. Here, the people who fought against National Socialism

22. *Spiegel* interview with Wolfgang Ross, NPD representative in the Bavarian Landtag, Number 7/1967, p. 28.

become not heroes, but traitors; this is in fact the NPD position. Those who emigrated from Nazi Germany to fight the dictatorship from abroad, as did Willy Brandt, are attacked by the National Democrats as traitors who abandoned the "my country right or wrong" principle of blind patriotism. The same is true of the men of the "20th of July," who, on July 20, 1944, tried to overthrow the National Socialist dictatorship through an assassination attempt on Hitler's life.

Once again, the NPD brands victims of Nazi terror as the "true" criminals, making the National Socialist dictatorship the victim of traitors and cowards. Once again the NPD line in small gatherings is likely to be the most violent, as when NPD speaker Hans Moschiedler says simply: "Emigrants [from the Third Reich] and resistance fighters [from within the Third Reich] are traitors."[23]

However, the demands of the official NPD newspaper, *Deutsche Nachrichten* are not much milder:

Therefore after twenty years of oppression and illegal partition we demand a general amnesty [for Nazi crimes] through a legislative act. We are struggling for justice against the continuation of the policy of annihilation, of revenge, and insatiable retribution. We are fed up with being on the pillory of the world. We will see to it that those who betrayed the fatherland in its moment of need and who during the war worked abroad against the embattled Germany are brought to the pillory.[24]

The same condemnation is laid by the NPD upon the group of men who tried to assassinate Hitler during the war. In its list of standard answers for NPD speakers, the NPD position on the men of the 20th of July attempt is given:

How does the NPD stand on the 20th of July? There have always been mutinies. The mutineer always had the choice between success and execution. Treason on the other hand was always an ignominious crime. It is not clear why those who committed treason during the last war, to the benefit, for example, of the Soviet Union are honorable men, while those who today commit treason for the benefit of the Soviet Union are sentenced (with right) by the federal court.[25]

23. NPD speaker Hans Moschiedler, in *Spiegel*, Number 20/1967, p. 122.
24. Lothar Kühne (then NPD chairman in Niedersachsen) in *Deutsche Nachrichten*, Number III/1965.
25. "Einheitliche NPD Aussage," 1966.

The NPD proudly claims that it is the only party, "which refuses to accept men and women . . . who have committed treason."[26] This question—of the possibility of citizens legitimately opposing authority—has a special place in NPD propaganda, since in the Bundesrepublik every soldier in the Bundeswehr retains the right to refuse an order which he knows to be illegitimate. Captain Wolfgang Ross, now an NPD legislator in Bavaria, denies that any soldier can be given this moral responsibility, and he therefore places any such actions as the 20th of July attempt in the category of simple treason:

> *Spiegel*: Will you and the NPD, if you could decide, forbid celebration of the 20th of July?
>
> Ross: Forbid, no, that is a very hard word. We would omit any celebration. One cannot praise rebellion. How many soldiers are able to recognize when they may refuse the unconditional obedience of the soldier?[27]

Walter Stockerl, an NPD candidate for the Bundestag in 1965, put it more simply: "Treason is treason. Why were the oppositionists too cowardly to kill Hitler with a pistol?"[28] To get an impression of the support for this favorite NPD theme we examine the response to the proposition: "People who as emigrants worked from abroad during the war against a struggling Germany should no longer be considered Germans." In other words, any German who escaped from the Third Reich and who fought to overthrow the Third Reich should no longer be considered a German because he betrayed his country. Fully 35 percent of all interviewed in nationwide surveys agreed with this proposition, 49 percent disagreed and 16 percent gave no opinion. Surprisingly enough, although this proposition is aimed directly at SPD leaders Willy Brandt and Herbert Wehner, as many as 30 percent of those giving the SPD as their party preference agree with this statement. Once again, as with most of these propositions, among major sectors of West German society it is the white-collar employees who support this proposition least. (It may be well to note that others beside NPD speakers have labeled emigrants who fought against the Third Reich from abroad as ex-Germans; Kai Uwe von Hassel, a prominent CDU/CSU leader, once stated: "I don't renounce nationality and citizenship

26. *Spiegel*, Number 15/1966, p. 42.
27. In *Spiegel* interview with Wolfgang Ross, NPD legislator in the Bavarian Landtag, *ibid.*
28. *Ibid.*

on account of personal or other advantages. I cannot give up this membership when it seems personally dangerous to me, and then join it again when the risk has passed."[29]

The picture presented here of NPD propaganda themes regarding nationalism and the National-Socialist past shows that the NPD is trying to rehabilitate both the legitimacy of a strident nationalism and the reputation of the Third Reich. It attempts to do this at the expense of those who fought against Hitler and who suffered under the Nazi regime. A conspiracy of foreign powers and internal collaborators has combined to suppress Germany and to keep it divided. Germany is being betrayed now as it was during the Third Reich. Only the NPD has the true interests of the fatherland, of the German people, at heart.

The survey information indicates that there is a relatively large audience which is potentially receptive to these strident nationalistic appeals and to defense of the National-Socialist past.

Another type of NPD appeal seeks to arouse feelings against certain groups which are considered alien to the German culture and inimical to it. The NPD seeks to capitalize on a deep-seated xenophobia (Fremdenfeindlichkeit—a dislike of anything foreign) which is focused mainly against Americans, foreign workers in Germany, and Jews. Connected wth this xenophobia is the NPD's claim that foreign influences are destroying or polluting German culture. In short, the NPD wishes to get rid of all foreign influences in West German society: "Germany for the Germans," as the NPD Manifesto states.

The most threatening of these for the NPD is the United States. The NPD sees Americans threatening to monopolize and pollute German culture. NPD chief von Thadden, at the November, 1967, national convention in Hanover, diagnosed the problems of modern West German society thus: "The American preoccupation with sex and crime is corrupting German cultural life."[30] The Bundesrepublik, according to von Thadden, is in a "state of national emergency" and, because of its alliance with the Americans, its people are "exposed to a wave of criminality and sex that may be a tradition in America because of the Wild West."[31]

Americans are trying to make the Bundesrepublik a vassal state

29. In *Spiegel*, Number 20/1967, p. 122.
30. Excerpts from an article by Wellington Long, *Boston Herald Traveller*, November 12, 1967.
31. *Ibid.*

for Americans; this is nothing new, says the *Deutsche Nachrichten*. Americans have been to blame for the world's miseries, including of course Germany's, since at least 1939:

> If Hitler fired the first shot against Poland in 1939, then it must also be stated that he was ready in 1939 and 1940 to end the European war and to prevent a world war. Roosevelt, however, torpedoed all peace attempts, urged on the Euroepan war, and then widened it into a world war. This crime against world peace rests since then like a curse upon American policy. The "American century" has become the misfortune of mankind.[32]

After the collapse of the National-Socialist regime, Americans installed a puppet government in Bonn to carry out their wishes, according to Fritz Thielen, then chairman of the NPD:

> Spiegel: You accuse the Bonn parties in your founding manifesto of pursuing alien foreign interests.
>
> Thielen: We state very clearly that the fulfillment of American desires is not a German policy.[33]

Americans are not satisfied to have a servile puppet regime in Bonn, say the National Democrats. They are, again with the help of local collaborators, gradually taking over control of the West German economy. Giant U.S. firms are driving the German-owned competition out of business and are forcing them to sell out to Americans.

A 1966 NPD handbill, titled "Numbers that No One Believes," explains:

> Right now, giant U.S. concerns are beginning gradually either to finish off the German competition or to get them in their own hands. The method they use is quite simple: favored by a rate of exchange falsely set by the government and favored by the federal tax system, they buy up businesses in Germany, which they then . . . incorporate into the fortresses of their organizations. Americans proceeded in a similar way when they exterminated the Indians. . . . Today the Bundesrepublik has become the "Golden West" of the U.S.A. . . . What state capitalism does over there is done in our country by giant Anglo-Saxon concerns, except that with them the tribute carries the name of "dividends," which then, tax free, are

32. *Deutsche Nachrichten*, Number 37/1966.

33. Excerpts from a *Spiegel* interview with NPD chairman Fritz Thielen, Number 15/1966, p. 42.

used for new investments, until the German middle class, even the entrepreneurial middle class, is destroyed and finally the Germans don't own a single stone in their own country.[34]

Even the German *Wirtschaftswunder*, or economic miracle, of the 1950s and 1960s is, according to the NPD, a ploy to enslave the German people:

> The share of foreign capital in German firms, largest of which belongs to the Americans, it not about DM 50 billion, while German capital is participating in foreign firms with only about DM 7 billion. Decide for yourself, please, if it is an exaggeration to speak of the danger of foreign control of the German economy. . . . Germans as workers, employees, and consumers—Americans as the big-salaried entrepreneurs. That is the reverse side of the so-called economic miracle, which our people will only realize when it is too late.[35]

Once again the NPD turns to a conspiracy theory, this time a plot of the Americans to buy out German firms in order to control the German economy. The NPD's goal is, according to its manifesto, "to guard against foreign control by foreign capital and against the selling out our basic industries to world concerns." The NPD goal is a complete autarchy, or self-sufficiency, of the German economy from all outside economic sources. The implications of this demand for complete economic independence will be examined later; the NPD itself is reluctant to discuss rationally whether an attempt at economic autarchy would be even possible and, if so, whether it would be of advantage to the German people. The NPD simply arouses a blind reaction against a presence which is admittedly both obtrusively visible and extensive.

This anti-Americanism applies also to the Bundesrepublik's military ties with the West. The NPD sees West Germany's ties to NATO as proof of the Bonn government's sellout to the Americans. With regard to the defense of Western Europe, the NPD sees the Bundeswehr and the Bundesrepublik as cannon fodder for the Americans to throw against any Russian invasion.

Americans have suddenly given up the conception of the "forward defense" and have given the Bundeswehr, which in the meanwhile represents the largest NATO contingent, the role of fighting de-

34. NPD handbill, "Zahlen, die keiner glaubt," 1966.
35. "Musterrede E" for NPD speakers.

laying actions with conventional weapons. This means that our German divisions are assigned merely to win time for Americans, and it is still an open question, whether the Americans, in view of their engagement in Vietnam, would strike back in Europe at all. In any case the war would roll over West Germany twice, and it takes little imagination to realize that then there would be nothing more in Germany to defend.[36]

As the NPD states in its manifesto, the goal is independence for Western Europe:

The German people on this side and on the other side of the wall and the barbed wire do not want our country to become a showplace of war between brothers. They will not fight for foreign interests. They want unity, peace, and freedom. Germany's unity in freedom, however, can only be achieved in a self-sufficient Europe which possesses sufficient defense power to protect its independence.[37]

The NPD is willing to see West Germany as one part of a European defense system, as long as this system is independent of American direction. Thus, when the NPD states that Germans do not want to fight for "foreign interests," it is "American interests" which are meant.

The greatest part of the NPD's propaganda is aimed at the threatening "Americanization" of the Bundesrepublik. Americanization threatens the traditional small businessman as well as traditional cultural values. In a sense the American has replaced the Jew as the scapegoat for what is wrong in West German society. Much of the NPD's appeal is to a similar cultural backlash against the continuing urbanization and modernization of West German society and industry that the NSDAP preached in the 1920s and 1930s. The symbol of this cosmopolitanism, of course, was the Jew. In anti-Semitic literature the Jew epitomized the evils of city life and the manipulations of finance capital. Now it is the American, and Americanization, whch represents the continuing breakdown of traditional, nonurban and nonindustrial life styles in the Bundesrepublik. Much of what the NPD decries as the influences of Americanization is actually only the necessary result of modernization, but an extra measure of emotionalism is attained by blaming a foreign element, the American, in the same way that another element, the Jew, was previously blamed.

36. *Ibid.*
37. Preamble to the NPD "Manifest."

To test the resonance of this anti-American appeal made in NPD propaganda, we may examine the survey responses to the following statement: "Germany shouldn't depend so much on the Americans. Americans only want to exploit Germany." Fully 42 percent of all interviewed in nationwide surveys in early 1967 agreed with this statement, while 47 percent disagreed and 11 percent gave no opinion. This proposition received noticeably less than average support among white-collar employees, among those under twenty-four, and among people with more than a grade-school education. It received some of its greatest support from workers, both skilled and unskilled. In all sectors of West German society, however, this basic NPD theme of anti-Americanism has a large, receptive audience. Many Americans have written recently about the "Americanization" of Europe, and especially of West Germany, assuming that this continuing adoption of Americanisms and the large American economic presence in West Germany was widely acclaimed and unopposed.[38]

It is now clear that there is a reverse side to this process which produces a deep resentment of anything smacking of American paternalism or dominance; the NPD, in many ways, embodies this reaction.

Americans are not the only foreign devils to be excoriated by the National Democrats, however. There are also the *Gastarbeiter* (literally, "guest workers"), foreign workers drawn to West Germany by the surplus of jobs which were available until 1966, when the present economic slowdown began to take effect. Approximately one-and-a-half million Gastarbeiter—chiefly Italians, Spaniards, Greeks, Yugoslavs, and Turks—were employed in West Germany at the peak of the importation of foreign workers. In many areas these Gastarbeiter created ethnic ghettos for familiarity and protection; conflicts between foreign workers and the local German population were bound to occur, and resentment against the Gastarbeiter was never far below the surface. Surveys taken in early 1966 by the INFAS Institute showed that a majority of Germans held some prejudices against foreign workers.[39]

Majorities of Germans thought that Gastarbeiter meant higher crime rates, that Gastarbeiter were after German women and girls—

38. See, for example, Professor Peter H. Merkl, *Germany Yesterday and Tomorrow* (New York: Oxford University Press, 1965), especially the chapter "Americanization Apace."

39. INFAS Research Report "Deutsche und Gastarbeiter" (Bad Godesberg: 1966).

with all the connotations of that thought—that there were already too
many foreign workers in West Germany, and that no more should be
let in. Little appreciation was shown for the fact that these Gastarbeiter provided the labor for positions not being filled by Germans,
that the foreign workers helped to keep the Wirtschaftswunder going,
in situations where labor shortages would have hampered growth.

The NPD's basic position on the Gastarbeiter is given in the
party manifesto: "The German worker has a first-priority right to a
guarantee of his job against foreign labor"[40]; or as the business manager
of the NPD in North Rhine-Westphalia put it, "We are basically
against the Gastarbeiter."[41] Fritz Thielen, then chairman of the NPD,
in reply to the question whether foreign workers should be sent pack-
ing: "In any case, I would hire Germans first, before foreign workers.
Long-term contracts with foreign workers confirm the danger, that Germans where possible will become unemployed, while foreigners here
still have jobs and bread."[42] As far as the supposed harmful effects of
Gastarbeiter on German society, the NPD party newspaper has no
qualms about stirring up the already considerable tensions between the
Germans and the foreign guests: "The claim that crime is not increased
by foreign workers, has been refuted by a hole in the public relations
work of the police who found 10 pistols, 9 mm caliber, 400 rounds of
ammunition, a gas gun, 2 sledgehammers, 4 axes and a special trunk for
ammunition transport in a camp for Turkish Gastarbeiter and also in
their private apartments."[43] This NPD propaganda theme, which denounces all non-German influences within the culture of West Germany and which of course reserves to the NPD the definition of what
constitutes German culture, has a focal point: to claim that "German
culture" is being destroyed by alien elements. This primal appeal calls
up all of the latent prejudices against Americans, Jews, Gastarbeiter,
and any elements within the boundaries of West Germany considered
by some to be destructive, in various ways, of the traditional German
culture. As an appeal from the far right of the political spectrum this
should come as no surprise to most Americans. Die-hard segregationists
in the American South, and leaders of the white backlash in the North,
have always cried out that "outsiders," the equivalent of foreigners,

40. NPD "Manifest."

41. In *Spiegel*, Number 15/1966, p. 40.

42. *Spiegel* interview with NPD chairman Fritz Thielen, Number 15/
1966, p. 42.

43. *Deutsche Nachrichten*, January 7, 1967.

have been responsible for attempts to destroy the status quo in their areas; likewise, this "alien" influence has been seen as conspiratorial and illegitimate by those tied to the maintenance of the traditional system of values. These "outsiders" are held responsible for all things deemed undesirable in their society by the backlash forces.

The question in West Germany is: What is the strength of this cultural backlash? Is there great support for the NPD backlash against "continuing destruction and foreign domination of our culture,"[44] which calls for some patriotic action to defend German culture?

It would appear that here the NPD has one of its potentially most fruitful propaganda subjects. No less than 58 percent in nation-wide surveys in early 1967 agreed with the statement: "An end must be put to the destruction of our people by foreigners."[45] Only 23 percent dissented from this proposition of generalized xenophobia. Here, as with most other prime NPD themes, support was widely distributed through all segments of West German society. Only white-collar employees (with 49 percent approval) and the university-educated (with 43 percent approval) were noticeably weaker in their support for this statement. This generalized statement allows the bearer to fit his own frustrations into the complexities, problems and changes within today's Bundesrepublik. The NPD merely focuses these frustrations onto a convenient scapegoat with whom the bearer is least likely to identify or sympathize: the foreigner. The National Democrats do not need to say how or what they will do to end the problems and difficulties of modern Western society as evidenced in the Bundesrepublik; they need merely point an accusing finger at the already suspect outsider. And any Germans who attempt to defend the outsider or his influences on German life also become traitors and collaborators with an alien enemy.

Under the heading of "destruction of German culture" the NPD moralizes against the new "sex wave" (*Sexwelle*); the spread of immorality and pornography through television, radio, and film: and the spread of crime and corruption through the Bundesrepublik. In addition, the mass media are responsible for the spread of this "moral decay." The NPD manifesto states:

44. *Deutsche Nachrichten*, Special Issue, Number VI/1965.
45. The use of the word *Volk* connotes the culture of the people as well as the people themselves. Thus, the statement asserts that an end must be put to the destruction of German culture (folkways) through foreign influences.

We need a free and responsible media system which is appropriate to the worth of a traditional nation of culture. Therefore we demand that destructive public opinion monopolies in television, radio, and film be removed. An unscrupulous clique which systematically undermines and holds in contempt our national, moral, and customary values can no longer be tolerated. The shocking increase in crime is a result of this uninhibited activity. Our women and children must no longer be free prey for violent criminals.[46]

Television, radio, and film are to blame not only for crime in the streets and the planned undermining of traditional morality; they are responsible also for the new approach to sex, and for the new roles opening up for women in West German society: "Our young people today, with the permission of extra-familial authorities, are exposed to merchants of sex, and the destructive influences of a depraved environment. However, they need and want pure and respectable standards. We demand, therefore, elimination of public immorality which does daily damage, especially to the values of womanhood."[47] Fritz Thielen, as chairman of the NPD, was especially concerned with upholding the traditional image of the woman in West German society. Undermining of this traditional stereotype can be blamed, he feels, on the unchristian leadership of the federal government: "When no longer the wife and mother, but rather the prostitute, is the feminine ideal among our people, then I ask myself where the government gets the courage to claim that this state is run according to Christian principles."[48] Again from Herr Thielen: "One really gets sick when one sees on every magazine cover a nearly naked girl. I want the mother, not the whore. Gentlemen: we are concerned that these pictures systematically undermine moral and traditional values. There only crimes of the most vile and brutal form are reported."[49] The NPD inveighs against the new sexual revolution which is taking place not only in the Bundesrepublik but in all Western societies. Without drawing too close a parallel, the Nazi doctrine of puritanism and righteousness was a similar backlash against the roaring-twenties trend in the Weimar Republic.

This cultural backlash carries over also into the field of modern

46. NPD "Manifest."
47. *Ibid.*
48. Fritz Thielen, in *Spiegel*, Number 27, 1966, p. 31.
49. In *Spiegel*, Number 15/1966, p. 43.

art and music, seen by the NPD as the alien, imported products of diseased minds. In particular, the NDP "Standard Speech H" devoted itself to the denunciation of all modern art forms:

> In the graphic arts we no longer experience . . . the representation of the beautiful and the sublime, but rather the products of sick fantasy which then, in addition, are heaped with cultural honors. There is an unmistakable intention to produce in our people a universal schizophrenia—that is, a split personality—convincingly strengthened by the products of sex and criminal literature.[50]

Not only painting and sculpture, but music also has become one of the decadent arts in modern Germany, again with the help of the establishment. "How far the foreign domination of our people has proceeded right before our eyes! When, for example, we hear music programs on German radio, we must slowly come to the conclusion that there never was a Beethoven, a Schumann, a Mozart, or a Schubert. For those who control music, the history of the art of sound seems only to begin with jazz and beat."[51] Just exactly what kind of art appeals to National Democratic tasks may be implied from Fritz May, chairman of the NPD in Rheinland-Pfalz and head of the NPD legislative delegation in that state: "This modern art should fade away; the works of art which were created under Hitler, however, correspond perfectly to my ideal of beauty."[52]

A favorite NPD target in the field of literature is Günter Grass, author of several best-seller novels and perhaps the best-known representative of the left intellectuals in the arts. What would happen to such writers and artists if the NPD had the power to decide? While the NPD professes to uphold the principles of the democracy, it would appear that speaker Josef Truxa at least would limit the right of free speech and publication to those approved by the NPD: "The television and radio networks are destroying German culture. Günter Grass should be given no possibility of appearing in the press, radio, and television. The NPD will follow the people's feelings and seek to prevent such occurrences."[53] The NPD claims that schools, in addition to mass media and the modern arts, are destroying such traditional

50. "Musterrede H" for NPD speakers.
51. *Ibid.*
52. Fritz May, NPD chairman in Rheinland-Pfalz, in *Spiegel*, Number 15/1966, p. 40.
53. NPD speaker Josef Truxa at an NPD meeting in Munich, May 18, 1965.

values of German society as dutiful respect of children for their parents and country. "The decay of morality begins for our young people in school. . . . When I think of the rejection of their own nationality which is taught to my children in school. . . . These young people who have no chance to compare are influenced against their own people, their own history, their own fathers."[54]

Again, the NPD blames the "problem of the generations"—the searching questions which the youth of Germany poses to its elders who followed the Nazi banner—on an instrument of the establishment, the schools. It refuses to see any relationship between the atrocities of National-Socialist Germany and the demands of a good part of the youth to search out the reasons and causes of this terrible chapter in German history. Actually, from much available evidence, it would appear that the German school system in large measure neither aids the young in forming an objective picture of the history of the Third Reich, nor encourages them to pose searching and critical questions about the past.[55]

Yet, the NPD has to find a scapegoat for the problems of West German society, for otherwise it cannot seek out the true causes without necessarily repudiating the National-Socialist past. The NPD propaganda line is based upon a rehabilitation of the Third Reich, so it is inevitable that the National Democrats must propound irrational conspiracy and treason theories which leave the realities, both of the present and the past, buried under a stream of name-calling and finger-pointing.

Another plank in the NPD platform is the charge of widespread moral corruption and spiritual decay within establishment circles. The first section of the NPD manifesto denies the moral legitimacy of the present administrative structure as a whole: "We must defend ourselves against the ever widening corruption in those circles which have taken possession of public offices. The true reward for an official is not money and power, but the knowledge of legal fulfillment of duty and the resulting esteem for the servant of the state."[56]

To test the potential appeal of this NPD theme of moral decay and destruction of German tradition and culture, I shall examine the

54. Cited from an interview with NPD chairman Fritz Thielen in *Spiegel*, Number 15/1966, pp. 43–44.

55. See, for example, the description and analysis given in the article "Rechts ab zum Vaterland," Part IV, in *Spiegel*, Number 21/1966, pp. 86–87.

56. Section I, NPD "Manifest."

survey responses to a group of strongly worded propositions which closely parallel the National Democrats' propaganda line. The first proposition includes the NPD's generalized condemnation of the mass media as corrupting influences, and the threat of action to end this supposed undermining of public morals: "It is intolerable that all moral values are systematically despised in television, radio, and film." This blanket condemnation receives approval from 47 percent of the population, and disagreement from only 31 percent, with 22 percent undecided or unwilling to express an opinion. This proposition received a plurality of agreement from every important sector of the West German social structure, with the single and important exception of the white-collar employees. Even the relatively small group of the university-educated agreed with this basic NPD theme by a margin of 48 percent to 43 percent. In addition, although this proposition receives relatively less support among the younger age groups then among the older, it still receives at least a plurality among all age groups.

Next we examine responses to a pair of questions about the public feeling towards such institutions of present-day youth as the miniskirt and long hair styles for young men:

1) "One must be ashamed of oneself as a German, to see in our country, in broad daylight, youths with Beatle haircuts and miniskirts."

2) "One should finally take steps against the unkempt youths who unabashedly walk our streets with Beatle haircuts and miniskirts."

To the first statement 44 percent of those interviewed in nationwide surveys were in agreement; 47 percent were opposed; the rest, undecided or unwilling to give an opinion. As one might expect, there was considerably less agreement here from the lower age groups, as well as from white-collar employees, who rather consistently have shown themselves relatively less inclined to agree with these NPD propaganda themes. In addition, only 20 percent of the university-educated agreed with this first statement. However, this first proposition asks whether the respondent himself feels ashamed as a German that such things as Beatle haircuts and miniskirts can be seen in the Bundesrepublik. The second proposition, on the other hand, does not elicit a mixture of moral indignation and shame, but calls forth a different mixture—that of moral indignation with the threat of some unnamed punitive action. This second statement, in an INFAS survey taken in the state of Niedersachsen in early 1967, received agreement from an overwhelming majority (69 percent), with disagreement expressed by only 25 percent.

In regard to the NPD charge that the Bundesrepublik's leadership is decadent and corrupt, we can estimate the strength of this claim from the fact that in the above mentioned Niedersachsen survey 45 percent of those interviewed agreed with the statement: "The wild orgies of the ancient Greeks and Romans were child's play compared to certain goings-on today, in circles where one would least expect it." Only 25 percent disagreed; and a surprisingly high 30 percent declined to give an opinion.

If the present government, party structure, and mass media seem to be corrupting and destroying the German cultural heritage, then where would the NPD lead the Bundesrepublik? I have offered the hypothesis that in this respect the NPD resembles the NSDAP as a cultural backlash against the loosening of traditional mores and behavioral bonds. NPD outcries against the mass media's "destructive influence," and their demand for the "removal of public immorality," is matched very closely by several passages from the NSDAP 25 Point Program of 1920: "We press for the rightful struggle against the conscious political lies and their spread by the press. . . . We demand the rightful struggle against the trend of art and literature, which exercises a destructive influence on our people's culture. . . ."[57] We have seen that in art, in literature, in all forms of publication and communication, the NPD today—as the NSDAP in the 1920s and 1930s—charges that the present establishment, of the Bonn and Weimar Republics respectively, are actually conspiring to destroy the moral fiber and culture of German society. We have seen that NPD leaders such as Fritz May look to the National-Socialist regime as the period which corresponds to their own tastes in the arts, and we have heard from other NPD spokesmen that the NSDAP was composed of the "best elements" in Germany.

How many people agree with the NPD that National Socialism, despite some faults, was still a regime which should be praised for its maintenance of its own brand of puritanical morality and social dis-

57. For a more elaborate point-by-point comparison of the 1965 NPD Manifest with the NSDAP's 25 Point Program of 1920, see Fred Richards, *Die NPD*, pp. 151–160.

cipline? How many people still see National Socialism as a worthy social experiment, albeit carried out badly by Hitler and the Nazi leadership?

To attempt to answer to these questions, we first look at the response to the question "Do you consider National Socialism to be a good idea, which was carried out badly?" This was asked in a representative nationwide survey in October of 1948.[58] A healthy majority replied in the affirmative, 28 percent replied "no," and 15 percent were undecided. In other words, despite the totalitarian suppression of all basic freedoms, despite the planned extermination of scapegoat minorities, and despite the destruction for which the Nazi regime was responsible in October of 1948 57 percent of the German people living in the three western occupation zones still felt that these facts were only errors of execution. Despite incidental errors, the basic National-Socialist concept was seen as a worthy goal. A basic part of the National-Socialist ideal was the Nazi demand for a return to a strict authoritarian code of morality which was continually being eroded in modern Western society.

Almost twenty years later, in the spring of 1967, another nationwide survey by INFAS asked people whether they agreed or disagreed with the following statement: "National Socialism had its good side also. At least then order and morality prevailed." The results were very similar to those for the first question above; fully 56 percent of all interviewed agreed with the statement, 27 percent disagreed, and 17 percent gave no opinion. Although this statement received strong support in every sector of the social structure, there were some interesting differences which are worth looking at. For example, it is clear that agreement with the proposition that the Third Reich represented a moral society of law and order increases as one moves towards higher age groups. This would be expected in any cultural backlash sentiment which basically expresses alienation from the changing mores and which calls for a return to a posited set of mores said to exist in some past era. It is not, then, surprising that this appeal has less support among the younger generation; to the contrary, it is surprising that it has so much support among people who never lived under the type of morality and order offered by the Third Reich.

Also noticeable is a slightly higher level of support among

58. Elisabeth Noelle and Peter Erich Neumann, *Jahrbuch*, 1947–1955 volume, p. 134.

groups whose social position and mores have eroded most in the post-war period of the Bundesrepublik, namely, small businessmen and practicing Catholics. The small businessman has found it increasingly difficult to uphold the capitalist entrepreneurial morality in the face of large scale competition, and of organized labor. The community of practicing Catholics finds its coherence and completeness diminished, and the traditional morality of the Church increasingly questioned and modified. On the other side of the coin, the rising middle-class, white-collar employee—child of postwar Western society—finds himself relatively more in agreement with the diversification of life styles, since he is usually part and parcel of these changes. Therefore his tendency to support the whole NPD arsenal of cultural-backlash themes is noticeably less. The percentage approval of white-collar employees for the above proposition was distinctly lower than for all other occupation groups, although at 49 percent it still was near majority.

It would appear that only at the very top of the educational ladder is the tendency to support backlash themes markedly lower. Only among the university-educated, who comprise a mere 4 percent of the survey sample, was there a majority (56 percent) which disagreed with the statement viewing National Socialist Germany as a state in which morality and order prevailed.

The NPD—as champion par excellence of behavioral codes which undoubtedly are being eroded by further development of the Bundesrepublik as a modern, urbanized, industrial democracy—has a large audience which can be said to be similarly concerned over the course of this development.

We have noted the xenophobic element of the NPD appeal, certainly related to the charge that traditional German culture is being destroyed by alien influences. But these undermining influences are not seen by them as large-scale social movements and adjustments within the development of a modern industrial democracy; rather they are seen as a part of an internal conspiracy to destroy West Germany. There is an inner enemy at work, and this enemy is the Communist. The NPD propounds a theory that although the KPD (*Kommunistische Partei Deutschlands*) has been banned, and although the Bundesrepublik is a firm ally of the West, the establishment is secretly run by Communists who are softening the West German population for a Bolshevik takeover. Within the establishment and within intellectual communities, according to the NPD, this takeover has already occurred.

In the standard speeches prepared for NPD speakers this theme of threatened betrayal of the nation to the Communists is elaborated. The mass media are so Communist-infiltrated that there no longer exists real freedom of expression:

> There would be a free expression of opinion only if everyone in Germany really could state his political views unhindered in word, letter, and picture—the fact is that we Germans in the Bundesrepublik do have greater political freedom than inhabitants of the Soviet zone. One sees, among other things, television and radio commentators who hardly bother any more to conceal their communist leanings, campaign for understanding for the foreign policy of the Kremlin evening after evening, and at the same time heap scorn, insult, and contempt upon all efforts of the Bundesrepublik.[59]

A major goal of this presumed conspiracy, of course, would be the silencing of all patriotic organizations, principally the NPD. The NPD—which has gone on the record as saying that Günter Grass, for one, should not be allowed to publish or to speak on radio or television—now appears as the defender of freedom of speech. The situation is so bad, however, says the NPD, that the Bundesrepublik is no longer a true democracy, but rather a television-democracy, in which Communist-leftist intellectuals pull the strings. Their eventual goal is a Communist takeover, after brainwashing of the populus has been completed. The NPD shouts that West Germany is falling into the same trap that was prepared for the Russian people. Only if the Volk wakes up and listens to the NPD can it be saved.

> The so-called left intellectuals have achieved this and are opening to communism the only possible way, as Lenin had recognized. He had realized too that the Russian people, especially peasants and workers, rejected communism and that only the rootless, decadent class of intellectuals, also present in Russia—who constantly spread seeming truths, perversions, and utopian promises—could accomplish the brainwashing which makes communistic robots out of a free people. . . .
> We speak the language of a normal and healthy people, and one day this people will prove itself stronger than the fungi which have planted themselves in the cracks of our nation.[60]

59. "Musterrede A" for NPD speakers.
60. *Ibid.*

It is clear that the NPD sees the mass media as the main organ of a colossal conspiracy to brainwash the German people, to destroy their resistance, and to prepare the way for communism.

But there are other traitors at work within the Bundesrepublik, says the NPD. There are the *Bonner Parteien,* who are selling out their country to alien interests. Speaking at an NPD meeting in Munich on May 21, 1965, the NPD laid the accusation of disloyalty to the national interests indiscriminately on all three Bonn parties: "They make possible the predominance of foreign powers and the destruction of German culture. The pig swill of a Günter Grass is permitted by the state, but the German-conscious literature of, for example, a Hans Grimm is barred from any kind of promotion. We must follow German-conscious men, in order to continue our great tradition."[61] We have seen how the term "licensed parties" (*Lizenzparteien*) is used by the NPD to imply that these parties were set up by the Western allies to look after Allied interests, and not the national interests of the German people. The NPD presents a bizarre picture of a simultaneous betrayal of the West German people both to communism and to the West, principally to the United States. On the one hand, the "licensed parties" supposedly enable the great American concerns to destroy German-owned firms and buy them out through false exchange rates; on the other, these same Bonner Parteien are accused of supporting a mass media campaign designed to bolshevize West Germany. The NPD sees West Germany simultaneously being sold out to East and West, just as Nazi Germany was "sold out" by those who fought the National-Socialist dictatorship from Moscow and London:

> There is not the least reason to deny the right of participation to those who, to be sure in error, and ill-used, at that time [the Third Reich period] demonstrated the finest human characteristics. For the rebirth of the German nation these people are better to use than those, who then went over to the National Committee of Free Germany in the Soviety Union or practised their work of destruction over London radio.[62]

Then as now, in the NPD view, good, upstanding Germans stayed at their posts, loyal to their country. Now, as their country is again being betrayed to outsiders—both East and West—loyal Germans must rally to the new defender of true German interests, the NPD. The choice

61. Comments cited from an NPD meeting in Munich, May 21, 1965.
62. "Musterrede B" for NPD speakers.

is simple: the NPD is loyal to Germany, the "licensed parties" are not. These "facts" may not make sense, but the appeal does not rest on facts. It rests on a basic uneasiness over the close alliance with, and frequent dependence on, the United States or the Bundesrepublik while simultaneously attempting, however haltingly, to improve its relations with Eastern Europe. The emotional basis for this NPD theme is a suspicion that the German people are being "used" by foreign interests, that Germany is the playing field for foreign powers on which the Germans themselves are mere pawns, and finally that the federal government in Bonn is not really upholding German interests.

We can test the strength of this sentiment by noting the surveyed response to the statement: "Germany now needs energetic leaders, who think first of their own people." This is, of course, a somewhat milder formulation of the basic NPD "sellout" or "betrayal" theme. Yet the implication is clearly present, that the present leadership of the Bundesrepublik is not defending the interests of the German people as it should. More damning yet, this fault of the present leadership is not laid to incompetence or to mistakes, but to the suspicion that this leadership does not have the real interests of the German people at heart.

A strong majority (62 percent of all interviewed in nationwide surveys) agreed with the above statement, giving more than a two-to-one ratio of agreement to disagreement (28 percent of all interviewed). Support for this NPD theme was strongest among those over twenty-four years of age, among Catholics, among retired people and skilled workers, and among the less educated. The proposition received at least a plurality, and usually a strong majority, in every major sector of West German society with the sole exception of the university-educated, who disagreed with the theme by a margin of 52 percent to 43 percent.

Doubtless the response to this basic NPD appeal would have been weaker if the formulation had included a direct accusation of disloyalty by the Bonner Lizenzparteien to the German people; yet the implications were there, not far below the surface.

A concomitant feature to the NPD's complaints about the destruction of traditional mores and social patterns is the call for restoring the social discipline which once prevailed in Germany. This theme is especially directed at the need, according to the NPD, to save the youth from the "corrupting influences" mentioned earlier and to train them in the spirit of service and sacrifice for the fatherland. Section VII of the NPD manifesto proclaims:

> Germany needs a youth, conscious of duty and sincerely educated, in order to resist threatening enslavement through communism and the atheistic thrust downward into the masses.
>
> We demand for the German youth in the hard competition of the systems of our time, a uniform cultural and educational system which supports every gifted person without regard to money or origin, and which preserves for him his proper place in the order.[63]

It is also clear that this sense of duty, which the NPD feels must be instilled in youth, involves a return to the militaristic values which stressed unquestioned obedience to authority as an integral part of sacrifice for the fatherland. The military tradition of Germany must be restored, says the NPD, with the rehabilitation of the National-Socialist past as a prerequisite for restoring German militaristic values. "The valiant performance of German soldiers of all times must be the example for the federal army. Military service is a service of honor. The soldier must know, what values are at stake and that no one expects him to serve as a mercenary for foreign interests. As long as fathers are publicly and without punishment branded as criminals, the sons cannot be good soldiers."[64] Here again, the call to restore the former social position of the military and to instill militaristic traditions in West German youth masks a much broader appeal to rehabilitate the Nazi past. The military is seen by National Democrats as a special elite class which should be free from democratically elected civilian authorities. In addition, it is charged, the military cannot fulfill its traditional role unless certain basic changes are made within the social order, one of which would be reversal of the present public judgements of the Third Reich. This is spelled out rather explicitly in a *Spiegel* interview with Wolfgang Ross, an officer in the Bundeswehr and NPD member of the Bavarian Landtag, for whom military discipline in the federal army is "absolutely too slack":

> *Spiegel*: In several divisions of the federal army, reveille is no longer called in the morning. Is this too much against discipline for you?
>
> Ross: Most certainly. What can you do then with a man who shows

63. Section VII, NPD "Manifest."
64. Section I, NPD "Manifest."

up late. . . ? You can't punish him, because he will say: Just a minute, I wasn't awakened, and was unable to get myself up.

Spiegel: A few units also are experimenting with letting soldiers go to meals individually, instead of in ranks. This also displeases you?

Ross: Some say the soldiers were led to meals like a herd of animals. But, then, our fathers, grandfathers, and forefathers were only cattle, too. In my opinion, if an army is to have discipline and striking power, everything must be regimented.

Spiegel: Will you take a stand on this as an NPD politician, and as a military expert of your party?

Ross: For this, and besides, reestablishing the worth of German soldiers is my most pressing task.

Spiegel: Do you mean that the federal army should have higher social respect?

Ross: Yes, of course.

Spiegel: Different from others?

Ross: Yes; the opinion prevails in many places that an officer doesn't count for anything. . . .

Spiegel: Isn't that so?

Ross: No; without question he belongs to an elevated class. That was so always in German history.[65]

This NPD emphasis on regaining the social discipline of the past belongs to the treasure chest of cultural backlash themes. It evokes the same patterns of response as those given to statements viewing National-Socialist Germany as a society in which morality and order prevailed. For example, the proposition, "Above all young people need hard discipline, strict leadership, and the will to struggle for family and fatherland," found agreement from 59 percent of all interviewed, disagreement from only 30 percent, and no response from 11 percent in nationwide surveys. As with the other slogans, this formulation found greatest agreement in those social sectors whose mores and positions had been most eroded during the twentieth century, specifically small businessmen and practicing Catholics. Again, middle-class, white-collar workers and the younger generation, more consonant with

65. Excerpts from an interview with Captain Wolfgang Ross, NPD legislator in the Bavarian Landtag, *Spiegel*, Number 7/1967, p. 26.

changing social patterns, tended to agree less with such backlash appeals.

We now pose a crucial question for understanding the NPD propaganda goals. Up to this point we have listed charges of treason, conspiracy, sellout, moral corruption, and cultural decadence made by the NPD against the modernizing sectors of West German society and, in particular, the political establishment of the republic which, in NPD eyes, is fomenting these developments. How then, after all these charges have been made, can the NPD still say that it is loyal to the republic—to the parliamentary democracy which permits the social freedoms and the changes in mores and life styles which the National Democrats so despise? Yet, of course, the party must proclaim a loyalty to the system it so clearly opposes, or risk being banned as a subversive party dedicated to the overthrow of the constitution and the republic.

Indeed, the NPD does announce its approval of parliamentary democracy in its *Annotations to the Manifesto and Principles of the NPD*, but with a special accent and flavor:

> We National Democrats affirm parliamentary democracy out of conviction. It has proved itself as the order which meets the freedom of the individual as well as the necessities of humans living together. Parliamentary democracy guarantees voluntary cooperation of the franchised and responsible citizen. It overcomes the submissive mentality and creates the insoluble unity of people and state. . . .
>
> Therefore we demand the guarantee of the basic freedom of enfranchized people by introducing the plebiscite and referendum.
>
> For full realization of the sovereignty of the people we demand also direct election of the head of state [*Bundespräsident*] by the people. Not last we National Democrats demand democratization of the elections to parliaments in the federal government, in the states and in the communities, guaranteed by the constitution as universal, free, equal, and secret elections. In the prevailing constitutional situation there is no equality of votes.[66]

The aim of NPD propaganda here is twofold: first, to reassure the audience, especially the federal authorities in Bonn, of the NPD's support, "out of conviction," of parliamentary democracy; second,

66. "Annotations to the Manifesto and Principles of the NPD," given out by the NPD national committee, 1966 (mimeograph).

however, to raise in the same breath the charge that the political system of the Bundesrepublik is not in fact a true democracy. Once more the National Democrats are telling the people that they have been hoodwinked. They, just as the NPD, want a true democracy, but instead they have been given something else. This "something-else" government, it is implied, does not allow the people to express their will directly, or to enforce the people's will on the government. Therefore the NPD must demand certain changes in the system to assure the realization of a true popular democracy, in which the people—not special interests or professional politicians—hold sway.

The NPD, however, is not really interested in reforming the political system so that it may be a "true" parliamentary democracy; rather, as will become clear, it seeks to remove the parliament as a deliberative body. The NPD, for all its claims of support for parliamentary democracy, actually espouses a system which is termed a people's democracy (*Volksdemokratie*). In a Volksdemokratie the parliament is short-circuited and important decisions are made through plebiscites, thus the NPD emphasis on introducing the plebiscite. Let us examine at some length a speech made by Professor Doctor Ernst Anrich, chief ideologist of the NPD, on "the German democracy." This speech, made at the party conference of 1966, was labeled by the National Democrats as their "ideological groundwork."

> The state stands above the individual and above the masses living at any moment; it represents the whole Volk; but the state can be protected only by the living, above whom it stands. . . .
>
> We reject the management of the constitution by the present ruling parties not because the constitution is democratic, but because it is not democratic enough. We are convinced, and in this sense we are true radicals, that things must be basically altered in the relationship among the real elements of the constitutional political system, the Volk, the individual, and the state.[67]

The plot begins to unfold. In NPD ideology, the state comes before the individual, and the individual is important only in that he is called upon to "man" the state—a euphemism for being ordered by the state to sacrifice himself to it. The present system, we learn, is in fact rejected, but only because it is not "democratic" enough. In fact, the

67. Speech by Professor Dr. Ernst Anrich (chief ideologist of the NPD), "Die deutsche Demokratie," announced as the ideological basis of the NPD at the Karlsruhe party conference in 1966.

NPD feels it is so far from democratic that things must be radically reordered as follows:

> A new pulse of German life can only be reached if . . . the people in its whole being, in its totality . . . are freed and made the living foundation of the reconstruction. Should that be the honest demand of the NPD? . . . Yes! Full democracy, that is our honest pursuit and demand. With no doubt that national sentiment would also return. . . . The courage to move to full democracy and to . . . a people's democracy will not lead to egoism and pressure for removal of freedom, but rather, when the three elements are brought into correct order, will have a moralizing effect. . . . In short, we believe that courage to build a people's democracy is the prerequisite for the establishment of that state which in this historic hour is the steady task of our Volk: the founding of a national democracy.[68]

The NPD ideology has now moved from affirmations of support for the parliamentary democracy of the Bundesrepublik to a call for a people's democracy; but this people's democracy, or full democracy, is only a transitional phase on the road to a national democracy. There is, however, no explanation of the difference between a full democracy and a national democracy. Presumably, if one has already achieved a full democracy, one cannot get any more democratic, only less. The suspicion arises that the NPD is simply playing with the word "democracy," attaching different adjectives which may in practice negate the substance of democracy.

What is clear above all is that the NPD seeks to weaken the role of parliament as a deliberative and legislative body. The National Democrats despise the competition of social interests and the political compromises characteristic of a pluralistic democratic system, and it is clear that this clash of interests within the Landtag and Bundestag are deplored by the NPD as weakening the national fabric. In the NPD ideology there are only three elements: man, the people (Volk), and the state. Once these three elements are brought into the "correct order," there should be no social conflict. Thus labor, big business, church, political party, and various minority interests are not seen by the NPD as legitimate elements competing for influence. All of these special interests only destroy the unity of the German people.

Professor Doctor Anrich, having called for the founding of a

68. *Ibid.*

"national democracy," goes on to repeat the NPD demand for introducing the plebiscite, abolishing the 5 percent clause which prohibits
splinter parties from gaining seats in the legislatures, and abolishing
the rule that before a government can be voted out in the Bundestag
a new majority must be found. Each demand should be considered
both in its relation to the parliamentary democracy of the Bundesrepublik and with an eye to its historical role with respect to the Weimar
Republic and the Third Reich.

First of all, it is clear that if one wants to decrease the role of
the parliament, one can rely on the plebiscite mechanism for direct
approval of executive proposals. In the historical context, of course,
the plebiscite was a mechanism favored by Hitler to stamp approval
on actions of the Nazi regime, actions which had already been taken,
rendering the plebiscite meaningless as a method of control. The
plebiscite mechanism, with its wider opportunities for manipulation,
has often been used by nondemocratic regimes to provide a show of
public approval without allowing an organized opposition to campaign
against the government policy.

As for NPD demands concerning the 5 percent clause and the
requirement for a new parliamentary majority to be present before the
old government can be voted out, these too are aimed at splintering
the parliament into many small and ineffective parties and making
easier the overthrow of the governing parliamentary coalition. Again,
in the historical context of Weimar, it was just such a severe splintering of political factions and the overthrow of coalition after coalition
(with no requirement to find a replacement), which helped to weaken
the Weimar parliamentary democracy.

Ideologist Anrich continues his list of NPD demands, which
are at the same time a blanket condemnation of political parties as a
basic and legitimate organizing mechanism of a pluralistic democracy:

5. A reformation of the election law, so that it will be more possible to vote for men and not lists. . . . Parasites of the party bureauc-
racies will disappear from the lists, as will some of the lobbyists.
Members of parliament would be more like messengers of the people.

6. A tightening up of the working habits in the Bundestag. Formerly, the Reichstag met only a few weeks a year. The result was the
people could send men who kept their permanent occupations, who
were independent from the pressure of reelection, the party bureau-

cracy, and party cliques. They could be true representatives of the people. Today, the Bundestag works throughout the year. The result: Membership in parliament has become itself an occupation ... and the member not representative of the people because he is cut off from his vocation and from the lifestream of the people. Further, he becomes dependent on his party, because his financial situation depends on reelection. .... The present situation inhibits formation of a steadily changing, truly democratic elite. The development of the correct type of representative, however, is as crucial for democracy, and remains as decisive, as the training of officials and military officers for the state and the army was for Prussia.[69]

In other words, the NPD aims to depoliticize the institution of the Bundestag.

A picture of the NPD's basic posture towards the parliamentary democracy of the Bundesrepublik now begins to emerge. So far, all NPD demands for the establishment of a "real," "full," and eventually a "national" democracy have had one main feature—to weaken the role of the Bundestag and to render it ineffective as the basis for constituting a government. If the Bundestag were to be filled with many splinter parties which could combine to bring down governments, but could not agree on upholding them; and, if in addition the Bundestag were to meet only briefly without ample time for debate and resolution of pending problems, then real direction of governmental power must come from another source, if from anywhere at all. NPD ideology has provided for this too, in the form of special powers to be given the federal president, a proposal which harks back to the "enabling law" of the Weimar constitution which was used by Hitler to rule without parliament and to destroy the republic.

The present system does not allow for such a situation but the National Democrats, in their desire to emasculate the Bundestag and increase the possibility of one-man rule, advocate a new "enabling law." The NPD suggests abolishing the 5 percent clause, which would

69. *Ibid.* An interesting additional note to Prof. Dr. Anrich's ideological groundwork for the NPD is that he made a similar speech on January 18, 1934, entitled "Folk and State as the Basis of the Reich," in which he praised the destruction of the Weimar Republic by the National-Socialist dictatorship. More than thirty years later, he is still giving the same speech, except that now he claims to be a "convinced democrat." That Anrich has learned nothing about democracy in the last thirty years is as symbolic a sign of the NPD's basic disposition as can be found.

(as previously mentioned) increase the probability of a Bundestag packed with small splinter parties, such as existed in Weimar. A government could then be brought down in the Bundestag without a new governmental majority to replace it. In the hoped-for event of parliamentary deadlock, NPD's "enabling law" would allow the President to rule alone.

The NPD ideology seems to be directed (perhaps wishfully) towards placing the Bundesrepublik into a historical view parallel to that of the Weimar Republic. The National Democrats would see the Bundesrepublik as a second Weimar and would submit it to the same dangers which helped to destroy Weimar. All of this, of course, is prefaced by the NPD with professions of loyalty to parliamentary democracy, then to the search for a true, full people's democracy, and finally towards founding a national democracy.

Democracy is not a concept for the NPD. When Herr Thielen, then chairman of the NPD, said that "we accept the rules of the game of democracy,"[70] he was only encapsulating the view, shown in so many other appeals of the National Democrats, that democracy is at best a game with a certain set of rules, but lacking any substance beyond these *Spielregeln*. The NPD, as we have heard, would see no contradiction between democracy and a prohibition on the publication of the works of Günter Grass, to take one oft-mentioned target of NPD venom. Indeed, the NPD implies that its pledges of loyalty to democracy, while made "but of conviction," are meaningless unless one defines what the content of democracy is supposed to be. As Peter Lauer, member of the NPD national committee, states: "But can the empty concept 'democracy' replace what to earlier generations the *Volk* meant. . . . He who says 'democracy,' must also be able to state its content and prove what it is. For there are parliamentary, presidial, socialistic 'democracies'; people's 'democracies,' authoritarian 'democracies,' and even 'chancellor' democracies."[71] Lauer then goes on to repeat the NPD line that, while the NPD supports democracy, the Bundesrepublik is not really a democracy now, certain changes must be made, and so on.

To summarize the NPD's view of parliamentary democracy in the Bundesrepublik, we can say with some surety that the NPD's ap-

70. *Spiegel*, Number 15/1966, p. 42.
71. Peter Lauer, NPD national committee member, "The Young Generation Today and Tomorrow," a speech given at the NPD party conference, 1966.

peals are aimed at basic changes in the system, all of which would tend to subvert that parliamentary democracy. The NPD seeks to remold the "Bonn republic" in the image of the Weimar Republic, with all its potential weaknesses. In this way, the NPD hopes to arrive at a "national democracy" which will have a "moralizing" effect upon West German society. We have seen from other NPD appeals what is meant by "moralizing" effects. The NPD morality is based upon a cultural backlash against the pluralization of life styles and mores in a modern Western society. It is based upon an explicit denial of basic freedoms, especially of speech and of the press, to representatives of new life styles and moralities. It rests upon the rehabilitation of the National-Socialist past, on a strident nationalist and militaristic disciplinarianism, and a support of traditional prejudices against scapegoat minority groups.

Once again we must ask the crucial question: How much attitudinal support does the NPD view of the parliamentary democracy of the Bundesrepublik have among the people? How many people, for example, view the Bundestag with disapproval and would prefer, as the NPD proposes, to see a strong leader at the top who could act independently with all the power of the government concentrated in his hands? To test this we examine survey replies to the statement: "Instead of the Bundestag, we need a man at the top now who can act decisively." This strongly formulated statement received agreement from 37 percent of all people interviewed in nationwide surveys conducted by INFAS in early 1967. In disagreement were 48 percent of all those interviewed, with 15 percent unable or unwilling to give an opinion. Although 37 percent is not a majority, it is a surprisingly, indeed very disturbingly, large minority to be explicitly dissatisfied with the basic institution of West German parliamentary democracy, and to wish to see it replaced by some form of strong-man leadership. In fact, within certain major sectors of West German society this proposition held a plurality. Among the retired, and unskilled workers along the occupational dimension, among those who did not graduate from the public schools (Volksschule), and among those who give no party preference, the weight of opinion was on the side of the above proposition. Once again, it is among the chief beneficiaries of the modern industrial system—the white-collar employee and the university-educated—that one finds least agreement with such antiparliamentary appeals.

But this call for a strong-man leadership to replace the inter- and intraparty competition of interests within the Bundestag is only one facet of the NPD's image of its "full democracy." NPD ideology lays heavy emphasis on the idea of the Volk viewed as a whole having priority over the interests of the individual or of any particular social subgroupings (i.e., "special interests"). This ideology (*Volksideologie*) has no place in which the rights of minorities can be heard or maintained against the will of the Volk. According to the NPD line, the will of the Volk is best expressed through plebiscites, not by parliamentary debate and compromises. Parliamentary competition of interests only serves to divide the Volk, which must always preserve its unity. The Volk must act as a unity through plebiscites which support decisive actions of the leader, who is not hindered in carrying out the will of the Volk by considerations of interparty competition. This is what the National Democrats call a *Volksdemokratie,* transitional step towards the eventual goal of a "national democracy," whose content we can only guess at from its projected "moralizing" effects on West German society.

How many people agree with the NPD theme of absolute sovereignty of the Volk over all minority interests? How many would, as the NPD has often called for, deny the right of dissent from convention and from majority opinion to the individual? To get a measure of the feeling that the interests of the individual must be subordinated —by force if necessary—to the interests of the Volk, we need only look at the responses to the following statement: "The good of the whole people stands above the interests of the individual. Whoever does not want to conform should be locked up." A stronger or more explicit formulation of the abandonment of individual freedom according to the Volk ideology would hardly be possible. Yet fully 28 percent of all interviewed agreed with the statement, explicitly denying the rights of the individual which do now exist in the Bundesrepublik (57 percent disagreed, and 15 percent were unable or unwilling to give a reply). The pattern of responses in terms of the social structure of the group surveyed was similar to the pattern found for other such questions of attitude concerning intolerance, antidemocratic, and cultural backlash issues.

While it is encouraging that 57 percent did disagree with this explicit formulation of the denial of individual liberty, let us remember that in specific situations, in which the support or denial of freedom is actually being tested, pluralities and perhaps majorities can be found to back statements calling for deprivation of liberty for a given minority group. Thus, for example, 45 percent approved of a statement calling for imprisonment of homosexuals (against 41 percent who disapproved). This 45 percent included many individuals who would not agree with a general denial of personal liberty but who were quite ready to deny such liberty to specific minorities.

It would appear, then, that National Democrats can expect a friendly response from over one-fourth of the voting populace to their Volk-ideology slogans, and a sympathetic ear from slightly under two-fifths of the people for NPD charges against parliamentary democracy. In addition, the NPD may be able to find near majorities on individual issues which involve denial of freedom to specific groups—a denial of freedom which would undermine the substance, if not the formalities, of a democratic society in the Bundesrepublik.

We have now discussed the major emotional appeals of NPD propaganda. We have described them in terms of their basic "themes" —namely, rehabilitation of nationalism and the National-Socialist past; virulent xenophobia towards all things non-German; denunciation of the decline in traditional morality and values; the supposed sell-out by the enemy within; the call for a return to militaristic, authoritarian discipline; and the NPD demand for "true democracy," in terms of its Volk ideology.

From the above discussions, we conclude that the NPD has a larger number of sympathetic listeners than it has, to date, been able to convert into votes for the party. We have, in fact, said nothing about the relationship between agreement with NPD propaganda appeals and casting one's vote for the National Democrats; this will be analyzed in the next chapter. We have only established here that the NPD is certainly not alone in its views, that a large number of people, sometimes a majority, are favorably disposed towards attitudes represented by right-radicals.

One factor not discussed until now is the question of whether the established parties (SPD, CDU/CSU, and FDP) have espoused similar attitudes, in certain areas, and may therefore have preempted the NPD. If this is true, the answer to the NPD's limited tapping of the number of sympathetic listeners may be due to the fact that the other parties have already grabbed off the lion's share of such listeners with similar appeals. However, it is certain on the face of it that the

NPD, in some of its emotional appeals, essentially holds a monopoly position, at least as a party at the national level. For example, no other party charges that the Bundesrepublik is not a true democracy, nor proposes such changes in the political structure as does the NPD. No other party claims that the Bundesrepublik is being sold out, or its moral fiber destroyed by an inner enemy. (It is true, however, that the CDU/CSU has not always refrained from trying to question the SPD's loyalty by referring to its Marxist past.) No other party has called for rehabilitating the National-Socialist past, nor has any other party put forward so menacing a nationalistic appeal as the NPD, although here the variations have been great. All three established parties have supported the West German policy of close ties to the United States and the West in general, and have not displayed the strong xenophobic traits which run through NPD statements. And while individual leaders of the CDU/CSU, SPD, or FDP have expressed concern over the social changes taking place in the Bundesrepublik, these three parties have not seen this as the dissolution or destruction of German culture and certainly not as a conspiracy against German culture. This is not to say that individual leaders of established parties, nor local party organizations, have not espoused nationalist values nor deplored the decay of traditional social values and once accepted truths, nor stirred up old prejudices and distrusts. Indeed, considering that, as the above discussion has shown, a goodly number of West Germans agree with these themes, it would be truly amazing if no one with similar attitudes held a position within any of the major parties and had expressed his views. But for the SPD, CDU/CSU, and FDP these views do not constitute the party program, as they do for the NPD, nor do they represent the basic thrust or emotional direction for any of the three. In all three, the party leadership does not see problems or their solutions in the same light as does the NPD leadership, and in no major area of its appeals does the NPD really repeat the appeal of any of the present parties in the Bundestag. In this sense, the NPD stands alone and is quite correct in announcing itself as an opposition not just to a policy or a set of policies, but instead to the present political system which now prevails.

Having covered the basic NPD emotional pitch, I would like to spend some time now on the actual NPD program, so far as one actually exists. In fact, this "program" is far less important than the emotional appeals in explaining the success of the NPD. Most NPD voters cannot name any points in an NPD platform, and for good reason. The National Democrats are seeking to build an image as a national opposition based not on program points, but on a series of strident charges and stirring slogans. To a certain extent it would be out of character indeed for the NPD to write a real program which dealt with specifics and details, for if the National Democrats ever dealt with facts and issues, they would lose much of their appeal. They would be playing the same game as the other parties, the so-called *Lizenzparteien,* and they would be forced to support some interests or some groups over others. This would tarnish their claim to representing the whole Volk, as opposed to certain special interests. Any real program would recognize that German society is made up of different groups with differing interests; also it would be an admission that such groups have a legitimate right to be represented and heard. The NPD much prefers to make pronouncements about the needs and the desires of the German Volk, which it claims to embody. This is not to say that National Democrats do not hold any special interests above others; they most certainly do. But these class prejudices are muted in favor of suprainterest group slogans, where all individuals and interests are subordinated to Volk interests as interpreted by the NPD. Any struggle by the party with the specific NPD solutions to the problems facing West German society would either reveal only too clearly the antidemocratic underpinnings of the NPD ideology or would place National Democrats into the same category as other political parties. In the first instance, the NPD would run the risk of being banned; in the second, it would lose its image as opposition to the political system itself. The party cannot afford to do either. In a very real sense, then, the NPD must wait for the political system itself to be changed before it can reveal any program, for many NPD solutions to the social ills it perceives are unacceptable within a democratic political framework. It must proclaim its desire to alter radically present society without actually stating how it would do this.

Nevertheless, the NPD has on occasion given some general programmatic points which are worth discussing, for they do add some light as to the kind of situation that the National Democrats are striving to create.

It was stated earlier that the NPD, in claiming to be the voice of the Volk, denounces all representations or lobbyists for special interests. The NPD's social or economic policy renounces all ideological formulations which lend support to one class of society over others. "In economic practice all doctrines of the capitalist, liberal, and Marxist brand have proved themselves insufficient. . . . The goal of the National Democratic economic policy is the synthesis of entrepreneurial freedom and social obligation.[72] This "synthesis," however, is heavily weighted towards the small businessman, the petty bourgeois, who finds his situation ever more difficult in a modern industrial society.

> To recognize that only a highly intensive heavy industry, with strong capital backing, can assure competitive success for German goods on the world market must in no way lead to restriction of. . . middle-class industry—of handcrafts, of the shop, or of small and medium-sized industry.

> The middle-class economy is a vital sector of our economy. Because it is less crisis-prone, it guarantees stability for the whole economy. . . . Maintaining the strength of the self-employed middle class is necessary in order to keep it from being turned into a mob, and in order to protect a mature people [Volkstum]. . . .[73]

Presumably the NPD is advocating a very thorough system of economic protectionism for the small businessman against open-market competition by large-scale firms, both foreign and German, which extends also to the self-employed farmer who had, like the small businessman, found his position deteriorating, especially with the continual lowering of tariffs agreed to within the European Common Market. This has resulted in a rising tide of discontent among independent farmers, and demands for protection against foreign competition. The NPD seeks to manipulate that discontent with its call for maintenance of the farmer's social position regardless of economic and market conditions.

> Germany needs a healthy agriculture for the defense of its political independence. . . . The agricultural sector, therefore, needs a guaranteed income in order to insure its continuing existence in our industrial society.[74]

> Therefore, through energetic representation in the Common Market, we demand also an end to that unfair competition which over and over is prejudicial towards our farmers, despite their diligence.[75]

72. "Annotations to the Manifest," 1966.
73. Ibid.
74. NPD "Manifest," 1965.
75. "Annotations to the Manifest," 1966.

The NPD shows this antiunionist side in its social policy as well. It would like to see unions function as organs of the state, not as protectors of worker interests, and certainly not as political influences.[76] In the interests of serving the state, the NPD recommends measures to restrict the workers' right to strike: "The NPD recognizes the strike as well as the lockout as last resorts in labor disputes. . . . The NPD rejects strikes and lockouts for political reasons. The government and parliament must have the legal right to deny the right to strike and lockout from time to time in instances of threatening external danger, and for other vital reasons."[77] These measures are in keeping with the NPD Volk ideology which sees no legitimate interests below the level of the Volk and its embodiment, the state. The individual must face the state alone as a political figure; all independent intervening groupings, such as unions, associations, and competing parties are seen as divisive and destructive of Volk unity. This applies in particular to unions, which the NPD denounce as being run by Communists.

Along with NPD proposals of a protectionist policy for the small businessman and the farm owner, the party also has advocated a Germanization of all basic industrial sectors, especially energy sources. The NPD's view is that, while it may be more economical and efficient to import basic raw materials and fuels, the true goal should be a situation of economic autarchy in which Germany would be self-sufficient and therefore independent of foreign suppliers. "The use of our own energy sources (especially coal) has priority before importation. The same goes for all other minerals. Coal, iron ore, ferrous metals, oil and gas from native soil are 'cheaper' in the long run than the corresponding imports. They are indispensable for the maintenance of our industrial production in times of crisis!"[78] The NPD's aim is to cut West Germany off from the world economy, to force it to try to exist on its own. The NPD makes no attempt to analyze the possibility, let alone the practicality, of such a move, partly because such an attempt at autarchy would be an economic catastrophe, and partly because such an attempt is basically seen as a political rather than an economic goal: "We are defending against alien control by foreign capital, against the sell-out of our basic industries to world concerns. The protection of our own independent energy sources is

76. NPD "Manifest," 1965.
77. "Annotations to the Manifest," 1965.
78. *Ibid.*

indispensable. They alone can guarantee political freedom of action."[79]

In summary, we can say that the economic policy of the National Democrats would lead towards economic isolation of West Germany as a means of gaining "political freedom of action." The NPD, as a part of this attempt at autarchy, would set up a system of protective barriers for certain favored classes against both foreign and internal competitive pressures. In doing this, it would restrict also the growth of large-scale German firms at the expense of small businessmen, and would restrict the rights of workers to strike in "certain instances."

This NPD penchant for isolative independence carries over to its proposed foreign-policy line. The party expounds, as we have seen, a strident nationalism and a fervent desire for reunification. However, the NPD can give no positive proposal as to *how* reunification is to be achieved. Instead, they castigate the government for not pursuing an energetic enough policy towards reunification; likewise they denounce the government for relying on Americans to achieve reunification. Though unable to formulate a specific reunification proposal, the NPD proposes only a casting off of West German's alliances to the United States and a self-reliance (although perhaps with some West European support), in approaching Moscow on this issue.

An active policy [of reunification] instead of a passive one is the demand. This means also that to Moscow will go no ambassadors who want to be silent or must be silent, but instead those who constantly speak about the German question. And this theme must no longer be left to their colleagues among the Western powers. . . .

Such an active policy would be practiced in close coordination with those West European neighbors who view the German, and therefore the European, division as a danger because while our old continent certainly can still live with the present situation for a while, it gives up its future thereby. A Europe, under American hegemony, integrated by technocrats, will not be fit for this task, but only a Europe whose nations have made up their minds on independent action.[80]

Thus, an NPD prerequisite for a more vigorous reunification effort involves breaking West German ties to the U.S., and developing

79. NPD "Manifest," 1965.
80. Adolf von Thadden, "The Courage to Find New Paths," a foreign-policy statement at the party conference of the NPD at Karlsruhe in 1966.

a European position, somewhat along the lines suggested by de Gaulle. This Gaullist thread runs through much of the NPD view of military and foreign policy.

For example, the NPD uses the French position within the Common Market specifically to justify a similar stance by West Germany.

> The NPD approves of the economic cooperation of the countries of Western Europe, which has begun in the Common Market. . . . A political integration we reject. In practice it has been shattered already by French policy. Germany especially should not submit to a political integration which would politically tie our hands and, for example, could make the question of German unity an object of decision for a Strasbourg Parliament.[81]

The denial of any political integration role for the Common Market, along with the proposed restrictions mentioned earlier in regard to EEC agricultural policy, leads me to believe that, despite lip service to this overwhelmingly successful institution, the NPD's foreign policy is essentially antithetical to both economic and political cooperation or integration.

Another plank in the NPD's isolationist platform is its demand for an end of German foreign aid to developing nations.

> We are paying billions at foreign command in distant lands, which serve neither German nor European interests. Pressing tasks of our own development are being neglected.[82]

> In regard to development aid, it must once and for all be quite clearly established that we Germans do not have the least obligation to give money to Africa. We did not, as did the Americans, bring into the country African Negroes whose descendants have now loosed the greatest race war of all times, the outcome of which is still in doubt. We also did not, like the English and French, exploit Negroes and Indians for centuries; rather, in the short time that Germany possessed colonies at all, we only invested money in these colonies. It follows that we have not the least moral obligation to give to these lands money which we could use very well in Germany for our own purposes.[83]

81. "Annotations to the Manifest," 1966.
82. NPD "Manifest," 1965.
83. "Musterrede E" for NPD speakers.

The National Democrats do not note that most West German aid is in the form of loans to be repaid, and that goods and equipment to be bought with this aid money are almost always West German goods. Rather, they try to picture this aid as further evidence of blackmail practiced upon the Bundesrepublik by foreign nations. That such aid might actually serve both the long- and short-run interests of the Bundesrepublik does not enter into the NPD view, for once again their goal seems to be the complete withdrawal of West Germany from that world community which the party feels has treated the German people so badly.

The basic thrust of the NPD's foreign-policy line is to cut all alliances to the West which the party sees as entangling and, at the same time, stifle West German activity in the world community, as embodied in its foreign-aid program.

In the field of military policy, the NPD presents two goals: first, to reestablish the military in its prewar pattern; and, second, to cut West German commitments to NATO in favor of a strictly European defense system.

As I have already said, in its propaganda on the military establishment, the NPD seeks to view the military as an elevated class in society which lies outside the realm of democratic practices and procedures. The NPD, speaking out in its "Military Memorial of the NPD Party Committee," explicitly announces its intentions:

> The NPD turns sharply against the scurrilous defamation of soldiers of the old Wehrmacht, especially the officers. . . . Joy in responsibility, outstanding ability, untiring care, and the faultless personal example were, earlier, and are today the prerequisites for military leadership. The NPD therefore rejects democratic procedures which, carried over to the military realm, must lead to the disruption of order and discipline.[84]

The aim—as expressed earlier in the NPD call for a return to the social and military discipline of an earlier time—is to extract the military from its connections with the democratic system and to make it an autonomous body in which the authority of command is no longer questioned, either within or without the military.

The second basic aim of the NPD with regard to military policy

84. Article 4 of the "Military Memorial of the NPD National Committee," given out by the NPD national committee (mimeograph).

is to disengage West Germany from the NATO alliance. This is related to the NPD's views on reunification, for which the party sets disengagement from entangling alliances as a prerequisite.

> We National Democrats do not see the value of a policy of borrowed military strength. We are convinced that a war in Europe would lead to Germans fighting Germans, the federal army [of the Bundesrepublik] against the national people's army [of the DDR], and both in the service of the interests of foreign powers. . . . The task of a German foreign policy must be to prevent this war and to extricate both parts of Germany from the military blocs, in order to make reunification possible. We National Democrats are not at all doctrinaire pacifists, who would first lay down all their weapons and then deliver themselves to the mercy, or lack of mercy, of the conditions of the heavily armed Communist bloc. We know that we must negotiate with the Kremlin, that however it would be suicide to begin negotiations with the Communists without military security.[85]

The NPD alternative to NATO therefore is a heavily armed West Germany. This new West German military posture, however, would still belong to a West European defense system with its own atomic defense force on the lines of de Gaulle's *force de frappe*. Adolf von Thadden, at the second party conference of the NPD in Karlsruhe, summarized the party's proposals for a new military alliance posture:

> 1. Not a fear of NATO, but a general fear of the Third World War has preserved peace for Europe until now.
> 2. Europe will maintain itself and maintain its security so long as there is in Europe, above the system of solid cooperation, a deterrence power which is immediately credible, because it must be used with certainty in any really imaginable case. . . .
> 3. Europe is economically strong enough, in its creative economic capacity as well as in its productive industrial potential. It has all the prerequisites for a continental power that modern history demands for an independent course. Thus it would also be militarily credible. This would be a factor which could decisively assure peace in the world.
> 4. Europe's security is not being furthered by the disarmament talks since a true—that is, a nuclear—disarmament is not in sight. No one is angered at the Soviet Union or the U.S.A., when they both

85. "Musterrede E" for NPD speakers.

with a shrug refuse to renounce their atomic potential. But this doesn't mean that Europe must still renounce its own deterrent potential.[86]

Here again the influence of Gaullism is seen in the NPD view of Western Europe as a new great power which needs only to loosen its ties to the United States. The NPD is willing to join Gaullist France in its policy of reducing American influence in Europe; that is, the NPD's only intended international cooperation comes with regard to a common opponent, the United States. Thus the NPD proclaims in the preamble to its manifesto: "First Germany, then Europe. Germany for the Germans, Europe for the Europeans."[87]

In the areas of cultural policy, the NPD's slogans decrying crime, immorality, and the corruption of youth by the modern mass media are the most emotional, and the least revealing. The NPD says that "our women and children must no longer be free prey for rapists," but seldom do they say what policy they would actually adopt to combat such activity. The party has called for the return of the death penalty and castration for sexual offenders.[88] (It should be noted that this motion was passed over Chairman von Thadden's objections and was later abandoned on a technicality.) Nevertheless, this sort of attitude towards the problem of crime and punishment is representative of the party leadership.

But at the bottom of the modern immorality, encompassing a multitude of themes such as increased crime, the sex revolution, the searching attitudes of the youth, and the public condemnation of the National-Socialist past, the NPD sees the influence of the cultural leadership of the Bundesrepublik—modern artists and musicians; writers such as Günter Grass and Heinrich Böll; the television and radio establishment; the publishers of certain illustrated magazines; and the whole community of "left-intellectuals" in general are the real targets of NPD slogans. The NPD, as discussed earlier, has stated that it would "seek to hinder" such people from publishing, appearing on television or radio, or speaking in public generally. Naturally the party is in no position openly to advocate the censorship and abridgement of basic freedoms implicit in such a statement. Yet the direction which NPD policy would take is unmistakable, as is the party's attitude that

86. Adolf von Thadden, "The Courage to Find New Paths."
87. NPD "Manifest," 1965.
88. *Newsweek*, November 27, 1967, p. 51.

censorship is a necessary function of the state. The NPD feels that the state should ban or censor certain writers and left intellectuals such as Grass; an NPD state also would encourage and promote the Volk ideology through the works of ultranationalist writers such as Grimm.

To aid in the rebirth and strengthening of its Volk ideology, the National Democrats do advocate several steps towards restoring to respectability that time in German history when this was the state ideology—the period of the Third Reich.

First and foremost, the NPD would end the search for, and trial of, Nazi war criminals.

Second, the party would end all reparations, both to nations and to individuals who hold claims against the Third Reich.

Third, an NPD-led West Germany would deny German responsibility for the outbreak of World War II.

The NPD's cultural policy, though very unspecific, also would aim at an educational reform which would slant the educational system more towards explicit support of the Volk ideology and the denial of past German responsibility for the horrors of the Third Reich. Former NPD chief Fritz Thielen often denounced the school system for "influencing the young against their own people, against their own history, and against their own fathers."[89]

The NPD solution to this situation is hinted at in the party manifesto: "Germany requires a true picture of history for the future. We are fighting against the glorification of treason and the charge that Germany is to blame for all misfortunes in the world."[90] History presumably would be rewritten for the school system to match the party's views of the "true picture of history."

At the university level, too, the party seeks changes which emphasize teaching the supremacy of the Volk over all subinterests: "The NPD strives for a study reform by means of which more value would be given to educational points of view than heretofore. Therefore we welcome the establishment of student fraternities, in which young academics should learn that they cannot go through life as conceited odd fish, but that they must be prepared for tasks which will demand from them responsibility for countless fellow men."[91]

89. *Spiegel*, Number 15/1966, p. 44.
90. NPD "Manifest," 1965.
91. From a report by the Academic Working Circle of the National Democratic Party of Germany (NPD).

122   PROPAGANDA AND IDEOLOGY

While many details of the cultural policy of the NPD remain
to be spelled out by the party, it is clear that they all have one goal in
common: to overturn the judgments of the National-Socialist era
which have been made by present literary, intellectual, and political
leadership of the Bundesrepublik. To overturn those judgments, indeed to reverse them, the NPD in some fashion would have to restrict
or overturn the leadership of the mass media system which has grown
up in postwar West Germany. Whether this could be done within a
democratic framework is doubtful; whether the NPD would intend to
try it within such a framework is even more doubtful. Again, the means
which the NPD would advocate to achieve the general goals which it
postulates cannot be spelled out explicitly by the party for fear of running afoul of the law which bans activities of parties judged hostile to
the democratic system.

V

The National Democratic Party Voter Profile

The preceding chapters have related to the history of the NPD, its development as a party, and the nature of its appeals to citizens of the Federal Republic. If taken at face value, the surveys shows that the NPD propaganda slogans have a far greater potential audience than the NPD has been able to recruit for voting purposes. But who actually votes NPD? Are they a sharply defined group which can be isolated from the groups in West German society that support the establishment parties, or is the NPD a Volkspartei in miniature—that is, a party with roots and support in all sectors of West German society? Again it is difficult to answer with categorical absolutes, especially since the NPD, a new and still developing party, has gone through several stages in building a voter following in the various states of the Federal Republic where elections have been held since its founding. Many theories have been propounded as to which groups form the core support for National Democrats, and which groups are "immune" or "relatively immune" to their appeals.

Two groups often cited as poor targets for NPD propaganda are union-organized workers and practicing Catholics. The theory is that ties to these large social organizations provide barriers to NPD appeals, even though, as we have seen, opinions of union members and practicing Catholics are no less in accord with the scapegoat and conspiracy propaganda of the NPD than opinions of other social groups.

Presumably, then, it is not because the Catholic church or the unions have had any great success in breaking down prejudices and antidemocratic attitudes among their memberships, that a lower NPD-potential is claimed for these groups. Rather, the theory is that practicing Catholics and union workers already have basic political reference points, the CDU/CSU and the SPD, respectively, to which they look for answers to their problems, and whose leadership they accept. In times of crisis, personal or national, these organizations should serve as integrating factors to provide the worried, the alienated, the frustrated with a sense that they still belong to the larger society, and that they are still being protected and sheltered by these large social organs.

To examine these hypotheses and to analyze further the NPD's voter profile, it is necessary to construct from survey data an estimate of those people who are going to vote for the National Democratic Party. This task is complicated by the fact that, since the NPD has been labeled a neonazi or neofascist party by the press and by most authorities, few people are willing at this time to state openly that they will vote for the NPD.[1] That is, when the question of vote choice is asked in a direct manner, a very small percentage will identify themselves as supporters of this very controversial party. The few who are willing to be so identified constitute a minority of the actual NPD support and represent therefore a poor overall estimate of total NPD vote strength. However, this problem can be overcome by asking, in an indirectly formulated question, whether the respondent *might* vote for the NPD. The percentage voting in the affirmative are then classified as "potential" NPD voters, and they are taken to constitute the NPD potential as a percentage of the total population being surveyed. This NPD potential has served as a very accurate indicator both of the actual NPD vote and of changes over time in support for the NPD. In terms of the social composition of potential NPD voters, it can be

1. This is a problem of survey research not limited to such parties as NPD, but faced whenever one attempts to get a survey estimate concerning a controversial group, issue, or personality—or even, often a noncontroversial minority group. For example, the percentage of people surveyed willing to identify themselves as FDP voters is also a severe underestimate of actual FDP strength, although not as striking as with the NPD. Similarly, in the United States, it is widely accepted that the percentage of people who identified themselves as Goldwater supporters in polls prior to the 1964 California primary led to a consistent underestimate of Goldwater's actual strength, because of the controversial nature of the candidate.

shown that this potential corresponds closely to statistical breakdowns by age and sex of actual NPD voters provided after Landtag elections by the statistical office of the Land. Thus in the following analysis it is this group of potential NPD voters which will be taken to represent the social composition and total strength of the voter following of the right-radical party, the National Democrats.

Let us turn first to union members. Here also are included wives and dependents of union members, who are assumed to have similar political outlooks as actual union members. In other words, we are measuring the leanings of that community which has ties to the union movement. The findings here are not at all clear-cut. From several nationwide surveys taken in the Federal Republic it appears that the proportion of potential NPD voters who are in the union-movement community has decreased since the summer of 1966, at which point the union community was proportionately represented among potential NPD voters. Other surveys in Hamburg, and later in Hessen and Niedersachsen, also show that the union community is less than proportionately represented among the NPD following. (See Table V.1.) An exception here is Bremen, a strong SPD center with a large union community, which nevertheless is proportionately represented among potential NPD voters. The evidence here seems to indicate that, while the union community leans less to the NPD than average, it is by no means immune to NPD appeals.

The results are little different if we restrict our definition of the union community to male union members (See Table V.2.), leaving out dependents who may be rather removed from actual union influence, and women union members on whom the political inclination of the husband may be expected to have greater influence than that of the union. The NPD is slightly less attractive to male union members than it is to men in general, but even this is not consistent in all surveys.

The conclusion here is that unions represent a fairly ineffective barrier to the recruitment of NPD voters, despite the very hard stand taken by the union leadership against the NPD, and the measures taken by the union leadership to weed out NPD members within union ranks. The question is whether unions are fulfilling the role of defender of their membership's interests and integrator of union members into the larger society. In the final analysis it must be this functional viability of the unions, rather than their polemics against the

TABLE V.1

NPD POTENTIAL OF UNION MEMBERS (INCLUDING FAMILIES)
(in percent)

Nationwide surveys	All interviews	April–June 1966	Dec. 1966	Jan.–Feb. 1967
		Potential NPD voters		
Union ties	33	34	26	31
No union ties	67	66	74	69
Hessen surveys		July–Oct. 1966		
Union ties	38	33		
No union ties	62	67		
Niedersachsen surveys		Oct.–Dec. 1966		
Union ties	33	29		
No union ties	67	71		
Bremen surveys		Aug.–Dec. 1966		
Union ties	43	43		
No union ties	57	57		
Hamburg surveys		April–June 1966		
Union ties	39	29		
No union ties	61	71		

SOURCES: Representative surveys of the Institut für angewandte Sozialwissenschaft, Bad Godesberg (INFAS). Nationwide: April–June 1966, 2078 persons; December 1966, 1602 persons; January–February 1967, 1670 persons. Hessen: July–October 1966, 2138 persons. Niedersachsen: October–December 1966, 1908 persons. Bremen: August–December 1966, 3015 persons. Hamburg: April–June 1966, 1521 persons.

NPD, which will determine whether union workers will continue to be attracted by NPD slogans.

Another group thought to be a poor target for NPD propaganda is the community of Catholics with close church ties. Here the distinction among Catholics is between practicing Catholics, that is, those who regularly attend mass, and those who are nominal, or non-practicing Catholics.

The contention is that those with close church bonds should be less attracted to the NPD appeals because they already belong to an integrative social mechanism, the Catholic church. Evangelical churches are not seen as such an integrating force, since they do not generally attempt to build as cohesive and complete a social entity as is true for the Catholic community.

TABLE V.2

NPD POTENTIAL OF MALE UNION MEMBERS
(in percent)

Nationwide surveys	May–June 1966	Dec. 1966	Jan.–Feb. 1967	April–June 1967
Male union members as a proportion of all males	38	35	33	34
Male unionized potential NPD voters as a proportion of all male potential NPD voters	37	23	32	25
NPD union men as a proportion of all union men	7	9	11	10
NPD men as a proportion of all men	7	14	11	7

SOURCES: Surveys of INFAS, Bad Godesberg. May–June, 1966, 2078 persons; December, 1966, 1602 persons; January–February, 1967, 1679 persons; April–June, 1967, 2283 persons.

Surveys taken in the Federal Republic indicate that, to about the same degree as among union workers, practicing Catholics lean to the NPD less than the average. That is, practicing Catholics tend to be more reticent about expressing support for the NPD, but here again there are exceptions, most notably in Niedersachsen, where a poll in December of 1966 showed an overrepresentation for practicing Catholics among potential NPD voters. (See Table V.3.) This survey in Niedersachsen calls for closer examination for two reasons.

First, Catholic respondents who expressed the possibility of voting NPD came from the small number of *Landkreise* (roughly, "counties") in Niedersachsen which are overwhelmingly (over 80 percent) Catholic. In these very areas the Catholic community is most closed and most tied to the CDU as the political expression of their will. In these districts of Niedersachsen, the CDU vote percentage closely approximates the Catholic percentage of the population. One would expect that, if the theory of the Catholic church as a barrier against NPD recruitment is correct, it would be most visible in the most closely knit Catholic communities. But in these communities the NPD-potential among practicing Catholics was over 20 percent, or more than the NPD-potential among Protestants in the same area.

The second reason that this is interesting is that in the state election in Niedersachsen on June 3, 1967, the NPD was not able to convert these survey expressions of support into actual votes.

In the intervening six months between this survey and the election the situation had changed radically, and the NPD was no longer as attractive as it had been at the height of the economic and political crisis at the end of 1966. In June 1967, the NPD was still an outcast party in an overwhelmingly Catholic community with close ties to the church. Yet the surveys from December, 1966 show that even in the most cohesive Catholic community the NPD is seen as a protest party; an expression of support for the NPD is recognized as

TABLE V.3

NPD POTENTIAL IN RELATION TO RELIGIOUS AFFILIATION
(in percent)

Religious affiliation	All interviews	Potential NPD voters	
		April–June 1966	Dec. 1966
Nationwide surveys			
Practicing Catholics	29	22	18
Other Catholics	16	14	21
Practicing Protestants	11	9	9
Other Protestants	40	52	46
Others or no confession	4	3	6
		June–Aug. 1966	Oct.–Dec. 1966
Niedersachsen surveys			
Practicing Catholics	12	5	14
Other Catholics	5	8	4
Protestants	79	84	78
Others or no confession	4	3	4
		July–Oct. 1966	
Hessen surveys			
Practicing Catholics	17	11	
Other Catholics	14	12	
Protestants	64	70	
Others or no confession	5	7	

TABLE V.3 (*continued*)

Bremen surveys		Aug.–Dec. 1966
Practicing Catholics	3	3
Other Catholics	7	8
Practicing Protestants	9	11
Other Protestants	75	71
Others or no confession	6	7

SOURCES: Surveys of INFAS, Bad Godesberg. Nationwide: April–June, 1966, 2078 persons; December, 1966, 1602 persons. Niedersachsen: June–August, 1966, 1926 persons; October–December, 1966, 1908 persons. Hessen: July–October, 1966, 2138 persons. Bremen: August–December, 1966, 3015 persons.

a protest against the frustrations and worries of West German society. It may be that over a period of time the NPD, through its presence in the state and community legislatures, will gain a certain aura of respectability. This may make it easier for those in the Catholic community who at present sympathize with the NPD actually to vote for the party. But at present, at least among practicing Catholics, this threshhold of social acceptability does not seem to have been reached.

This is illustrated by Figure V.1 which measures the percentage vote for the NPD against the percentage of Catholics in the population for the thirty-five largest cities in the November, 1966, state elections in Hessen and Bavaria. Clearly the NPD vote is lower in predominantly Catholic urban areas.

In conclusion, then, the NPD is underrepresented among practicing Catholics, although with some exceptions, and with some indications that this underrepresentation may decrease over time. In addition, if one combines both practicing and nominal Catholics to form the total Catholic community, the underrepresentation of the NPD tends to disappear.

What about the educational level of the NPD voter? Does the NPD appeal mainly to those with a lower education, who may not realize the implications of the NPD's appeals for democracy in the Bundesrepublik? Does higher education afford a barrier against the attractions of right-radical propaganda? Often in the study of totalitarianism and dictatorship it is assumed that people with higher edu-

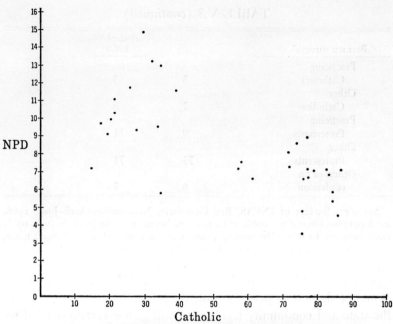

Fig. V.1. *NOVEMBER 1966 STATE ELECTIONS*

Each of the 35 largest cities in Bavaria and Hessen is represented by one point, which is plotted to compare the vote percentage received by the NPD to the Catholic percentage of the total population of that city.

cation are less attracted to simplistic views of society.[2] Certainly in most right-radical movements there is a strong current of antiintellectualism. Certainly, intellectuals are held suspect by the NPD, and are in many cases spoken of as traitors who are selling out the German people to the communists or to the Americans.

Available survey information seems to refute the thesis that higher education by itself is a barrier against voter recruitment by the NPD. In the Bundesrepublik as a whole, potential NPD voters are distributed almost exactly as is the population in general with respect to education. In some surveys taken at the state level, mainly in Hamburg and Hessen, the NPD clearly is overrepresented among the more highly educated. (See Table V.4.) The Hamburg survey may be

2. See, for example, Nelson W. Polsby, "McCarthyism at the Grass Roots," in *The Meaning of McCarthyism* (Boston: D.C. Heath, 1965). Polsby reviews the general finding that supporters of this American rightist phenomenon were more likely to have a lower educational level than the average of the whole population.

TABLE V.4

NPD POTENTIAL IN RELATION TO EDUCATION LEVEL

(in percent)

Educational level	All interviews	Potential NPD voters	
		April–June 1966	Dec. 1966
Nationwide surveys			
Grade school:			
without diploma	35	31	36
with diploma	41	42	40
Trade or middle school	19	22	19
University degree	5	5	5
Hessen surveys		July–Oct. 1966	
Grade school:			
without diploma	35	30	
with diploma	39	36	
Trade or middle school	19	23	
University degree	7	11	
Niedersachsen surveys		Oct.–Dec. 1966	
Grade school:			
without diploma	38	38	
with diploma	40	38	
Trade or middle school	17	18	
University degree	5	6	
Bremen surveys		Aug.–Dec. 1966	
Grade school:			
without diploma	26	21	
with diploma	42	43	
Trade or middle school	24	25	
University degree	8	11	
Hamburg surveys		April–June 1966	
Grade school:			
without diploma	23	17	
with diploma	43	31	
Trade or middle school	25	39	
University degree	9	13	

SOURCES: Surveys of INFAS, Bad Godesberg. Nationwide: April–June, 1966, 2078 persons; December, 1966, 1602 persons. Hessen: July–October, 1966, 2138 persons. Niedersachsen: October–December, 1966, 1908 persons. Bremen: August–December, 1966, 3015 persons. Hamburg: April–June, 1966, 1521 persons.

somewhat misleading, however, since it was taken in the spring of 1966, at which time the NPD was still unknown to many Germans with lower education. This may in turn account for underrepresentation of the NPD among these groups in earlier surveys. This factor will be covered in more detail in a later section.

Another thesis concerning education and right-radicalism states that NPD-type movements should be attractive to people with special problems of status frustration.[3] One example usually given is the highly educated man who is nevertheless at the lower end of the income scale, whose economic status is in conflict with that expected within his educational peer group. Another is the man whose educational achievement lags far behind his economic level. This thesis pictures the self-made economic success as being insecure and frustrated in his economic peer group, most of whom have had more education. The right-radical movement, which presents simplistic, conspiratorial answers for the troubles of society, is seen as a potential outlet for these frustrations.

Actually, the findings of two different groups of surveys indicates that neither of these two groups with assumed status conflicts leans in particularly great measure to the NPD. It would appear that frustrations in attainment of expected status—either economic or social, in relation to one's education—do not necessarily lead to increased susceptibility to NPD appeals.

In conclusion, educational level does not appear to be correlated in any way with NPD votership. NPD support is drawn from all educational levels in proportion to their representation in the whole population.

Two dimensions along which the NPD following does differ from the general population are age and sex. This is confirmed not only by survey results but also by official election statistics.

The NPD votership is made up of 60 percent men to only 40 percent women, though the total voting population runs about 46 percent men and 54 percent, women. This overweight of men is caused by the greater reluctance of women to associate themslves with any party which is considered radical. Thus, on the far left, the voter following of the DFU (*Deutsche Friedensunion*—German Peace Union) consists of 54 percent men and only 46 percent women. Even the

3. See Ira S. Rohter, "The Righteous Rightists," in *Transaction* (May, 1967).

SPD, with its past reputation as a radical party, is stronger among men than women, whereas the conservative CDU/CSU following has a noticeable overweight of women. (See Tables V.5a–c.)

The NPD following is overrepresented also in the 45–60 age group among men and in the 30–60 age range among women. The NPD advertises itself as a party popular among the youth of the nation and there is no doubt that many young people have been attracted to the NPD; there is also no doubt that its rallies are well attended by

TABLE V.5a

NPD VOTE/TOTAL VOTE, BY AGE AND SEX: BUNDESTAGSWAHL, 1965
(in percent)

Age group	Men		Women	
	All voters	NPD voters	All voters	NPD voters
21–30	19.8	14.5	16.7	13.0
30–45	30.9	28.7	28.6	31.5
45–60	25.1	33.7	28.2	32.7
60 and over	24.2	23.1	26.5	22.9

TABLE V.5b

DISTRIBUTION OF VOTE, BY SEX: BUNDESTAGSWAHL, 1965
(in percent)

Sex	NPD	CDU/CSU	SPD	FDP	DFU	Total
Men	59.6	41.3	51.2	47.7	53.7	46.2
Women	40.4	58.7	48.8	52.3	46.3	53.8

TABLE V.5c

NPD VOTE/TOTAL VOTE, BY AGE AND SEX: LANDTAGSWAHL, HESSEN, 1966
(in percent)

Age group	All voters	NPD voters
21–30	16	14
30–45	29	30
45–60	28	34
60 and over	27	22
Sex		
Men	46	60
Women	54	40

SOURCE: Results of the representative federal statistics for 1965, in *Wirtschaft und Statistik*, Issue 2, 1966; results of the representative state election statistics for Hessen, in *Staat und Wirtschaft in Hessen*, Issue 12, 1966.

the young. Yet much youthful attention comes from curiosity, not from agreement with NPD goals. The greatest support still comes from that generation actively involved in the World War II on the fighting fronts. The 45–60 age group were in their "best years" during the Third Reich. This age group, more than any other, had its fortunes bound to those of the Nazi regime. Interesting also is the constancy of the age and sex distributions of the NPD voter following despite the more than threefold increase in the NPD vote from the federal election of September 1965 to the state election in Hessen in November 1966.

In conclusion, the NPD has a great overweight of men in its following, along with an overweight in the 45–60 age group. This indicates that, despite its claims to be a party for the young, the NPD continues to be most attractive to men who were, so to speak, at their prime of life during the period of the rise and fall of the National-Socialist dictatorship.

One might imagine that supporters of a protest party, a party which seeks to gather behind it the frustrations and worries of the people, would include more people who, for one reason or another, had not shared in the West German economic miracle of the fifties and sixties. One might hypothesize that these people, who had watched the West German economic recovery but had not benefited from it themselves, would be fruitful targets for the NPD.

However, at least objectively, the income distribution of NPD supporters is very like that of the general population. In fact, the NPD potential is slightly higher among upper income levels, which seems to belie any theories of the economically deprived as an important basis for NPD support.

This is, however, the absolute and objective side of the economic dimension. When the question of the respondent's economic situation today as compared with two years ago is asked, it becomes clear that the NPD potential is more than twice as great (19 percent) among those whose personal economic situations, seen subjectively, have deteriorated as among those who have improved. (9 percent). (See Table V.6.)

Similar results were obtained when the question concerned future economic expectations. Here the NPD's greatest potential lay among those who thought that their economic situation, regardless of its present level, would decline in the coming year.

TABLE V.6

NPD Potential/All Interviews, by Economic Status and
Expectations: Nationwide

(in percent)

| | | Potential NPD voters | |
Income group	All interviews	Total	Percent of the group
less than 400 DM	10	9	12
401 to 800 DM	37	35	12
801 to 1200 DM	27	28	14
over 1201 DM	11	14	16
no answer	15	14	12
	100	100	
Judgment of own economic situation better than 2 years ago	18	12	9
the same as 2 years ago	59	59	13
worse than 2 years ago	23	29	19
	100	100	
will get better	16	15	12
will remain same	52	40	10
will get worse	32	55	18
	100	100	
worse than 2 years ago and will get still worse	11	20	23

SOURCES: Surveys of INFAS, Bad Godesberg. Nationwide: December, 1966, 1602 persons, with 205 potential NPD voters.

The greatest NPD potential (23 percent) was reached among that (still small) group of people whose subjective economic outlook had declined in the past two years and was expected to continue to decline in the coming year. Nearly a quarter of these thoroughly pessimistic types saw the NPD as the outlet for their anxieties.

These results from national surveys were confirmed by surveys in Hessen, Niedersachsen, Bremen, and Hamburg, with one exception. In Bremen there was no greater NPD potential among those whose economic situation, viewed subjectively, had declined in the past two years, although the NPD potential was higher among those with pessimistic future expectations.

It would seem, then, that the NPD following does not differ

from the general population so much in its objective present income distribution, as in its subjective economic outlook. NPD people are more likely to have suffered an economic decline or to expect to suffer personal financial deterioration in the near future.

There is much controversy over the occupational makeup of the NPD following. In an early study of the occupational structure of the NPD in Hamburg at the end of 1965, the INFAS Institute in Bad Godesberg reported that the NPD's chances were lowest among workers, retired people, and, most interesting, the self-employed.[4] The NPD potential was reported highest among white-collar employees. However, this study was probably not representative for the Bundesrepublik even at that time. To the contrary, a series of national surveys by INFAS (See Table V.7.) have shown that the NPD potential has consistently been higher than average among self-employed businessmen and farmers, climbing to a maximum of 21 percent in November, 1966. We have seen that much of the NPD's emotional appeal is to the small businessman and the small independent farmer, whose market position in the continuing modernization of the West German economy is ever more difficult to maintain. It is therefore not at all surprising to find a greater-than-average response from this group. Surveys from other sources confirm the attractiveness of the NPD to the self-employed.[5]

The second greatest potential for the NPD comes from the unskilled worker group. This seems not to have been true at the beginning of 1966, when the West German economy was still on the upswing; but, as the economic crisis deepened, hitting unskilled workers harder than most other occupation groups, some of the resulting discontent found an outlet through the NPD. There are some indications, however, that unskilled workers even at the beginning of 1966 were a relatively sympathetic target for the National Democrats, provided that they had heard of the NPD and recognized it as a protest party.

A survey taken in the spring of 1966 in Niedersachsen shows that unskilled workers and retired people were much less likely to have heard of the NPD as a new protest party than were other occu-

4. INFAS Research Report, "Rechtsstimmen unter der Lupe."
5. See, for example, Elisabeth Noelle-Neumann, "Wer Wählt die NPD," in *Politische Meinung*, Volume 12 (1967); also, Erwin K. Scheuch, "Dei NPD in der Bundesrepublik," in *Die neue Gesellschaft* (Number 4, 1967).

TABLE V.7

NPD Potential by Occupational Groups in the Bundesrepublik
(in percent)

Occupation	April 1966	May 1966	June 1966	Nov. 1966	Dec. 1966	Jan. 1967	Feb. 1967	April 1967	May 1967	June 1967
Retired	5	2	4	9	9	9	4	5	6	5
Self-employed	9	6	9	21	17	13	14	11	12	8
White-collar employee	6	5	7	11	8	9	11	8	10	7
Skilled worker	9	1	5	14	13	10	9	9	8	9
Unskilled worker	7	6	8	17	16	10	7	11	9	14
NPD Potential for the total population	7	4	6	14	12	10	9	9	9	8

SOURCES: Surveys of INFAS, Bad Godesberg. Nationwide: April, 1966, 735 persons; May, 1966, 779 persons; June, 1966, 564 persons; November, 1966, 761 persons; December, 1966, 841 persons; January, 1967, 847 persons; February, 1967, 832 persons; April, 1967, 764 persons; May, 1967, 739 persons; June, 1967, 780 persons.

pational groups. (See Table V.8.) Even when this factor was not taken into account, the potential for the new right-radical party was greatest among unskilled workers, but when the NPD potential was taken among the fraction of those who had heard of the NPD, the NPD potential jumped from 13 to 26 percent. This indicates that unskilled workers were slower to hear of the NPD, having in general a lower level of media consumption. But, once they had heard of the NPD, their leaning towards it was stronger than average and of course was helped by the declining economic situation and the increasing forecasts of recession in the Bundesrepublik.

As for skilled workers and white-collar employees, their NPD potential stays around the average in most of the surveys, with few meaningful deviations.

The one occupational group which has shown a constant less-than-average NPD potential is that of retired people. Several factors probably explain their reluctance to support a radical movement. Perhaps most important among these is that of a stable existence; also, the elderly, who overwhelmingly make up the ranks of the retired, are relatively more reluctant to support any movement which seeks a radical revamping of society. Then too, most elderly retired persons arrived at their basic political outlooks before the Nazi takeover, and

TABLE V.8

Knowledge of the NPD and NPD Potential among Occupational
Groups in the Bundesrepublik and in Niedersachsen
(in percent)

Bundesrepublik	Having heard of NPD as a right-wing party	NPD potential among whole occupational group	NPD potential among those having heard of NPD
Retired	44	3	3
Self-employed	50	7	10
White-collar employee	65	6	8
Skilled worker	56	3	2
Unskilled worker	33	7	13
Niedersachsen			
Retired	32	7	17
Self-employed	51	12	18
White-collar employee	64	8	11
Skilled worker	56	10	15
Unskilled worker	37	13	26

Sources: Surveys of INFAS, Bad Godesberg. Nationwide: May–June, 1966, 1343 persons. Niedersachsen: May–July, 1966, 1926 persons.

their formative years were by no means dominated by the radical doctrines of National Socialism, as were those of the 45–60 age group of today, whose years of maturation were spent in large measure under a totalitarian system.

One occupational group not mentioned so far is the military which, in terms of numbers, represents a very small proportion of the voting population. It would naturally be of great interest to know just how strong the NPD voter following is in the *Bundeswehr* (Federal Army). There are conflicting views about the extent of NPD influence within the military establishment. On one hand, the General Inspector of the Bundeswehr, General de Maiziere, stated in early 1967 that "the National Democratic Party has achieved no breakthrough into the Bundeswehr."[6] According to Maiziere's figures, only 386 members

6. *Spiegel*, Number 7/1967, p. 32.

of the Bundeswehr were NPD members. Maiziere explained that less than 1.5 percent of the NPD membership consisted of military men. He added that the highest rank among 31 soldiers put forward as NPD candidates at that date was that of captain and, when an officer is elected, he is put off the active-duty list, so that he no longer has any influence on the troops. The average age of NPD military candidates was a little over 30 years.[7] Maiziere's figures, however, do not tell the whole story. It is true that the greatest discontent within the professional military comes from the lower ranks of younger officers who are dissatisfied both with their own social prestige as soldiers and with what they consider the "sloppiness" of discipline in the Bundeswehr. This is reflected in the average age of NPD military candidates. The NPD also concentrates much of its propaganda, as we have seen, on the military virtues of the German people and to the refutation of the charges of German responsibility for the war. They propagate "stab in the back" theories which seek to explain the loss of the war in terms of treason at home. However, the small number of revealed NPD members in the Bundeswehr does not mean that National Democrats have not been successful in attracting soldiers to their banner. It was apparent that in the Bavarian state elections the NPD did very well in towns with large military garrisons. In one of the military ghettos, Sonthofen, the NPD actually got 60 percent of the vote. At that time NPD candidate Ross, a captain in the army, estimated that the NPD had the support of approximately 20 percent of all soldiers stationed in Bavaria.

A more recent study by Heribert and Marianne Schatz with the aid of Professor Rudolph Wildenmann shows that previous to the appearance of the NPD, the Christian Democrats were heavily overrepresented in support among the military and the Social Democrats, underrepresented.[8] While this is still true, it appears that in a short time the NPD has gained 25 percent of all soldiers as potential NPD voters, that is, soldiers who have already voted for the National Democrats or who expressed the possibility of doing so in the future.

Thus it would seem that the NPD's voter potential within the armed forces is higher than for all other social sectors; while this should not be a cause for immediate alarm, it is a factor to be closely watched for in future developments.

7. *Handelsblatt*, February 8, 1967, p. 2.
8. From a report in *Spiegel*, Number 8/1968, p. 24.

To summarize, the National Democrats, despite a decided anti-union bias and an equally strong call for protection and special privileges for the small businessman and small independent farmer, seem to be able to draw support from all occupation groups. Certain strong points and weak points, as noted above, can be rationally explained by the nature of that occupational group. But in the main the NPD's support among various occupational levels is far more proportional than that of the SPD, CDU/CSU or FDP. Along this important dimension, then, the NPD again gives an image of being a Volkspartei in miniature, a party whose appeal is to the German people, not to any particular set of occupational groups.

Almost one of every four citizens of the Bundesrepublik is officially classified under *Flüchtlinge* and *Vertriebene;* that is, people who have emigrated, fled, or been expelled from those areas, once part of the Third Reich, which now lie outside the boundaries of the Bundesrepublik. This includes not only the DDR (*Deutsche Demokratische Republik*), but also the Sudetenland in Czechoslovakia and those parts of East Prussia, Silesia, and Pomerania incorporated into Poland and the Soviet Union. As discussed earlier, many of the earlier right-wing parties in the Bundesrepublik were chiefly voices for such refugees and emigrants. The main interest of their clientele was reunification of Germany and recapturing "lost" German soil and lost properties. The numerical and political strength of the refugee and emigrant parties has dwindled as a result of assimilation of these people into the Bundesrepublik, the incorporation of many of these groups into the other major parties, and the inability of these single-issue parties to survive over the long run. From the first electoral debut of the National Democrats, there have been stories of particular support for the NPD by refugees and emigrants. One much-cited example is the emigrant settlement of Neu-Gablonz bei Kaufeuren, in Bavaria, a former stronghold of the refugee party, BHE.[9] In the local elections in early 1966 the NPD got 8.9 percent of the votes cast in the entire city of Kaufbeuren, to which the refugee settlement belongs. Fully 55

9. The much-used example of Neu-Gablonz bei Kaufbeuren is cited in INFAS "Rechtsstimmen unter der Lupe," pp. 5–6; by Klaus Liepelt, "Anhänger der neuen Rechtspartei," in *Politische Vierteljahresschrift*, Number 2/1967, p. 244; and by Dieter Thelen, "Die Wähler der Nationaldemokratischen Partei Deutschlands (NPD)," in Irving Fetscher et. al, (Frankfurt am Main: Europäische Verlagsanstalt, 1967), p. 167.

percent of the NPD votes came out of Neu-Gablonz, although this settlement contains only 34 percent of the voters of Kaufbeuren.

Another analysis of some 14,000 surveys in February of 1966 by the Allensbach Institut für Demoskopie also indicated that refugees and emigrants were overrepresented among NPD supporters, although not by much.[10]

Even more stories of the refugees as a main vote reservoir of the NPD were inspired by the fact that in Hessen the NPD replaced the BHE, major right-wing exponent of the refugee cause, in the state parliament after the November, 1966, elections. The district-by-district election results, however, failed to disclose a correlation between the NPD gains and the BHE losses, both in Hessen and later in Bavaria.[11] In addition, as Table V.9 shows, the representation of refugees and emigrants among NPD supporters is approximately proportional, being in some areas a little higher and in others a little lower, but significantly so in neither.

This is true even when one divides refugees and emigrants into two groups, those belonging to a refugee organization and those who do not. One might have speculated logically that in the membership of refugee groups, the feeling of being a refugee would have been stronger than among nonorganized refugees. Presumably the resentments and therefore the potential support for a party such as the NPD would be greater among organized refugees, with the organization serving to keep the saliency of refugee issues high. But in fact this seems not to be so.

It has been suggested that in some refugee settlements old traditions have been preserved, and that the NPD was able quickly to gain a foothold in these communities through personal contacts with refugee organizations.[12]

However, as a whole, refugees and emigrants from Communist-controlled areas do not seem to lean disporportionately to the NPD. This is not to deny that certain segments of the refugee organizations and the refugee press have a special receptivity to the NPD propaganda, for they certainly do.

There is no doubt, for example, that the *Sudetendeutsche*

10. Richards, *Die NPD*, p. 67.
11. Klaus Liepelt, "Anhänger der neuen Rechtspartei," p. 242.
12. *Ibid.*, p. 244.

TABLE V.9

NPD POTENTIAL/ALL INTERVIEWS: REFUGEES (EMIGRANTS) AND
WEST GERMANS, 1966

(in percent)

		Potential NPD voters	
Nationwide surveys	All interviews	April–June 1966	Dec. 1966
Member of a refugee organization	6 ⎫		5
Other refugees and emigrants	16 ⎬	24	19
Native West German and others	78 ⎭	76	76
Hessen surveys		July–Oct. 1966	
Refugees and emigrants	20	22	
Native West German and others	80	78	
Niedersachsen surveys		Oct.–Dec. 1966	
Refugees and emigrants	24	22	
Native West German and others	76	78	
Bremen surveys		Aug.–Dec. 1966	
Refugees and emigrants	21	17	
Native West German and others	79	83	
Hamburg surveys		April–June 1966	
Refugees and emigrants	19	22	
Native West German and others	81	78	

SOURCES: Surveys of INFAS, Bad Godesberg. Nationwide: April–June, 1966, 2078 persons; December, 1966, 1602 persons. Hessen: July–October, 1966, 2138 persons. Niedersachsen: October–December, 1966, 1908 persons. Bremen: August–December, 1966, 3015 persons. Hamburg: April–June, 1966, 1521 persons.

Zeitung, an organ of the organized German refugees from the Sudetenland areas of Czechoslovakia, gave the NPD its endorsement short-
ly before the state election in Bavaria in November of 1966.[13] But that
does not prove that refugees and emigrants as a community are especially receptive to the NPD. There is a difference here between appeal and
impact; and repeated survey evidence shows that the impact of NPD
appeals on refugees is no greater than on nonrefugees.[14]

As far as residence is concerned, once again the NPD shows
remarkably little under- or overrepresentation as to where it draws its
support. An analysis in early 1966 by the Allensbach Institute indicated that the NPD did somewhat better in small and medium-sized
towns than in villages or large metropolitan areas.[15] However, a later
analysis by INFAS in November and December, 1966, at the height
of the economic and governmental crisis of confidence, shows that
NPD supporters are distributed along the residence dimension in the
same proportions as the total population. (See Table V.10.)

However, this is only part of the story. In the smallest villages
it appears that there is a sort of community decision as to whether the
NPD is a socially acceptable party or not. For example, in *Regierungsbezirk* (administrative district) Mittelfranken in Bavaria the National
Democrats garnered 12.2 percent of the vote in the November, 1966,
state elections. Mittelfranken contains 836 *Gemeinde*, or communities, with an average voting population of 400 people. But in those
49 communities in which the NPD got over 25 percent of the vote,
more than twice their average for Mittelfranken, the average voting
population was only 140. In other words, the NPD's biggest successes,
percentagewise, were made in the smallest villages, in which community opinion had decided that it was socially acceptable to vote NPD.
It is also interesting to note that every one of these small NPD strongholds was predominantly Protestant, although Bavaria as a whole is
predominantly Catholic. However, in those small villages where the
community consensus came down against the NPD, it became very
difficult for the NPD to get votes. Thus, in the 267 communities
where the NPD got less than 5 percent of the vote—less than half
their average for Mittelfranken—the average voting population was

13. For a good description of right-radical tendencies within the refugee
and expellee press, see Edgar Weich's "Gibt es einen 'Rechtsradikalismus' in der
Vertriebenenpresse?" in Irving Fetscher et. al., *Rechtsradikalismus*, pp. 95–124.
    14. *Ibid.*, pp. 96–97.
    15. Richards, *Die NPD*, p. 76.

TABLE V.10

NPD POTENTIAL/ALL INTERVIEWS IN RELATION TO SIZE OF
COMMUNITY: NATIONWIDE
(in percent)

Size of Community	All interviews	Potential NPD voters
less than 2000	24	24
2000–20,000	25	26
20,000–100,000	22	24
over 100,000	29	26

SOURCES: Surveys of INFAS, Bad Godesberg. Nationwide: December, 1966,
1602 persons.

only 155, or little more than the size of the pro-NPD villages. Of these
267 communities 164 were predominantly Catholic and 103 predominantly Protestant.[16]

It appears, then, that in larger cities and towns community
opinion cannot bring as much social pressure to bear on the individual
as in these small villages. This mechanism of consensus voting works
both ways. If the village is receptive to the NPD at all, it is likely that
the NPD will get a larger-than-average percentage of the votes there;
if the NPD is generally not socially acceptable, very few will dare to
go against the community consensus and vote NPD. It is difficult
enough to belong to a suspect minority grouping within the greater
mobility and anonymity of the larger cities, but within the small village such deviation is far more open to community discipline.

The National Democrats, if they are a real Volkspartei, albeit
in miniature, should also have relatively comparable strengths in the
various regions of the Bundesrepublik. It might be expected, of course,
that for a relatively new party like the NPD there would be areas
which their organizing had not yet reached. One would also, perhaps,
expect a slightly higher potential for National Democrats in the predominantly Protestant states of the North as opposed to the predominantly Catholic states of the South. Some analyses have shown
very significant regional differences, as for example, the one presented
in February, 1967, by Professor Hans Maier.[17] According to this study
the NPD strength was distributed as follows: West Berlin 1 percent,

16. *Wahl zum Bayerischen Landtag am 20. November 1966*, Issue 277a,
(Munich: Bayerisches Statistische Landesamt, 1966).
17. Richards, *Die NPD*, p. 70.

Schleswig-Holstein, 6 percent, Hamburg and Bremen 7 percent, Hessen and North Rhein-Westphalia 9-10 percent, and Niedersachsen, Bavaria and Baden-Württemberg 14–17 percent. When presented in this form this data is somewhat misleading, for it is not clear whether the NPD is relatively strong or weak in Bremen as opposed to Hamburg, unless we know the voting populations of both. What is more revealing is the NPD potential in the various regions of the Bundesrepublik, as a percentage of the voting population for that region. In addition, since at any given time election campaigns may be going on in some states and not in others, the NPD potential may be temporarily higher in regions with active campaigning. Therefore, we should look at several surveys over a period of time to get a better perspective of the fluctuations in and relative strength of the National Democrats in the major regions of the Bundesrepublik. As Table V.11 shows, at any given point in time there may indeed be large differences across regions in the NPD's potential. For example, the NPD potential in the southern region of West Germany in January of 1967 was 15 percent, probably as a result of the bandwagon effect of headlines after the elections at the end of November in Bavaria. This compares to only 8 percent for the southwestern region at that same time. However, only two months earlier, the same two regions had NPD potentials of 13 percent and 15 percent respectively.

Therefore we would have not been wise to conclude from our January surveys that the NPD potential was basically—that is, lastingly—almost twice as great in the southern states of the Bundesrepublik as in the southwestern states. Viewing the four regions, plus four individual states in which surveys were run concurrently, we see that in all regions the NPD potential at some time during the period November, 1966 to January, 1967 reached a peak of from 13 to 18 percent, and then generally fell off to a range of 6 to 10 percent by March, 1967.

It would seem, then, that the NPD had reached in all regions of the Bundesrepublik a potential of around 15 percent during the crisis months of late 1966. This is perhaps the best indication that no region or state is immune to the propaganda of this new right-radical group. More than that, it would not be an overstatement to say that the National Democrats can regard every region as potentially fruitful ground for the entrance of their party into state parliaments. This is not to say that the NPD will definitely get into all of the state parliaments, only that no political leader in the Bundesrepublik can

TABLE V.11

NPD POTENTIAL IN THE VARIOUS REGIONS AND STATES OF THE BUNDESREPUBLIK
(in percent)

Date of survey	Nation-wide	Northern states	North Rhine-Westphalia	South-western states	Southern states	Niedersachsen	Hessen	Hamburg	Bremen
April, 1966	7	—	—	—	—	10	—	5	—
May, 1966	4	5	4	4	4	9	—	5	—
June, 1966	6	5	12	5	5	12	—	4	—
July, 1966	—	—	—	—	—	—	—	—	—
August, 1966	—	—	—	—	—	—	8	—	6
September, 1966	—	—	—	—	—	—	8	—	6
October, 1966	—	—	—	—	—	14	6	—	13
November, 1966	14	14	13	15	13	13	10	—	11
December, 1966	12	12	11	9	14	18	12	—	8
January, 1967	10	7	9	8	15	12	12	—	10
February, 1967	9	9	7	9	11	11	9	—	8
March, 1967	9	9	6	10	9	9	10	—	6

SOURCES: Surveys of INFAS, Bad Godesberg, from April, 1966 to March, 1967.

proclaim that his state is "immune" to intrusion by the National Democrats.

When the NPD made its first electoral breakthroughs in the November, 1966 elections in Hessen and Bavaria, the claims were strengthened that most NPD voters represented a regrouping of voters of old, now mainly defunct, right-wing parties and dissatisfied right-oriented voters of the FDP. As early as the beginning of 1966 an analysis by INFAS of the NPD vote in the 1965 federal elections for the Regierungsbezirk Mittelfranken had strongly indicated that over 90 percent of the voters of this new party came not from the CDU/CSU and SPD ranks, but from former right-wing followings of the FDP, GDP, DG, and DRP.[18] The INFAS report correctly predicted also that the FDP, if it gave up as many votes to the NPD in the November state elections as it had in the 1965 federal elections, would not be able to top the 10 percent mark in Mittelfranken. And since this Regierungsbezirk was their only chance of getting over 10 percent of the vote in any Regierungsbezirk—necessary in Bavaria to gain any seats in the Landtag—it was therefore doubtful that the Free Democrats would make it back into the Bavarian parliament.[19]

At the November elections in Hessen the refugee party, BHE, was unable to gain entrance into the parliament, but the NPD gained eight seats; it was popular to say that the NPD indeed was bringing together voters of former right-wing parties. And, from the defeat of the FDP in the Bavarian state elections, it was similarly taken as confirmed fact that former FDP voters were a main source of NPD strength.[20]

However, if it were true in early 1966 that the NPD following was still composed mostly of onetime adherents of the FDP and earlier right-wing parties, this was certainly no longer so by the end of that year. By then the NPD following had reached into the former ranks of the SPD and CDU, to the point where fully 64 percent of *potential* NPD voters classified themselves as normal CDU or SPD followers. (See Table V.12.) Very few potential NPD voters actually favored or would admit favoring the NPD above all other parties.

18. "Rechtsstimmen unter der Lupe," p. 35.
19. *Ibid.*, p. 13.
20. With some dissent, on both counts, to labeling NPD voters as former rightist votes or rightist FDP voters coming from Prof. Erwin K. Scheuch in the *Süddeutsche Zeitung* issues of May 11, 1966, and December 30, 1966.

TABLE V.12

NPD Potential/All Interviews: Party Preference/Previous Voting Record, 1966

(in percent)

Nationwide surveys	All interviews	Potential NPD voters
Party preference		
CDU/CSU	38	26
SPD	41	38
FDP	5	7
Other parties	2	14
No answer	14	15
Previous voting record		
only CDU/CSU	27	17
only SPD	25	21
only FDP	1	1
only other parties	0	1
several parties	32	44
never voted	4	5
no answer	11	11
Hessen surveys		
Party preference		
CDU/CSU	26	23
SPD	48	39
FDP	5	12
Other parties	2	10
No answer	19	16
Previous voting record		
only CDU/CSU	16	11
only SPD	31	20
only FDP	2	3
only other parties	1	2
several parties	31	49
never voted	4	2
no answer	15	13
Niedersachsen surveys		
Party preference		
CDU/CSU	33	35
SPD	39	32
FDP	3	6
Other parties	2	8
No answer	23	19

TABLE V.12 (*continued*)

Nationwide surveys	All interviews	Potential NPD voters
Previous voting record		
only CDU/CSU	24	23
only SPD	24	14
only FDP	1	2
only other parties	1	2
several parties	32	37
never voted	4	2
no answer	14	20
Bremen surveys		
Party preference		
CDU/CSU	19	14
SPD	54	45
FDP	4	6
Other parties	2	12
No answer	21	23
Previous voting record		
only CDU/CSU	14	10
only SPD	37	24
only FDP	2	2
only other parties	1	3
several parties	29	45
never voted	4	5
no answer	13	11
Hamburg surveys		
Party preference		
CDU/CSU	22	28
SPD	59	29
FDP	3	6
Other parties	2	23
No answer	19	14
Previous voting record		
only CDU/CSU	15	15
only SPD	39	10
only FDP	2	2
only other parties	0	5
several parties	24	54
never voted	5	7
no answer	15	7

SOURCES: Surveys of INFAS, Bad Godesberg. Nationwide: Dec., 1966, 1602 persons; Hessen: July–Oct., 1966, 2138 persons; Niedersachsen: Oct.–Dec., 1966, 1908 persons. Bremen: Aug.–Dec., 1966, 3015 persons; Hamburg: April–June, 1966, 1521 persons.

Thus, while admitting that they might vote NPD (or had once voted NPD), they usually would not openly classify themselves as committed to the NPD. Indeed, FDP ranks were overrepresented in the NPD potential, as were the ranks of all other small parties (including those giving NPD as party reference), but together these two groups comprised only 21 percent of the potential NPD voters.

One may theorize that the NPD, in its first electoral appearances, was best known among right-wing groups, including right-wing elements of the FDP, which had always had identity problems because of the extreme right-left split within its ranks. Through the 1965 federal campaign and into early 1966 the NPD may have drawn predominantly from these vote reservoirs. However, the publicity given to the NPD during 1966, and its propaganda during the crisis at the end of the year, had brought it into contact with new vote sources; it had cut significantly into these new social areas.

Surprisingly enough, surveys taken at the end of 1966 showed a higher NPD-potential among nominal SPD followers than among CDU followers. Other surveys in Niedersachsen and Hessen show, however, that in individual states the NPD potential may be higher among nominal CDU voters as opposed to SPD voters. It is clear that the National Democrats are drawing the majority of their vote strength from nominal voters of the two major parties. This may be qualified in one respect. There is evidence to show that voters who have switched their votes between one of the two major parties and the small parties are more predisposed to vote NPD than constant voters of the CDU or SPD or voters who have switched their votes, but only between the two major parties.

This would indicate that many nominal SPD and CDU adherents have at some time in their past been dissatisfied with their attachment to that party, but have been reluctant to switch to the other major party. These marginal voters of the major parties have thus shown a previous dissatisfaction with both major parties, and a predisposition against the basic political configuration within the Bundesrepublik; in a crisis situation they could be expected to fall away from the major parties towards protest parties such as the NPD.

But these qualifications do not erase the fact that 21 percent of the potential NPD voters in the November, 1966 surveys were previously solid SPD rank and file who had, according to their own statements, voted solidly SPD in the past. (These statements, of course, may themselves be somewhat suspect. Some of these people may in fact have declined to admit voting a right-wing party previously. This would, however, probably not be a significantly large number of people.) Another 17 percent of potential NPD voters had been solid supporters of the CDU/CSU. Thus, by the end of 1966 it seems likely that not only were the great majority of NPD sympathizers being drawn from the two major parties, but nearly two-fifths of them formerly were firm SPD and CDU/CSU supporters.

To summarize, it appears that the NPD started out by collecting voters of the remnant right-wing parties and disgruntled right-leaning FDP voters. It continues to be relatively more attractive to these groups than to others; in addition it is somewhat more attractive to marginal voters of the SPD, and CDP, who have voted at least once in the past for small, usually right-wing parties. Yet the National Democrats have expanded to the point at which they are drawing support from previously firm backers of the major parties.

Up to this point nothing has been said about the connection, if any, between NPD voters and the votership of Hitler's NSDAP, and with reason. Perhaps no area of examination of the NPD so abounds with abuse and carelessness as the question, "Is the NPD a party of old Nazis (Ehemalige)?" Many sources have immediately labeled the NPD as a successor party to the NSDAP. Usually they point to the predominance of hard-core Nazi functionaries who run the party organization. In this respect they are undoubtedly correct, although one could, as the National Democrats themselves have pointed out, cite numbers of former Nazis within the party organizations of the FDP, CDU/CSU, and even (though to a lesser extent) the SPD.

All this is neither surprising nor new. But it refers to the NPD party organization, not to voters of the NPD. And it must not be assumed that since the leadership of this party is weighted heavily with men with Nazi pasts, so is its votership. First of all there are NPD voters between the ages of twenty-one and forty-five who voted neither for Weimar nor for the Third Reich before the outbreak of World War II. But even to brand those NPD voters over forty-five as old Nazis is unwarranted if for no other reason than that it is unprovable. There have been some, notably Professor Erwin K. Scheuch, who have warned loudly against equating the NPD voter with the NSDAP voter.[21] Professor Scheuch states that such an equation would not only be false but moreover might produce a reverse reaction which would only help the National Democrats.[22] Yet such cautions should not and must not be taken as the last word on the subject. Scheuch, for example, is scandalized at the risk of an unproven equating of the NPD votership with that of the NSDAP, but fails then to examine the relationship, whatever it might be, himself. The history of the Bundesrepublik does not arise out of a vacuum; inevitably interest will be drawn to comparisons of any extreme right-wing party with the National-Socialist movement of the past.

In this area of examination, surveys generally are not a very suitable tool of analysis, since few people will admit, at least during a short interview, that they voted NSDAP during the lifespan of the Weimar Republic—that is, when they still had a choice among competing parties. What is more often attempted is a comparison of the NPD vote in some district with the NSDAP vote in that district. It is not difficult to show that the district of Mittelfranken in Bavaria, the area of Grumbach in Rheinland-Pfalz, or the Island of Fehmarn in Schleswig-Holstein, which were early strongholds of the NSDAP, were also NPD strongholds.[23]

Dieter Thelen, in his study of NPD voters, makes a good many such comparisons to show that the NPD wins its greatest support from those same districts in which the NSDAP also achieved great electoral successes.[24] However, much of his work concerns a comparison of the NPD vote with the NSDAP vote in selected districts for the federal elections of 1965. In addition, his conclusion that NPD strong points coincide with earlier NSDAP strong points may be questioned, in that he presents only selected districts, but at no point gives any statistical correlation for any comprehensive collection of districts. One cannot

21. Erwin K. Scheuch, "Die NPD in der Bundesrepublik," pp. 292–301.
22. Ibid., p. 293.
23. A relative NSDAP stronghold is here considered as a district in which the NSDAP got a plurality or an absolute majority by 1930 or 1932 (when the NSDAP was able to get about one-third of the total votes in the whole Weimar Republic). The NSDAP received a 45 percent vote plurality in the July 31, 1932 elections on the island of Fehmarn in Schleswig-Holstein, and got fully 68 percent of the vote in the November 6, 1932 elections in the area of Grumbach in what is now the state of Rheinland-Pfalz.
24. Dieter Thelen, "Die Wähler der NPD," pp. 159–172.

show a statistical correlation between the NPD and the NSDAP in electoral strength merely by citing individual coincidences because, for those, there can somewhere be found examples of noncoincidence. Only a statistical measure taken over some comprehensive set of districts can give a defensible picture of the correlation.

I made such a correlation at the Institut für angewandte Sozialwissenschaft for two areas. The first was for the largest thirty-nine cities in Hessen and Bavaria, from which election data from the 1966 state elections were correlated with the returns for the federal elections in 1928, 1930, and 1932. The scatter-diagrams (See Figure V.2.) with their associated correlation coefficients demonstrate the growing correlation between the NPD success and the NSDAP success as one advances from 1928 to 1930 to 1932. This progression also coincides with the increasing crisis within the Weimar Republic. I do not believe that it is wrong to state that the November-December, 1966, period was also the greatest crisis in confidence, both economic and political, within the Bundesrepublik since its founding. Therefore, it is interesting to note that the greatest NPD-NSDAP correlation is achieved with 1932, most troubled of the three years for Weimar, and the November, 1966, period of crisis for the Bundesrepublik.

The second area is the 51 communities (*Gemeinden*) of the county (*Landkreis*) Dieburg in Hessen. The first example was for larger cities in Hessen and Bavaria, the second is for the smallest villages and towns in a single rural county. With a voting population of 74,800 the average voting population per community was about 1470. The 1966 state election results were here correlated with the state election results from November, 1931, again at the time of great and still growing crisis in the Weimar Republic. Once again the correlation between the NSDAP and NPD was a high .71, whereas, for comparison, the correlation between the SPD vote in 1931 and the SPD vote in 1966 for those same 51 communities was only .64. Thus the correlation between NPD and NSDAP, two separate parties, was higher than a similar coefficient for the SPD, with a continuous history spanning both eras. (Of course the SPD following also has changed over the years, and the SPD no longer has to compete with the KPD for support from the working class as it did during Weimar.)

Again, as in Mittelfranken, the NPD had its greatest success in the smallest villages. Four of the five communities with the highest

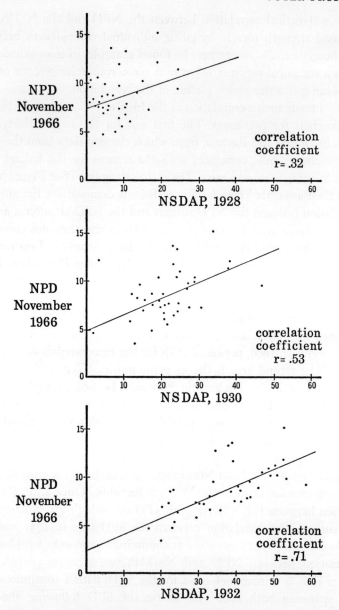

Fig. V.2. *NPD 1966 VERSUS NSDAP 1928, 1930, 1932*

The 39 largest cities in Bavaria and Hessen are each represented in
each chart by one point, which is plotted to show the vote percentage
received by the NPD in the November 1966 state elections compared
with the NSDAP vote percentage in 1928, 1930, and 1932.

NPD vote percentages had a voting population of less than three hundred people.[25]

What do these correlations mean? They certainly do not indicate that the same people who voted for the NSDAP in 1932 are now voting for the NPD, for those are only ecological correlations, not individual correlations. (It is theoretically even possible that none of the people who voted NSDAP are now voting NPD, although this is extremely unlikely.)[26] They do indicate that in those areas in which, during the most crisis-laden time of the Weimar Republic, the NSDAP achieved its greatest electoral victories, the NPD, in the worst crisis of confidence to date in the Bundesrepublik, also gained its greatest vote percentages. The importance lies not in the individuals involved, but in the mechanism of political mobilization by right-radical movements in periods of social crisis. The antidemocratic, or profascist, potential of such a mechanism depends on the socially determining factors which continuously shape people's attitudes and opinions. It is this set of socially relevant factors which will determine whether people, and which people, will be susceptible to right-radical appeals during times of unrest and change.

The NSDAP voters of 1932 can be replaced endlessly if the basic attitude-molding mechanisms of the society remain the same. To the extent that the same social relationships which created the potential NSDAP voters of 1932 still obtain, the same pattern of recruitment by right-radical parties in a crisis situation may also still be operative. These correlations may be taken as an indicator of the extent to which, despite all the tremendous dislocations and changes since World War II, those social mechanisms that produce susceptibility to right-radical appeals have survived in direct proportion to

25. The five communities with the top NPD vote percentages were the following, listed with their voting populations:

Community	NPD vote (percent)	Voting population (number)
Nomrod	18.7	72
Schlierbach	15.4	282
Harputshausen	14.4	253
Reinheim	14.2	3178
Messbach	13.9	55

26. For a more detailed explanation of the relationship between ecological and individual correlations, see W. S. Robinson, "Ecological Correlations and the Behavior of Individuals" (Bobbs-Merrill Reprint PS-243), *American Sociological Review*, XV, June, 1950.

their strength as measured in 1932. Of course the climate of crisis in the Bundesrepublik at the end of 1966 was mild compared to the social disintegration taking place in Weimar in 1932. Thus it should be no real comfort that the NPD was only getting 7 or 8 percent of the vote as opposed to the NSDAP's more than 30 percent in 1932.

We have discussed the structural breakdown of the potential NPD following and compared this structure with that of the population of the Bundesrepublik. The purpose was to see if the NPD votership represented a demographically isolatable group within the population; many people would like to see the NPD voter in such a light. Many journalists would like to see the NPD voter as a former Nazi, or Nazi voter, thus to dismiss the problems which are creating NPD votes and to socially scandalize NPD adherents. Many a socialist would like to see the NPD as a middle-class phenomenon, with the working class as a bulwark against the fascist tide. Others would like to view the NPD as a collection of the remnants of earlier right-wing movements, and assume that the same self-destructive divisions and splintering tendencies which proved fatal to such parties in the past will also catch up with the National Democrats.

However, we have seen such oversimplified images of this new force in the political scene of the Bundesrepublik fail to meet the test of objective verification. At best they are only relatively accurate. By that I mean that adherents of earlier right-wing parties are indeed relatively more sympathetic to the NPD and more easily and quickly recruited into its voter following. And yet these voters do not, at least since early 1966, form the majority of the NPD electoral supporters. Along most dimensions the NPD voter-structure varies only by a few percentage points from the structure of the whole voting population— less in general than for the three major established parties in Bonn.

If then, the NPD voter-structure can not be readily isolated along demographic lines, perhaps it can be sorted along attitudinal dimensions, or along some combinations of the two. Perhaps it is the opinions which people hold, rather than any one set of demographic factors, which predispose them to right-wing extremist appeals. In the earlier discussion of emotional themes of NPD propaganda, I tried to indicate the size of the potential audience receptive to each theme. I also demonstrated that such antidemocratic opinions are widely distributed through all classes and social backgrounds in West German society—though, to be sure, with some noticeable high and low points.

Here I would like to examine the opinions of potential NPD voters as compared with the general populace. Table V.13 presents a list of twenty-three questions, each representing an important NPD slogan or theme, which were tested in Niedersachsen in early 1967.[27] In twenty-one of these the potential NPD voters do exhibit a higher degree of affinity to extremist themes, but again the difference is often a matter of only a few percentage points. Only on one question does the majority of potential NPD voters fall on the different side of a theme from the majority (here actually the plurality) of the whole survey population. This question, testing the attitude towards Germans who fought the Nazi regime during the war, is aimed directly at SPD leaders Willy Brandt and Herbert Wehner, who spent the war years as emigrants fighting the Third Reich. The replies to this question split pretty much along party lines, with SPD followers overwhelmingly on the "disagree" side; the "agree" side came predominantly from right-oriented voters of the CDU, FDP, and from more right-wing parties.

It is interesting to note that questions on which the NPD people show the most noticeably higher levels of agreement with these right radical themes are those directly concerning the evaluation of the National-Socialist dictatorship, its legitimacy, and its crimes.

The question of whether those Germans who fought from abroad against Nazism should still be considered Germans (as opposed to traitors) leads this list. Obviously if one regarded (or regards) the National-Socialist regime as proper and legitimate, then those Germans who fought against this regime are seen not as heroes or freedom fighters but as traitors no longer worthy of the name "German." Since Brandt and Wehner of the SPD are anathema to right-wing voters in general, the question has a special poignancy for NPD supporters.

Did National Socialism have its good side also? Was it a regime under which law, order, and morality prevailed? Fully 65 percent of potential NPD voters said "Yes," as opposed to 49 percent of all interviewed. Perhaps more significantly, only 14 percent of all potential NPD backers and "No," whereas 34 percent of all asked did not see

27. Survey taken by INFAS in March of 1967 in the state of Niedersachsen, 633 cases. The results of this state survey differ only by a matter of percentage points from later nationwide attitude surveys. The substantive findings of the state and nationwide surveys are the same.

TABLE V.13

NPD POTENTIAL/ALL INTERVIEWS: ANSWERS TO STATEMENTS,
1967 NIEDERSACHSEN SURVEY
(in percent)

		All interviews	Potential NPD voters
1. "Germany now needs energetic leaders, who think first of their own people."	Agree	68	72
	Disagree	21	8
	No answer	11	20
2. "Germany should not depend so much on the United States. Americans think mainly of their own interests."	Agree	67	69
	Disagree	23	14
	No answer	10	17
3. "The undependability of the southern peoples [Spanish, Italians, and Greeks mainly meant here] lies in their blood. One should not depend all too much on them."	Agree	72	72
	Disagree	16	10
	No answer	12	18
4. "The best course for us would be to go along with France. Then we could get along without any American support."	Agree	33	37
	Disagree	50	40
	No answer	17	23
5. "Since human nature is unchangeable, there will always be war among peoples."	Agree	53	59
	Disagree	33	19
	No answer	14	22
6. "National Socialism had its good side also. At least then order and morality prevailed."	Agree	49	65
	Disagree	34	14
	No answer	17	21
7. "As long as the number of Jews really killed in the war is not established, one should not speak constantly of supposed German cruelties."	Agree	43	52
	Disagree	38	18
	No answer	19	30
8. "If they accuse us because of the concentration camps, the Allies also should be brought to account for their war crimes."	Agree	71	74
	Disagree	14	6
	No answer	15	20
9. "Things must be changed, so that the interest of individual groups no longer stand above the good of the whole people."	Agree	79	68
	Disagree	4	4
	No answer	17	28
10. "The working class never had it so good. Still higher wages would endanger the whole economy."	Agree	66	56
	Disagree	26	27
	No answer	8	17
11. "Instead of legislatures, in which there is much talk but little action, we need at last men who can act decisively."	Agree	62	66
	Disagree	23	12
	No answer	15	22
12. "Our people [Volk] are different from other peoples. Thus with right we can claim a special place in Europe and the world."	Agree	30	32
	Disagree	55	43
	No answer	15	25

TABLE V.13 (*continued*)

		All interviews	Potential NPD voters
13. "The claims to our eastern territories are undeniable people's rights. The winning back of this German soil must be worth every sacrifice to us."	Agree	46	51
	Disagree	37	27
	No answer	17	11
14. "Above all young people need strict discipline, directed leadership, and the will to struggle for family and fatherland."	Agree	65	66
	Disagree	19	13
	No answer	16	21
15. "Crimes against morality, such as rape and child molesting, require a stronger punishment than jail. Such criminals should be publicly whipped or worse."	Agree	83	77
	Disagree	11	5
	No answer	6	18
16. "German policy should see to it that foreign troops are withdrawn from our country."	Agree	47	51
	Disagree	34	23
	No answer	19	26
17. "People who as emigrants worked from abroad during the war against a struggling Germany should no longer be considered Germans."	Agree	34	53
	Disagree	45	21
	No answer	21	26
18. "It is high time to get rid of the claim that Germany was to blame for the outbreak of World War II."	Agree	44	56
	Disagree	36	17
	No answer	20	27
19. "Germany has already paid much too much money to the Jews as reparations. We should end the payments to Israel."	Agree	69	79
	Disagree	16	6
	No answer	15	15
20. "The wild orgies of the ancient Greeks and Romans were child's play compared to certain goings-on today, in circles where one would least expect it."	Agree	45	49
	Disagree	25	15
	No answer	30	36
21. "It is intolerable that all moral values are systematically despised in television, radio, and films."	Agree	46	57
	Disagree	29	14
	No answer	25	27
22. "An end must be put to the dissolution of our people through foreign influences."	Agree	58	64
	Disagree	20	8
	No answer	22	28
23. "One should take steps against the unkempt youths who unabashedly walk our streets with Beatle haircuts and miniskirts."	Agree	69	69
	Disagree	25	17
	No answer	6	14

SOURCE: Survey of INFAS, Bad Godesberg. Niedersachsen: Feb.–March, 1967, 633 persons.

National Socialism as a regime of law, order, and morality. This question might have gotten an even higher affirmative response had the second sentence been deleted. But the choice posed for the person was to decide not only if National Socialism had its good side, but whether it could also meet the second positive qualification. Here the potential NPD voters clearly see the National-Socialist past in a quite positive light which goes beyond a neutral or nonnegative standpoint.

Is it high time that Germans put an end to the claim that Germany was responsible for the outbreak of World War II? A majority of 56 percent of potential NPD voters said "Yes," and only 17 percent said "No," as opposed to 44 percent "Yes" and 36 percent "No" for the total survey population. NPD supporters, again, are more likely to see World War II as being forced upon the Third Reich. In this view National Socialism is seen as not responsible for the massive destruction wrought in Germany by the war, or for the division and occupation of Germany after the war.

Another question on which potential NPD voters differed from the average concerns the extermination campaign carried out against Jews during the war. Fully 52 percent of potential NPD voters agreed that as long as the exact number of Jews killed in the war is not established, one should not keep on talking about supposed German atrocities. Only 18 percent disagreed. Here again it appears that the NPD following, more than the population as a whole, would cloud the issue of the Nazi atrocities with argument as to whether the given numbers of victims are correct.

It would seem, then, that those who say they have already voted or might in the future vote NPD differ from the general population in their receptivity to NPD themes chiefly in their stand towards National Socialism and the Nazi past. It would appear too that, with this exception, the rest of the population also contains people who agree with the NPD themes in roughly the same proportions as do potential NPD voters.

However, I would qualify this with a look at the opinions of the small number of people who give the NPD as their true party preference. Here we see the opinion structure of the hard-core, self-admitted National Democratic voter who represents only a fraction of the NPD's actual votes. As Table V.14 demonstrates, such hard-core NPD adherents overwhelmingly agree with those right-radical propaganda issues. Even the most harshly formulated statement—

"The Jews have no claim to reparations. It would have been better if Germany had not given the Jews a cent"—received 47 percent agreement from hard-core NPD adherents as opposed to only 17 percent from the population as a whole.

A strongly formulated statement about needing one strong man, instead of the Bundestag, received an 84 percent vote of agreement from this small group; for the total survey population it found agreement with 38 percent of the people, discouragingly high but still less than half the percentage-approval among outspoken NPD followers.

Only when we analyze opinions of this small minority do we see the full agreement with the whole string of right-radical appeals.

In conclusion, it can be said that a very small number of ardent NPD supporters is in overwhelming agreement with the whole set of NPD appeals. The larger group of potential NPD voters shows a noticeably greater-than-average receptivity to NPD themes where such themes directly concern a judgment of National Socialism. On all such questions the potential NPD voters showed themselves more favorable towards the National-Socialist past and more intolerant of those who fought against, and/or suffered under, the Nazi regime.

Yet the potential receptive audience to all of these NPD themes far exceeds the NPD potential itself. That is, that group of potential NPD voters in no sense equals the group of people who basically agree with many, if not all, NPD slogans. At this time the NPD has only been able to mobilize a fraction of the people who, in their own outlook on society, agree in many areas with the National Democrats.

It would seem that we have reached an impasse of sorts. On the one hand, we have seen that along most ecological dimensions the NPD is proportionately represented; on the other hand, we have seen that, while National Democratic sympathizers agree somewhat more than the average with the various right-radical propositions, it by no means follows that holders of such opinions are NPD sympathizers. The results, along both ecological and attitudinal lines, are unsatisfying and rather inconclusive when taken separately. If anything, they tend to bolster the image of the NPD as a *Volkspartei*, as opposed to a class party (*Klassenpartei*) or special interest party (*Interessenpartei*).

In particular, the presence of large numbers of potentially

TABLE V.14

NPD VOTERS/ALL INTERVIEWS: ANSWERS TO STATEMENTS, 1967 NATIONWIDE SURVEY

		All interviews	Admitted NPD voters
1. "National Socialism had its good side also. At least then order and morality prevailed."	Agree Disagree	58 42	90 10
2. "Germany should not depend so much on the Americans. Americans want only to exploit Germany."	Agree Disagree	42 58	73 27
3. "Germany now needs energetic leaders, who think first of their own people."	Agree Disagree	62 38	100 0
4. "There are now and for all time different races and colors in the world. They will always fight each other. That is a law of nature."	Agree Disagree	32 68	42 58
5. "The Allies committed far more crimes during the war against the German people than ever were committed in the concentration camps."	Agree Disagree	34 66	63 37
6. "As long as the number of Jews really killed in the war is not established, one should not speak constantly of supposed German cruelties."	Agree Disagree	43 57	79 21
7. "Instead of the Bundestag, we need a man at the top now who can act decisively."	Agree Disagree	38 62	84 16
8. "Our people [Volk] are different from other peoples. Thus with right we can claim a special place in Europe and the world."	Agree Disagree	22 78	53 47
9. "The claims to our eastern territories are undeniable people's rights. The winning back of this German soil must be worth every sacrifice to us."	Agree Disagree	42 58	47 53
10. "Above all young people need strict discipline, directed leadership and the will to struggle for family and fatherland."	Agree Disagree	59 41	84 16
11. "People who as emigrants worked from abroad during the war against a struggling Germany should no longer be considered Germans."	Agree Disagree	35 65	74 26

TABLE V.14 *(continued)*

		All interviews	Potential NPD voters
12. "It is high time to get rid of the claim that Germany was to blame for the outbreak of World War II."	Agree	43	74
	Disagree	57	26
13. "The Jews have no rights to reparations. It would have been better if Germany hadn't given the Jews a penny."	Agree	17	47
	Disagree	83	53
14. "Sexually abnormal persons, as for example homosexuals, should be put under lock and key for life to protect the public."	Agree	45	68
	Disagree	55	32
15. "It is intolerable that all moral values are systematically despised in television, radio, and film."	Agree	47	79
	Disagree	53	21
16. "An end must be put to the dissolution of our people through foreign influences."	Agree	58	89
	Disagree	42	11
17. "One must be ashamed of oneself as a German to see in our country, in broad daylight, youths with Beatle haircuts and miniskirts."	Agree	44	68
	Disagree	56	32
18. "The good of the whole people stands above the interest of the individual. Whoever does not want to conform, should be locked up."	Agree	27	53
	Disagree	73	47

SOURCE: Surveys of INFAS, Bad Godesberg. Nationwide: April–May, 1967, 1503 persons.

sympathetic listeners who have as yet not been mobilized for political purposes by an organization such as the NPD is of special interest for the future of democracy in the Bundesrepublik. As seen earlier these anti-democratic attitudes, with minor exceptions, are present to a surprisingly similar degree in all sectors of West German society. Is there, perhaps, a catalyst which both makes these options politically relevant and directs the holders of such opinions into the camp of the NPD?

One such catalyst is suggested by the NSDAP-NPD correlations discussed earlier, which showed a connection between the level of crisis in both Weimar and the Bundesrepublik, and the level of correlation between the NSDAP and NPD vote percentages. The catalyst is the crisis situation in general, and perhaps the economic crisis may

be used as the most specific and most easily measurable crisis in question.[28]

The best indicator of the personally felt sense of economic
crisis is the question: "Do you expect your own personal economic
situation to improve, worsen, or stay the same in the coming year?"
When this question on economic expectation for the coming year was
superimposed upon any one of the opinion questions for the surveys
in Niedersachsen and Hessen, the differentiation in the NPD potential becomes very clear. As Table V.15 shows, this combination of an
ideological predisposition and a personal-crisis catalyst goes a long
way to explain the dynamic of NPD recruitment. While any one of
the NPD theme questions, mated with the subjective economic
expectation, produced the same basic differentiation of the NPD potential into visibly separate levels, it was found that the best differentiation was the stance of the respondent towards National Socialism
(i.e., "National Socialism also had its good side," etc. Other questions
directly relating to the Nazi past in general were also better differen-
tiators than others, although the differences were somewhat less.) For
respondents with a favorable predisposition towards National Socialism *and* expectations of personal economic difficulties, the NPD
potential soars to over 30 percent, although for those with an unfavorable disposition towards National Socialism, along with personal
economic worries, the NPD potential is a mere 4 percent (average
for the whole survey was 14 percent). For all subsequent surveys taken
in Niedersachsen and Hessen—two states in which the NPD had recently run electoral campaigns—the results were similar. (See Figures
V. 3 and V. 4.) In all, the NPD potential for the group having both
ideological and economic conditions fulfilled was in the neighborhood
of 30 percent. The next highest potential was recorded for the group
fulfilling the ideological but not the economic condition; that is, people who were favorably oriented towards National Socialism but who
did not express any personal economic worries. For the last two groups
who were both unfavorably oriented towards National Socialism, the
NPD potentials were the lowest and, on the average, interchangeably
close. (Though on individual surveys there were some differences,

28. Other ecological and attitudinal dimensions may be combined to
give higher and lower NPD potentials, but the number of cases for these potentials
dwindles rapidly; thus, additional variance reduction gained is minimal. See Klaus
Liepelt, "Anhänger der neuen Rechtspartei," for further combinations of various
factors to get higher and lower NPD potentials.

TABLE V.15

RIGHT-RADICAL ATTITUDES AND ATTITUDES TOWARD ECONOMIC EXPECTATIONS

1. "National Socialism also had its good side. At least then order and morality prevailed."

	Number of responses*	NPD potential (percent)
Agree, and own economic situation expected to get worse	124	32
Agree, but own economic situation not expected to get worse	474	13
Disagree (or no answer), and own economic situation expected to worsen	109	4
Disagree (or no answer), but own economic situation not expected to worsen	558	8
Agree, and own economic situation got worse	142	25
Agree, but own economic situation did not get worse	479	15
Disagree (or no answer), and own economic situation got worse	116	10
Disagree (or no answer), and own economic situation did not get worse	573	5

2. "Germany should not depend so much on the United States. Americans think first of their own interests."

Agree, and own economic situation expected to get worse	172	24
Agree, but own economic situation not expected to get worse	680	11
Disagree (or no answer), and own economic situation expected to worsen	61	5
Disagree (or no answer), and own economic situation not expected to worsen	352	9
Agree, and own economic situation got worse	189	24
Agree, but own economic situation did not get worse	677	11
Disagree (or no answer), and own economic situation got worse	71	7
Disagree (or no answer), and own economic situation did not get worse	376	8

3. "People as emigrants who worked from abroad during the war against a struggling Germany, should no longer be considered Germans."

Agree, and own economic situation expected to get worse	147	27

TABLE V.15 (continued)

	Number of responses*	NPD potential (percent)
Agree, but own economic situation not expected to get worse	593	12
Disagree (or no answer), and own economic situation expected to worsen	86	5
Disagree (or no answer), and own economic situation not expected to worsen	439	8
Agree, and own economic situation got worse	170	24
Agree, but own economic situation did not get worse	611	13
Disagree (or no answer), and own economic situation got worse	90	10
Disagree (or no answer), and own economic situation did get worse	452	6

4. "It is high time to get rid of the claim that Germany was to blame for the outbreak of World War II."

Agree, and own economic situation expected to get worse	115	24
Agree, but own economic situation not expected to get worse	453	15
Disagree (or no answer), and own economic situation expected to worsen	118	14
Disagree (or no answer), and own economic situation not expected to worsen	579	7
Agree, and own economic situation got worse	118	27
Agree, but own economic situation did not get worse	468	15
Disagree (or no answer), and own economic situation got worse	142	12
Disagree (or no answer), and own economic situation did not get worse	585	7

5. "Above all, young people need strict discipline, directed leadership, and the will to struggle for family and fatherland."

Agree, and own economic situation expected to get worse	148	25
Agree, but own economic situation not expected to get worse	686	11
Disagree (or no answer), and own economic situation expected to worsen	85	8
Disagree (or no answer), and own economic situation not expected to worsen	336	7
Agree, and own economic situation got worse	177	25

TABLE V.15 (continued)

	Number of responses*	NPD potential (percent)
Agree, but own economic situation did not get worse	698	12
Disagree (or no answer), and own economic situation got worse	83	6
Disagree (or no answer), and own economic situation did not get worse	365	7

* A few answers to questions were undetermined; these deleted cases cause the number of responses to be smaller than the total number of persons interviewed.
SOURCE: Surveys of INFAS, Bad Godesberg. Niedersachsen: Feb.–May, 1967, 1344 persons, with an NPD potential of 12 percent.

which of the two groups would have the lower NPD potential could not be predicted.)

As a test to see whether close church or union ties made any difference in this pattern, the survey populations were divided into two main groups—those with such ties to these major social institutions, and those without them. According to several theories, such organizations form a barrier to right-radical appeals.[29] The patterns of differentiation for both Hessen and Niedersachsen, however, remain remarkably undisturbed by the addition of this third factor to the ideological and economic ones. The differences are usually a matter of a few percentage points, although it can be conceded that these differences are always in the direction of lower NPD potentials for the groups with union or church ties. This should not be too surprising, since it was seen earlier that the extent of antidemocratic sentiment is not more than a few percentage points lower for members of one or both of these major social institutions than for nonmembers. It might still have been possible, however, that these established social institutions might have been able to keep such sentiments dormant or turn them away from an attachment to the National Democrats.

Hopefully, such social institutions would have the effect of integrating their members into society, to bear its trials and tribulations without turning against society in general. Hopefully, the Catholic church and the union movement, despite the antidemocratic leanings of a sizable block of their membership, would be able to give

29. Klaus Liepelt, ibid., p. 269; Richards, Die NPD, pp. 69–70; Helga Grebing, "Nationalismus und Demokratie in Deutschland," Irving Fetscher et. al., in Rechtsradikalismus, pp. 62–63.

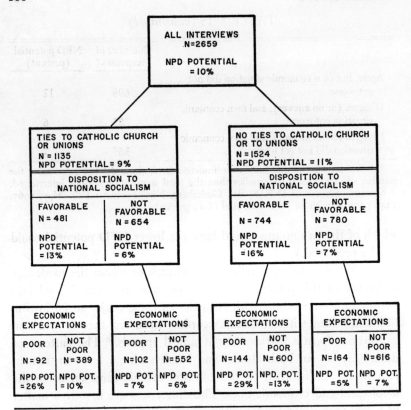

(CONDENSED FROM FIGURE V.3 TO THE TWO DIMENSIONS OF IDEOLOGICAL
PREDISPOSITION AND ECONOMIC EXPECTATIONS)

		ECONOMIC EXPECTATIONS	
		POOR	NOT POOR
DISPOSITION TO NATIONAL SOCIALISM	FAVORABLE	N=236 NPD POTENTIAL =28%	N=989 NPD POTENTIAL =12%
	UNFAVORABLE	N=266 NPD POTENTIAL =6%	N=1168 NPD POTENTIAL =7%

SOURCE: SURVEYS OF INFAS, BAD GODESBERG. NIEDERSACHSEN,
FEB.-MAY, 1967, 2659 PERSONS.

Fig. V.3. *NPD POTENTIAL IN NIEDERSACHSEN*

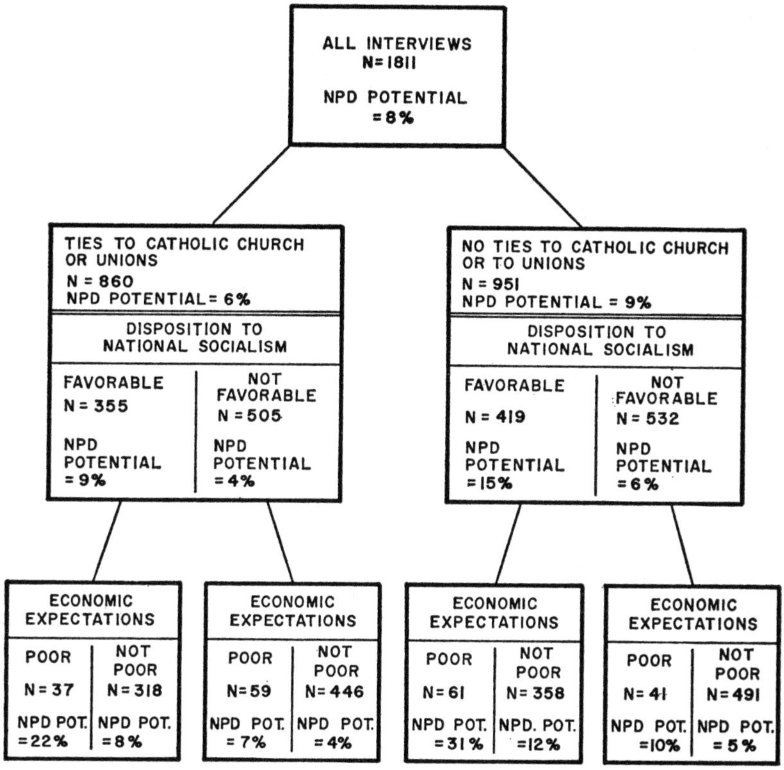

```
                          ┌─────────────────────┐
                          │   ALL INTERVIEWS     │
                          │      N=1811          │
                          │                      │
                          │   NPD POTENTIAL      │
                          │       = 8%           │
                          └─────────────────────┘
```

TIES TO CATHOLIC CHURCH OR UNIONS N = 860 NPD POTENTIAL= 6%		NO TIES TO CATHOLIC CHURCH OR TO UNIONS N = 951 NPD POTENTIAL = 9%	
DISPOSITION TO NATIONAL SOCIALISM		DISPOSITION TO NATIONAL SOCIALISM	
FAVORABLE N = 355 NPD POTENTIAL = 9%	NOT FAVORABLE N = 505 NPD POTENTIAL = 4%	FAVORABLE N = 419 NPD POTENTIAL = 15%	NOT FAVORABLE N = 532 NPD POTENTIAL = 6%

ECONOMIC EXPECTATIONS		ECONOMIC EXPECTATIONS		ECONOMIC EXPECTATIONS		ECONOMIC EXPECTATIONS	
POOR N = 37 NPD POT. = 22%	NOT POOR N = 318 NPD POT. = 8%	POOR N= 59 NPD POT. = 7%	NOT POOR N = 446 NPD POT. = 4%	POOR N= 61 NPD POT. = 31%	NOT POOR N = 358 NPD. POT. = 12%	POOR N= 41 NPD POT. = 10%	NOT POOR N = 491 NPD POT. = 5%

(CONDENSED FROM FIGURE V.4 TO THE TWO DIMENSIONS OF IDEOLOGICAL PREDISPOSITION AND ECONOMIC EXPECTATIONS)

		ECONOMIC EXPECTATIONS	
		POOR	NOT POOR
DISPOSITION TO NATIONAL SOCIALISM	FAVORABLE	N=97 NPD POTENTIAL = 28%	N=676 NPD POTENTIAL = 10%
	UNFAVORABLE	N=100 NPD POTENTIAL = 8%	N=937 NPD POTENTIAL = 5%

SOURCE: SURVEYS OF INFAS, BAD GODESBERG. HESSEN, APRIL–JUNE, 1967, 1811 PERSONS.

Fig. V.4. NPD POTENTIAL IN HESSEN

members a sense of support and comfort during periods of unrest. This support and comfort should give the troubled membership a feeling that someone cares about them, that they are not alone, that someone will help. Presumably the more alienated a person feels, the more likely he is to turn against the social establishment toward radical groups for answers to his problems, for an outlet for his frustrations, and for a sense of potency which membership in the establishment institutions does not give him. The numbers of both union members and churchgoers are declining in the Bundesrepublik, an indication of the already waning strength of these social institutions.[30] The evidence also seems to demonstrate the weakness of these mass organizations in keeping the NPD from voter recruitment within their ranks. It would appear that these organizations do not at present represent a very difficult hurdle for right-radical movements to overcome. It is not to say that these two major communities cannot or will not regain the relevance and relationship to their membership which they once held; it is not to say that the church or the unions are irrelevant to new forces at work within the Bundesrepublik. It is, in a sense, a warning to be heeded or ignored, a warning which says that the Bundesrepublik has passed from the era of postwar social reconstruction and economic rise to well-being. Old problems, submerged by the labors of reconstruction and by the presence of occupation powers, and new problems arising from the continued occupation and from continuing modernization of the West German economy, have surfaced and people will refuse to heed the old slogans of the postwar period. Dissidents of both right and left indicate that an increasing number of people no longer look to the present governing parties as forums and action organizations relevant to problems to which they seek and demand solutions. For example, the new wave of student activism, not only at the Free University of West Berlin but throughout the Bundesrepublik, decries the present social structure and the standard answers which do not seem relevant to the problems being posed. Many students, too, especially since the formation of the Great Coalition, have serious doubts about the ability to reform West German society in line with their ideals.

The preceding discussion has attempted to show the development of a three-way connection between antidemocratic sentiment,

30. Klaus Liepelt, "Anhänger der neuen Rechtspartei," p. 269.

a personal-crisis catalyst, and recruitment by the National Democrats. Now this must be modified by stating that although this relationship showed up very clearly in Niedersachsen and Hessen, for the Bundesrepublik as a whole it is not so strong. The general pattern is the same, but the NPD potential for the group which has both personal economic worries and a favorable disposition towards National Socialism is not nearly so high as was seen in Niedersachsen and Hessen. It may be that the NPD, through its *Landtagswahl* (state election) campaigns in Hessen and Niedersachsen, has been able to identify itself as the main outlet for frustrated and activated right-wing sentiments, whereas for the Bundesrepublik as a whole it has not. In the 1965 federal elections campaign the NPD had not yet achieved wide recognition as a focal point for such discontent, nor was the economic situation ripe enough to act as a catalyst for large numbers of people.

In every state election campaign since November of 1966, however, the NPD may be establishing this pattern of appealing to a basic favorable disposition towards the NSDAP past, mobilization of such sentiment through personal crisis, and attachment to the NPD as the outlet for the resulting dilemma.

The above-mentioned pattern of attachment to the NPD does not necessarily have to be positive. When asked why they voted NPD, the overwhelming majority of admitted National Democratic voters— a small percentage of the total NPD voters—give a negative reason for such a vote.[31] The most common answer is "out of opposition," a general opposition to the three parties who have governed in Bonn since the founding of the Bundesrepublik. Among other answers were: "The other parties aren't worth anything"; "I wasn't satisfied with the Bonn government"; "the NPD points the finger at the other [parties]." Only a few respondents said anything positive about the NPD itself, such as "They have good ideas," or "They stand for order and thrift."

This general impression that a vote for the NPD is a vote against something rather than a vote *for* something was in part confirmed by the few conversations and interviews I conducted with people who had indicated that they would vote NPD. Two respondents explicitly assured me that they did not want to see the NPD as a governing party. They merely wanted to "apply a hot iron" to other parties, to

31. *Ibid.*, p. 262.

the government. All of them viewed the three Bonn parties as a unit with little or no differentiation: They were the government, and the NPD was the opposition to the government. The FDP was never mentioned as the official parliamentary opposition to the Great Coalition of the SPD and the CDU/CSU. Rather, the FDP was still seen as a member of the government, and therefore incapable of expressing the problems which people felt. The NPD's program, or lack of it, was never mentioned; it was not important that the NPD had no real program. The NPD vote was seen as a threat to the government which would make it sit up and take notice of their problems. Two men to whom I talked were union members who had been SPD followers for many years. They told me that the SPD and the unions used to fulfill their need for a vocal opposition and support for their cause. But now the SPD was committed to the Great Coalition and, as one man said, "The unions are keeping their mouths shut."

It appears, then, that the clearest pattern of attraction to the NPD arises not from any of the usual ecological factors which go far to explain and isolate voter followings of the SPD, CDU/CSU and FDP. Union ties and Catholic church ties, often seen as institutional barriers to right-radical movements (here, the NPD) do not seem to be particularly effective in "immunizing" their followings from turning to the NPD almost as frequently as people with no union or Catholic church ties.

Rather, it is a combination of antidemocratic ideological predisposition and a subjective sense of personal crisis whch seem to lead most noticeably to support of the National Democrats. In addition, this support for the NPD is not necessarily based on a positive approval of the NPD or its "program"; often it represents an attraction of people who are dissatisfied and worried to a party which advertises itself as the "national opposition" to all three Bonn parties which have led the Bundesrepublik.

In this chapter I have tried to outline what seems to be the dynamic of the NPD vote mobilization. We have seen that the major long-run barrier to the NPD lies in people with basically democratic predispositions who stay within the accepted parliamentary democratic framework even in troubled times, whereas people holding antidemocratic opinions soon turn to extraparliamentary or antiparliamentary movements to express their protest. The first group of people seek to redress their personal grievances within the present social and political structure by influencing it from within; the second group is more likely to structure their protest against society and against the present political structure from without.

Somewhat discouraging in this respect is that the level of antidemocratic sentiment is not significantly lower among the eighteen to twenty-four year old group which had been raised almost entirely since the end of World War II and the collapse of the National-Socialist regime. It is clear that many of the prejudices and opinions which can endanger a democratic system had been passed down to a new generation despite the absence of a fascist regime at the top. It may be, as some contend, that these opinions are less dangerous now because they do not form an antidemocratic ideology but are merely broken-off pieces of the earlier National Socialist ideology;[32] this is, in part, true. Many people hold an odd and not necessarily consistent assortment of opinions: democratic, antidemocratic, and some which defy rigid classification. For example, one NPD voter whom I interviewed had just finished agreeing that instead of the Bundestag, what Germany needs is a strong man on top who can act decisively. "But not a dictator," he then added. A dictator was seen as someone who governed alone and independent of the will of the people, but a strong man on top was seen as someone who could incorporate in his person the will of the people without the factional struggle of the parliamentary system. What is desired here is a hero of the whole people who will not abuse his power or make the mistakes which would turn him into a dictator. This, as described earlier, is the concept of the *Volksdemokratie*, a sort of plebiscite democracy, in which only one interest, the interest of the German nation, has validity. The rights of competing interests, here seen always as "special interests," or of dissident individuals, are recognized not as valid but as suspect or even traitorous.

Such opinions, while not subjectively seen as antidemocratic or favorable to dictatorship, are certainly not classified as a bulwark for the pluralistic democracy of the Bundesrepublik, and form one long-run factor in the voter potential of right-radical movements such as the NPD. Only penetrating examination and reform of the opinions taught in the schools, the church, the unions, and the family can

32. *Ibid.*, pp. 269–271.

hope to significantly reduce this long-run antidemocratic potential. This has not been done up to this time. The fact that these opinions lie dormant in times of economic prosperity should be no satisfaction. Only the constant refutation of antidemocratic views, whether part of an ideology or just individual prejudices, can in the long run provide the attitudinal basis for a democratic system sure of its support in times of crisis as well as in times of peace and prosperity.

The above analysis has shown that, while the long-term potential of right-radical movements in the Bundesrepublik depends upon an attitudinal groundwork of antidemocratic opinions, the short-term factor in activating these opinions to electoral relevancy is this sense of personal, especially economic, crisis. The sense of present or impending economic difficulties brings with it the fear of loss of position, or status, within the social structure. This finding is by no means new, nor is the connection between the threat or actuality of decline in social status and proclivity towards right-radicalism.[33] It has often been pointed out that many leaders of right-radical organizations are people who held middle-class positions during the Third Reich and who, after 1945, suffered a sharp decline in social status. This includes not only Nazi party functionaries, but administrators and officials of the supporting organs of the totalitarian state, as well as professional soldiers. However, it has often been assumed that this right-radicalism is a product of the middle class, caused by the reaction of this class against the threat of being thrown back into the proletariat. One of the standard explanations of the NSDAP electoral successes in 1930 and 1932 states that the lower middle-class elements, who had been forced into the ranks of the working class by economic collapse, turned to the NSDAP as a rebellion against this loss of social position.[34]

I would argue that, if we look at the NPD following, the phenomenon of rebellion against loss of social position (or threat of such a loss) is by no means limited to the middle class, but is a more general phenomenon which applies as well to workers, skilled and unskilled, white-collar employees, and self-employed businessmen. Some defenders of the working class have argued that these workers who vote NPD

33. See, among others, H. Knütter, *Ideologien des Rechtsradikalismus im Nachkriegsdeutschland,* (Bonn: Röhrscheid, 1961), pp. 24–27.

34. Erwin K. Scheuch, "Die NPD in der Bundesrepublik," pp. 293–294.

are either displaced bourgeoisie or aspirant bourgeoisie—people with the middle-class mentality.[35] That this is not true can be verified easily by the NPD potential among union-organized workers who should be the core of the working-class consciousness, or among nonunion workers who consider themselves to be working-class people. That this is so can be seen also from the NPD potential among those who give the SPD, the party of the working class, as their party preference, or even more, from the NPD potential among those who have until now been steady SPD voters. Rather than middle- or working-class mentality, it is basic antidemocratic attitudes which cut across all demographic and class lines, providing fertile conditions for right-radical recruitment under conditions of personal distress.

We should note however, that it is the positions of the small businessman, the farmer, and the unskilled worker in the continuing rationalization of the West German economy which are most threatened—both in times of general economic prosperity and times of recession. To this extent we may say that since the catalyzation factor is more likely to be present among small businessmen, farmers, and unskilled workers, there should be a more constant susceptibility to radical appeals among these groups. (I say here "radical" appeals, since in earlier times the left-radical appeals of the KPD and SPD attracted protest votes of unskilled workers threatened by the new labor-saving dimensions demanded by further rationalization of the capitalist economy.) And in fact it was among these two groups that the highest NPD potentials were found, although they were only a few percentage points higher than the other occupational groupings.

In the absence of quick solution to the problem of the antidemocratic attitudes held by many people, the only real barrier to the mobilization of these attitudes on behalf of the National Democrats is the maintenance of a healthy economic environment which keeps the number of distressed people to a minimum and which gives people temporarily displaced by continuing modernization confidence that

35. See Helga Grebing, "Nationalismus und Demokratie . . . " in Fetscher et. al., *Rechtsradikalismus*, p. 62. Grebing claims that working-class NPD voters must have a mentality which related them, either positively or negatively, to the middle class, rather than to their own class. Thus, she attempts to maintain her image of the NPD as a middle-class phenomenon. Her argument is tautological: any worker who votes for the NPD is not really a worker; this presumably preserves the immunity of the working class from right-radical appeals.

there is still opportunity for them. To what extent this lies within the power of the government or the society to fulfill upon command is another question which cannot be answered here.

The question remains as how these antidemocratic leanings, activated by a personal sense of crisis, are transformed into votes for the NPD. Why should such protest votes not go to the CDU, SPD, FDP, or perhaps to the DFU on the far left? (There are some indications from the elections in Bremen on October 1, 1967 that some of these protest votes are going to the DFU, as the left-radical opposition to the social establishment.) They do not because these parties are the *Bonner Parteien* which embody the parliamentary democracy of the Bundesrepublik. They are seen as representing the satisfied interests of society. This is still not as true for the SPD as for the other two parties, although in the last several years it has become more and more so. The search is for a "true opposition" as opposed to a formal parliamentary opposition. This true opposition is to be an opposition not to a party or a coalition of parties, but to the system itself. Only the NPD, for all its claims to support the rules of the game (*Spielregeln*) of the democracy, fulfills a clear-cut image of an extra- or antiparliamentary opposition. The NPD strengthens this image by asserting that, while it supports the present democratic order, it would like to make a number of changes (see Chapter IV) which would bring about a "true democracy."

As for the DFU, the appeal of any far-left party is unavoidably tarnished by connections, real or imagined, to the Communists, largely discredited as a political force in the Bundesrepublik.

That leaves the NPD as the only party representing the opposition of the outsider to the satisfied complacency of insiders. The NPD is a symbol which is seen as threatening to the present establishment, a powerful outlet for the frustrations of impotence. The frustrated need to feel that their protests are not being disregarded; they need to feel that their protests are feared and respected for their forcefulness if not for the reason and justice of their cause. In a sense the NPD vote is an end in itself, a release of activated antagonisms against society. Thus the NPD voter does not have to say anything positive about the NPD itself. Nor is it necessary for the NPD to have a program—as opposed to slogans or propaganda—which is rationally aimed at relieving causes of the social frustrations which brought people to the NPD in the first place. The NPD is not a problem-solving organism; its function is seen more as a threat to force other problem-solving bodies, namely those in authority, to satisfy the demands of the protesters.

This use of the NPD as a political bludgeon against the establishment was explicitly seen by Rehwinkel, head of the farmers' organization (*Bauernverband*). His threats to turn to the NPD (see Chapter III) were meant to make it clear to the CDU, which farmers normally support, that they were not fooling about the seriousness of their demands.

This same picture was given by NPD voters whom I interviewed and by those in the surveys who gave their reasons for voting NPD. The NPD was not seen as one of many competing parties, but as an antiparty, a weapon against the Bonner Parteien.

The danger of the present situation for the three established parties in Bonn is clear. A significant, perhaps growing, number of people not basically committed to the democratic system in the first place, are finding an antiparliamentary outlet for their protests in the NPD. The role of the traditional parties, that of trying to solve problems within the present social framework, is being bypassed for more radical appeals. This is especially evident under the condition which now prevails, namely the Great Coalition of CDU/CSU and SPD. The FDP is at present too weak to provide any real opposition to the Great Coalition, and is simply not viewed as hostile to the present state of society in the Bundesrepublik. On the contrary, the FDP is the status symbol of the bourgeois block, and thus to many the height of self-satisfaction with the present social structure. The complete failure of the FDP to find a platform on which to oppose the Great Coalition is an index of its incapability to fulfill the role of government opposition.[36]

This role of real social opposition as opposed to parliamentary, official opposition, was filled in the fifties and early sixties by the SPD and the KPD. The KPD is now discredited and the SPD, having officially renounced all ties to Marxism at its Bad Godesberg conference in 1961 has now become a major partner of the establishment at the national level for the first time. In the absence of the SPD or any other

36. The FDP national party conference in early 1967 once again brought to the surface the deep split with the FDP; it was clear that the party could not at that time even agree on a successor to Dr. Mende as chairman.

party as a responsible social opposition committed to the democratic system, people who themselves have no special commitment to democracy but are searching for someone to voice their opposition, will continue to see the NPD as the fulfillment of their momentary needs.

The SPD, in some areas and under certain conditions, still has the image of a social protest movement. As mentioned earlier, the vigorous campaign of the SPD for the April 23, 1967 state elections in Schleswig-Holstein probably was responsible for the poor showing of the NPD there. It had been predicted that the NPD would be able to attract the votes of the many economically distressed (especially dike workers) in Schleswig-Holstein, but the returns indicated that most of these voters stayed with the SPD. Joachim Steffen, head of the SPD in Schleswig-Holstein, disassociated himself during the campaign as much as possible from the Great Coalition and led a powerful attack on the shortcomings of Lemke's CDU/FDP coalition government in Schleswig-Holstein. As a result, Schleswig-Holstein has been the sole example to date of an area in which the SPD gained votes during the period of the Great Coalition, at the same time that it was the poorest state showing for the NPD (5.9 percent) since its first electoral breakthrough in November, 1966. The connection is not coincidental.

There is also some evidence that the DFU (*Deutsche Friedensunion*), long an exercise in political futility on the far left, was able to attract some of these protest voters in the October 1, 1967 elections in the city-state of Bremen.[37] Nevertheless, the main benefactor of the political realignment brought about by the Great Coalition still seems to have been the NPD. In a situation in which social frustration and protest will be voiced one way or another, the strategy of bringing the two major parties into a coalition may provide a certain immediate stability, but as an enduring institution it deprives the democratic system of the flexibility necessary to keep this protest within its own bounds.

37. For further comment on the success of the DFU in the Bremen elections and its significance, see *Die Zeit*, October 10, 1967, p. 1.

VI

Potential for the Future

I have now looked at the NPD as the successor to several earlier right-wing movements, and I have related the electoral history of the party to date. I have examined its propaganda themes with the aim of presenting the world view of the NPD and the basic cultural backlash-motivations which are the foundation of this *Weltanschauung*. Finally, I have presented the demographic structure of the NPD voter-following and related this following to both the attitudinal and economic variables. In this chapter I will summarize these findings and try to present the basic factors which may determine the future potential of the National Democrats.

The NPD has gone through at least four distinct stages of development. The first stage involved the original formation of the party from the remnants of the BHE, DP, and DRP, under the nominal chairmanship of Fritz Thielen and under the actual control of Adolf von Thadden and his DRP apparatus. This event capped several years of fruitless attempts by increasingly weakened and fragmented rightist groups to achieve some sort of organization which would again provide an audible voice for the far right. Only when the political stock of earlier rightist parties hit bottom was this possible. Even then, the founding of the NPD was regarded in the Bundesrepublik as little more than just another hopeless attempt by the far right.

The second stage in the development of the NPD took place during the federal election campaign of 1965; during this period the NPD established itself both as a national party and as *the* right-radical party in the Bundesrepublik. Although the NPD won only 2 percent of the vote in the federal elections and thus failed to gain any seats, the party had conducted a nationwide campaign which established it as the only electoral vehicle with any hope of success within right-wing circles. The party still had not developed enough nationwide publicity to make itself a generally known commodity, but among those dedicated to the far right it had solidified its position as the "national opposition," an achievement symbolized by the self-dissolution of the DRP in December of 1965.

The year 1966 was to prove the breakthrough stage for the NPD as a vote-gathering organization. In 1966 the NPD achieved enough publicity to make itself known to over 90 percent of all voters and gain an image as a successful opposition party.

Early in 1966 the party achieved some local victories in Hamburg, Bavaria, and Schleswig-Holstein, enough to awaken the West German press to the possibility that the NPD might be able to play a significant role in the November state elections in Hessen and Bavaria. The chances were seen as good that the NPD would make it difficult for the FDP to maintain its delegation in the Bavarian Landtag, although it was still seen as doubtful that the NPD itself would be able to jump the 10 percent clause necessary to gain seats in the Bavarian Landtag.

With the NPD's surprisingly strong showing of 7.9 percent of the vote in the Hessen state elections on November 6, 1966, the NPD became front-page news in the Bundesrepublik. With the Erhard regime already on the way out, but its successor unchosen, the governmental crisis was reaching its peak. The economic crisis was growing, and the Bonn parties were unable to decide on a regime which would be able to act decisively to put the governmental budget in order and to restore economic confidence. Each day that this determination was put off increased public anxiety over the economic future—an anxiety, as we have seen, which redounded to the benefit of the NPD. The National Democrats were now beginning to be seen also by people outside the diehard rightist circles as the "real opposition" to what was viewed by many as the indecision of the CDU/CSU, SPD, and FDP. An NPD vote was taken by many to be a threatening protest to get the other parties moving.

The state elections in Bavaria on November 20, 1966, demonstrated again the NPD's vote-getting power in a crisis situation. In addition to garnering 7.4 percent of the vote in all of Bavaria and 12.2 percent in Mittelfranken, thus giving the NPD fifteen seats in the Landtag, the NPD succeeded in its announced goal of squeezing the Free Democrats out of the Landtag. The BP (*Bayern Partei*) was also unable to retain its seats in Bavaria, with the result that the NPD not only bolstered its image as a rising new political force but also visibly challenged the FDP for the position of the third largest party in the Bundesrepublik. Now the NPD had a recognizable party label, and was identifiable as a right-radical opposition to the Bonner Parteien. The fact that it had neither a real program nor well-known leaders did not seem to detract from its acknowledgement by many as "the opposition." Even after the Great Coalition of the CDU/CSU and SPD was formed, with Kiesinger and Brandt at the helm, there were dire predictions in the press, and hopeful predictions from the NPD, of great electoral victories in the coming state elections of 1967.

The fourth stage of the NPD's evolution began early in 1967 with the eruption of the power struggle between Thielen and von Thadden, as the latter was replacing members of Thielen's following with his own cadres in the party hierarchy. Thielen, finally realizing that he was being pushed out of the picture, decided to make a final stand against von Thadden, relying upon the help of the courts to strengthen his own position within the party. Thielen, however, had seriously misjudged both his own strength and the ability of court decisions to change the basic loyalties of the party apparatus. While the West German press wishfully predicted the splintering of the party into meaningless factions, as had been the fate of several previous right-extremist movements, a closer examination of the party structure would have revealed the emptiness of Thielen's threats to split the party. When, after several weeks as powerless chairman of the NPD, Thielen finally decided to withdraw and form his own *Nationale Volkspartei* (NVP), very few NPD members followed him. Whatever following Thielen had originally brought to the NPD remained substantially with the NPD and, although there were a few well publicized defections and foundings of new splinter parties, these were all statistically meaningless to the survival and maintenance of the NPD as *the* voice of the radical right.

The NPD's electoral showing in 1967 did not fulfill either the dire predictions made in late 1966 or the predictions of collapse made a few months later. The party's vote percentages (5.8 in Schleswig-

Holstein, 6.9 in Rheinland-Pfalz, 7.0 in Niedersachsen, and 8.8 in Bremen) confirmed the staying power of the party. The atmosphere of crisis which existed in the Bundesrepublik in late 1966 had passed, and the Great Coalition's popularity was on the rise after its initial successes in straightening out the budget and in establishing diplomatic relations with Rumania. A certain amount of economic confidence was being reestablished; with the decline of the atmosphere of anxiety, the great hopes of the NPD for even better showings than in Hessen and Bavaria faded. Yet the NPD was still able to gain entrance into four more legislatures in 1967, and thus by the beginning of 1968 the National Democrats held seats in six of the ten state legislatures.

Then, in the April elections in Baden-Württemberg, the National Democrats demonstrated that they had overcome their own internal difficulties and were continuing to build a solid voter base as an opposition force to the Great Coalition. Despite renewed prosperity, the NPD was continuing to channel into its voter following much of the reaction to the social evolution of West Germany. It, and not the Free Democrats, continued to benefit the most from playing the opposition role to the CDU/SPD government. Now the National Democrats could confidently look forward, as von Thadden predicted, to gaining seats in the September, 1969 Bundestag elections.

To examine the future potential of the NPD one must first look at the new era of West German politics which has now begun. The economic miracle is past. The German economy has long since passed the stage of reconstruction of the standard of living which had existed at the height of the Third Reich. The man most responsible for the direction of policy in the Bundesrepublik since its founding in 1949, Dr. Konrad Adenauer, has passed from the scene. The United States, main ally of West Germany, has turned its attention to another part of the globe, and the close alliance with and reliance on the United States is coming more and more into question. In short, the era of postwar politics no longer has an adequate answer to the new dissatisfaction within West German society. The NPD signals the CDU/CSU, SPD, and FDP that there are frustrations which a significant number of people feel are not being answered by any of the establishment parties. Student discontent on the left is a similar sign of alienation from the political process as now dominated by the three Bonn parties. These signs, both on the far left and the far right of the political spectrum, point to a certain disaffection with the present establishment and the need for an opposition voice to the establishment.

The Great Coalition represents the culmination of an effort by the SPD to gain entrance into the establishment ranks of the Bundesrepublik. In becoming a partner in the Great Coalition, however, the SPD inevitably gave up much of its role as social opposition to the status quo. It remains to be seen whether the Social Democratic Party can still maintain enough of its former identity within the Great Coalition to keep dissent channeled through a democratic party structure.

West German society is entering a new era of change and development. Postwar reconstruction is over, and the problems of further development are far more complex. Because West German society is beginning to act under its own dynamic rather than under the unavoidable pressures of postwar reconstruction years the consensus of the Adenauer era has begun to break down. The new changes in West German society are creating frustrations and demands which will be voiced in opposition to present trends. The form this opposition takes —an opposition which can formulate realistic solutions to these frustrations and which is favorable to a democratic, pluralistic society, or an opposition movement such as the NPD—can make a great difference in the level of conflict and crisis which will mark the continuing evolution of West German society.

The danger is that a rising percentage of frustrated voters, finding no champion within the democratic parties, may turn to the NPD which, as I have shown, is basically opposed to a democratic order of increasingly pluralistic interests. The NPD does not help formulate reasonable solutions to situations of social conflict. Rather it exacerbates and escalates them by offering simplistic, scapegoat, and conspiracy theories which make the application of more complex, less emotionally satisfying, and less totalistic remedies more difficult.

The success to date of the NPD already had adversely affected the ability of the political system to put forward new policy initiatives, namely in the field of foreign policy. The new *Ostpolitik* of the Kiesinger-Brandt government has been complicated by the continued presence of the NPD; while it may still be possible for the Bundesrepublik to improve its relationships and expand its contacts with the East European Communist states, every electoral gain for the National Democrats creates new difficulties. Thus, in one of the Bundesrepublik's promising foreign-policy initiatives of the post-reconstruction era, the NPD has already, by raising the specter of renewed German nationalism, demonstrated its power to hinder the effective formulation and executing of policy reform designed to meet the needs of the post-reconstruction years. This effect may soon become apparent in internal as well as external policy matters.

The major danger of the NPD is probably not the chance of its gaining control of the West German government, although this, of course, would be a disaster of major proportions. The present danger is that much social dissent, which stems from real frustrations, will be captured by a movement which does not offer realistic solutions to such tensions. Should the NPD be able to gather these people as solid adherents, the difficulty of reaching disaffected citizens of the Bundesrepublik with rational answers or attempts at reform would be increased. In other words, their positions of opposition would become more permanent, and their frustrations more difficult to alleviate, trapped as they would be within the fantasy world of right-radicalism.

With the SPD as a member of the Great Coalition, only the Free Democrats are available to challenge the NPD for the role of opposition; indications to date are that the FDP is unsuited to this task. There are several reasons for this almost built-in unsuitability.

First and foremost, the FDP—too long a member of the CDU/ CSU coalition—is still seen as a part of the Bonn establishment, part of the government, despite its new formal role as the only opposition party in the Bundestag. The FDP would have to alter its whole image radically in order to divorce itself from its past record as junior partner in the government coalition.

Another obstacle for the FDP is its self-proclaimed status as a minority party. The FDP has accepted itself as a minority party which does not seek to become a majority party. As such, it does not offer the same protest-potential vis-a-vis the government as does the NPD. The National Democrats claim already to be the voice of the people; they appeal to, and attract, support from all major social categories. The FDP has tended to see itself as the "conscience of the people," not as the embodiment of the people. It could play this role in previous years, when it held the balance of power between the CDU/ CSU and the SPD. Now, however, with little leverage against the Great Coalition, it seeks a new role. In its previous position of alliance with the Christian Democrats, the FDP represented a status symbol vote for Protestant middle-class voters who wanted to distinguish themselves from the heavily Catholic CDU/CSU without voting for the Social Democrats. As such, the Free Democrats held almost no attraction for either Catholics or the working class. They would have to escape this tradition in order to challenge the NPD for the votes of those seeking an avenue of protest.[1]

The data presented in the previous chapter demonstrate one condition under which the NPD could increase its influence and expand its voter potential, namely in a crisis situation. I have shown that for each of its propaganda themes the NPD has a far greater number of people who agree with these themes than the party to date has been able to mobilize into voter strength. Under an atmosphere of crisis—economic crisis appears here to be the most salient—voters who hold basically antidemocratic opinions based on the Volk ideology are shaken from nominal attachments to establishment parties and become available for recruitment by radical protest movements such as the NPD. In such a period of crisis, the NPD can reach beyond its usual base of support, which encompasses those elements and life styles uprooted by the continuing urbanization and modernization of the West German economy. In the Bundesrepublik this potential of right-radicalism is perhaps somewhat greater than in other Western industrial nations, due to the continuing attitudinal influences of the Third-Reich era. However, this basic phenomenon is present in every modern Western industrial nation—by the Poujadists in France; the George Wallace movement, and the John Birch Society in the United States; the neofascist MSI in Italy; the Social Credit Party in Canada; and the Austrian Freedom Party in Austria.[2] All of these movements share with the NPD certain basic elements of the Volk ideology, an opposition to modernism and a desire to return to a situation in which their social class played a larger or a more stable role in society. In general these movements have their roots in the ever dwindling num-

1. There are some signs that the FDP, in time, may remold itself as a more left-oriented liberal opposition. The efforts of the sociologist and former SPD member Rolf Dahrendorf, educational expert Frau Hamm-Brücher, and FDP treasurer Wolfgang Rubin, are aimed towards that goal. However, the new chairman of the party, Walter Scheel, describes himself as a man of the middle, and may not be amenable to a drastic revamping of the party's image.

2. See Irving Fetscher et. al., *Rechtsradikalismus*, for articles on the Goldwater and McCarthy movements in the United States and the new right-radical movements in France; also Hans Rogge and Eugen Weber, editors, *The European Right* (Berkeley and Los Angeles: University of California Press, 1965).

ber of farm owners, the small businessmen squeezed both by big labor and big business and, in addition, sometimes the unskilled laborer threatened by automation and the demand for ever higher skill levels to secure employment. In other words, the existence of the NPD in the Bundesrepublik is a normal sign of the continuing evolution of West Germany as a modernizing, increasingly more urbanized, industrial state.

The case of the NPD in the Bundesrepublik, however, shows certain characteristics which may present more problems for the Bundesrepublik than is true for similarly based movements in other countries. The first of these additional problems arises from the need for the final acceptance of the Bundesrepublic as the legitimate form of government. The Bundesrepublik was explicitly formed as a temporary solution pending the eventual reunification of Germany. Thus Bonn still is not seen as a permanent capital; in place of a constitution there remains the "Basic Law," which recognizes the temporary nature of the situation, and leaves the door open to NPD propaganda.

In addition, the basic border problem of Germany leaves much room for rightist speculation as to the final solution of that question.

The Bundesrepublik was founded under American auspices, and throughout its first twenty years has been closely allied to the United States. In a period when France in particular is demonstrating its independence from the United States, the government of West Germany has made only halting attempts to reexamine these ties. The government has yet to show those Germans who see the Bundesrepublik not only as a temporary but also an American creation that it is in fact an independent nation. This does not mean that the Bundesrepublik must pull out of NATO to declare its independence, nor that it has to adopt the strident anti-Americanism of the NPD. Yet, as I have shown, there is a large minority which feels that the West German government does not act in the interests of its own people first, but rather accedes to other (read American) interests.

While right-radicalism seems to be a distinguishing feature of modern Western societies, it does not find everywhere the opportunity which exists in West Germany to question the legitimacy of the whole political system, and the geographic boundaries within which it operates. In no other Western democracy is the geographical basis, and the circumstances, of the founding of a democratic system more recent and open to revision than in the Bundesrepublik. This must be so as long as the government of West Germany claims the right, as it now does, to represent also the citizens of the *Deutsche Demokratische Republik* (DDR), and in addition does not recognize the Oder-Neisse as the eastern frontier of Germany. Such open questions are ready fuel for nationalist propaganda themes.

The other outstanding peculiarity of right-radicalism in West Germany is the "unconquered past" of Germany. West Germany bears the heritage of an unsuccessful nationalism defeated in two bitter wars. There remain the attitudes of thirteen years of indoctrination into the Volk ideology under the National-Socialist dictatorship. In large measure, these attitudes have been passed on to a new generation. This should not be surprising; indeed, it would be extremely surprising if this were not so. The extent to which the attitudes of the Volk ideology were disseminated throughout all sectors of German society thus probably surpassed the spread of similar attitudes in other Western nations. The basic potential of the NPD, especially in times of social or economic stress, is higher than would be true in other Western industrial democracies. In short, the NPD, because of the setting peculiar to the German situation, has been able to recruit a voter following from social classifications which in other countries are not at odds with the system.

Since its birth there have been several methods proposed for dealing with the NPD. The first method tried was to ignore it and hope that it would fade away, as had previous rightist parties. It became clear during 1966 that this would not happen to the National Democrats, although there were revived hopes in 1967 that the new party would destroy itself with intraparty feuding. Since this hope has faded also, the West German establishment has at various times offered at least five different ways of dealing with the perceived challenge of the NPD.

Perhaps the most direct method (suggested by Herbert Wehner of the SPD, among others) is a simple ban against the National Democrats as a successor organization to the NSDAP, or the already banned SRP. Such successor organizations can be banned under the Basic Law as dangerous to the democracy. The trouble with this approach is that if the NPD were brought to court under such charges and found innocent, it would be a tremendous victory for the National Democrats against the Bonn establishment. In this regard, it has been considered highly doubtful that in fact sufficient grounds for such proceedings exist. Even if a conviction could be attained, the voter following and its disenchantment with the social system would remain, either to be voiced in another such movement or to be alienated entirely from political participation. Whether this latter possibility would be to the long-run benefit of the system is doubtful, since the encouragement of nonparticipation or imposed alienation is not a particularly purposeful way of dealing with people who after all are seeking redress from real frustrations. Many people feel that the Bundesrepublik already has used the power of the ban once too often, namely in 1956 in the case of *Kommunistische Partei Deutschlands* (KPD), and that a democratic system should be extremely reluctant to forbid any party.

A second, more subtle method for eliminating the NPD is the electoral reform to which the Great Coalition is already committed. As a condition of formation of the Great Coalition both the SPD and CDU/CSU agreed to carry through a revision of the present proportional representation system, at least at the national level. The exact form of the electoral changes has not been spelled out, and it was announced in January, 1968, that the reform will not take effect before the 1973 elections. The original intent of the reforms was to convert from the present proportional representation system to a single-member plurality system. At present a party which receives 5 percent or more of the vote gains a number of seats in the Bundestag proportionate to the size of the vote received by that party.

Were these electoral laws to be reformed so that single-member districts would exist, with a plurality necessary to elect a candidate from that district, neither the FDP nor the NPD would probably be able to gain any seats in the next Bundestag. Proponents of such a reform say that this would result in a two-party system, with either the CDU/CSU or the SPD commanding a clear majority in the Bundestag. At the state level, barring similar reforms, the FDP and NPD would still be able to campaign with some hopes of success, but at the national level their future would be extremely bleak. Of course such electoral reforms might be thrown out by the courts, or they might release enough resentment against the "electoral manipulation" of the Great Coalition so that the FDP and even the NPD might, in certain of their stronghold districts, be able to win pluralities and thus still win a few seats. The vote-getting power of these parties would be greatly diminished, however, and it would be increasingly difficult for them to hold the loyalty of their voter following. The argument that "a vote for the FDP or the NPD is a wasted vote" would be hard to overcome under the new electoral logic.

The idea of electoral conversion to the single-member district system has certain advantages which are independent of the side benefit of denying representation of the NPD in the Bundestag. For this reason, I feel it would be a mistake to perform such a conversion at a time when it would be viewed by many only as an obvious manipulation of electoral laws. It would seem much more to the benefit of the electoral reforms themselves to have them introduced during a period when such charges could not be leveled against them.

It appears now that the SPD is having very serious second thoughts about the desirability of such an electoral reform. Several studies seem to indicate that the SPD also would be at least a short-run loser under the new system. (Due to the distribution of SPD voters and CDU/CSU voters and the probable redistribution of FDP and perhaps NPD voters, the CDU/CSU would apparently emerge as the majority party.)

Still another method which has been partly applied in an attempt to weaken the NPD is the strategy of social condemnation of NPD membership and votership. In other words, the idea is that if one can make the NPD supporter a social outcast, very few citizens will risk such social castigation, remaining instead in the camp of the established Bonn parties. This spontaneous campaign, strong in some areas and weak or nonexistent in others, relies on the church, the unions, and public leaders to denounce the NPD and those who support it, to make NPD membership incompatible with Christian ethics or union membership. Another facet of this campaign seeks to deny meeting halls for NPD conferences.

Such measures are worse than useless; they gain sympathy for the NPD and set up the battle-line between the establishment and the disestablished, with the NPD as the leadership of the opposition coalition. Such actions as denying for NPD meetings halls which the party had already rented are not only open to court reversal, but also give the party further fuel for its conspiracy theories. The NPD may only gain sympathy for its cause through this approach; citizens whose attitudes lean towards the NPD propaganda line may only be driven closer to the National Democrats by such attacks. This tactic does not recognize the underlying frustrations and anxieties which originally give birth to right-radicalist protests. The result, I would contend, is a strengthening of the previously held attitudes and convictions which led people to the NPD in the first place.

A fourth suggested strategy—almost the opposite of the previously discussed social-castigation campaign—would attempt to civilize the NPD and mellow its radicalism. Here the theory is that with time, and no effort to suppress its activities, the National Democrats will lose at least a part of their fanaticism as they become an accepted, or at least tolerated, facet of the establishment.[3] As the party gains a small but fairly stable representation within state legislatures and perhaps the Bundestag, the NPD would be educated into the refinements and subtleties of parliamentary politics. Without a frontal attack upon them to help maintain their radicalism, the National Democrats, it is hoped, would be unable to keep up their high emotional pitch in the face of such mundane necessities as reelection and conformity to behavioral standards at their new status level. To put it more bluntly, the radicalism of the NPD may be able to be bought off by giving the party, and especially the party leaders, some of the status and recognition which it now lacks.

This approach concerns itself primarily with an attempt to disarm the leadership of the right-radicals in much the same way the SPD and the CDU/CSU were able to handle the leaders of several parties on the far right in the early 1950s. At that time Social Democrats and Christian Democrats formed coalition governments in some states with such parties, giving their leaders, usually the more moderate ones, ministerial posts within the government. As these leaders became accustomed to the benefits of office, they became also more and more dependent upon their major coalition partners, either the CDU/CSU or the SPD. In many cases the CDU/CSU and, less often, the SPD, were able in the end to convert these leaders to their own party, thus beheading right-wing movements and transferring much of the personal followings of these leaders to the major democratic parties.

Whether such tactics would work again is questionable. The earlier rightist parties of the 1950s clearly were caught in the era of the "economic miracle," and their leaders quite naturally sought to salvage their political careers by attaching themselves to more viable

3. In fact, the Austrian Freedom Party may provide an example of the rightist movement which has gained a rather stable voter following and has become in many senses an established fixture of the Austrian political scene.

electoral vehicles. It is not clear that the NPD's future will follow the same pattern, nor that its leaders, former DRP radicals, are as digestible by the major parties as were many earlier, more moderate rightist organizers.[4]

The fifth proposal for undermining the NPD advocates the takeover of certain NPD propaganda themes by a major party. This solution is seen as deflating the NPD by stealing its campaign thunder. The most prominent advocate of this approach is Finance Minister Franz-Josef Strauss, head of the Bavarian Christian Socialist Union (CSU), who had himself espoused a more nationally oriented policy line for many years. After the Bavarian state elections in November of 1966, Strauss, analyzing reasons for the NPD success, said "We are the idiots of the world," and explained that Germans have allowed themselves to be mistreated by other powers, especially the United States and France, without defending their own national interests. Strauss suggested that if one of the major parties were to follow a national course with certain national accents, people would not need to turn to the NPD. In a follow-up interview with *Spiegel*, Strauss again was asked for his analysis of the NPD success.

> In this connection I would like first to say a word about the NPD; it does not concern only a protest action against the real or supposed neglect in representing national interests or only a reaction to the rising and falling campaign of defamation against Germany. To analyze it as concisely as possible, it concerns first a resistance to developments which we like to call Americanization but which really are nothing more than the economic and sociological results of the second technical revolution. This second industrial revolution demands revisions in our economic structure, which means undoubted hardship for many occupations and for less adaptable sectors.
> Here one meets over and over the belief that one can stay with the good old times or should return to the good old times.[5]

Strauss added that a part of the youth was rebelling against the collective guilt being attached to them as Germans even though they had taken no part in the hisory of the Third Reich.

4. All evidence in the records of DRP leadership in the 1950s and 1960s indicates that these leaders, who now in large part form the NPD hierarchy, cannot be bought off, and are not acceptable to incorporation into the other established parties.

5. *Spiegel*, Number 1–2/1967, p. 18.

When the interviewer argued that no reasonable person attaches collective guilt to all Germans, Strauss replied: "The younger generation, at least, has this impression and reacts against it. I could cite specific example from a notable source, among others Lord Montgomery, who said that in the House of Lords it was secretly stated that in the future Germans would be the real enemy. It is a shock for young Germans to hear such things."[6]

I would quite agree with the first of Strauss's main points in his analysis of the NPD success. "Americanization," as mentioned earlier, has become a shorthand symbol for much that is wrong in West German society, as seen from the point of view of those who oppose continuing urbanization and modernization of the West German economy. The Jew has been functionally replaced by "Americanization" as the symbol of the cosmopolitanism or "modernism" which, in cultural-backlash terms, is seen as destroying the good, traditional values.

There are several dangers inherent in the approach advocated by Strauss. The greatest danger is that, rather than one of the established parties (for example, the CDU) taking over certain NPD themes, all parties would orient themselves more in the nationalist direction in order to prevent parts of the voter followings from wandering to a party with more nationalist tendencies. One result of this might be a gradual shifting of the whole political spectrum towards a more nationally oriented policy line. To some extent this has occurred already. But it might mean also that each Bonn party would try to be more nationalist than the others, in the expectation that the rising nationalist sentiment would gravitate to the most avowedly nationalist-minded party.

In such a situation the major outcome might be a new legitimacy for strident nationalist appeals which would not be in the interests of the Bundesrepublik. In such an atmosphere it would seem that the NPD would be the real victor, almost by default, in that its emotional appeals would have been accepted as a legitimate basis for political campaigning.

It would be very difficult actually to borrow certain NPD themes without encouraging wholesale public expression of the entire gamut of right-radical appeals. This would tend to lead politics away from

6. *Ibid.*

the problem-solving approach in government in favor of emotion-packed recruitment to the never-never land of the right-radicals.

The question is not whether the NPD's challenge must be answered. There is no question but that the protest symbolized by the NPD vote is to be taken seriously. But whether the Strauss proposal—that of answering the NPD in its own terms, and conducting political competition according to the rules of the National Democrats—is the most efficient response is doubtful.

As for meeting the challenge of right-radicalism, the Bundesrepublik has many advantages which the Weimar Republic did not have. The Bundesrepublik already is much more urbanized and industrialized than was Weimar.[7] Many agricultural areas of the old Reich, early Nazi strongholds, now are under Communist control, and the strength of the nonindustrial sector of society within West Germany has also declined sharply since the 1930s. Similarly, many Protestant areas which were more susceptible to right-radicalist appeals from the NSDAP are now outside the Bundesrepublik framework. West Germany's economy, despite the recent recession, is strong and has provided a steadily rising standard of living for citizens of the republic, whereas Weimar was forced to struggle within an era of worldwide economic depression.

Yet while it is essential to say that the Bonn republic definitely is not a second Weimar, there are certain basic problems which both republics have had to face, and which, until solved, expand the opportunities to right-extremist movements within any Western industrial society.

Of first priority is the acceptance of the Bundesrepublik as the geographic definition of a nation, as well as the permanent political system within which social forces must operate. This may or may not involve a recognition of the DDR as the legitimate political system of East Germany. It must involve a recognition of the boundaries of

7. As an index of the further industrialization of the West German economy, the number of agricultural workers and farmers has decreased from 5,020,000 in 1950 to 2,877,000 in 1966. Percentages for the continuing urbanization are:

Communities of:	1966	1950	1933	1910	1871
Under 2000	20.7	28.9	32.9	38.5	62.6
2000–5000	12.3	13.6	10.6	11.2	12.8
5000–20000	17.8	16.0	13.1	13.6	11.5
20000–100,000	16.4	14.2	13.0	13.8	7.6
Over 100,000	32.8	27.3	30.4	22.9	5.5

present-day Poland and Czechoslovakia. More important, it must give to the Bundesrepublik greater recognition as a nation than it has been accorded thus far. The Bundesrepublik must become the permanent political system for the citizens within its borders, not a temporary political structure which claims also to represent and legislate for people who do not live within its boundaries. Such claims by the government of the Bundesrepublik only encourage fantasy aims of groups such as the NPD. A dialogue of charges and counter-charges based on the different facets of these claims does not address itself to the more tangible problems which can be solved within the society of the Bundesrepublik.

The Bundesrepublik shares also with Weimar the problem of establishing final acceptance as an independent sovereign nation. Survey evidence indicates that a large number of citizens, far beyond the NPD votership, doubts the ability of the government to stand up under foreign pressure, especially from the United States. Advantages and disadvantages of the close alliance to the United States must be rethought, and the nature of the relationship must be altered. The American role at the birth of the Bundesrepublik and the constant military presence of the United States within the country—at first as occupation troops and later, formally, as defender of the NATO alliance commitments—and the limits to the sovereignty of the republic, lead many Germans to the suspicion that West Germany is still an occupied land under foreign domination; all too often the high-handed actions and statements of the United States government or the lack of response and initiative by the Bundesregierung have served to confirm these suspicions for many citizens.

One example concerns recent protests against the war in Vietnam by students and young people all over the republic. Although it is well known that several prominent political figures consider United States policy in Vietnam to be morally wrong, futile, dangerous, and wasteful, no political party until recently has spoken to this issue which obviously concerns many thoughtful citizens.

Günter Grass, writing on this subject, details the consequences of the lack of responsiveness on the part of the government or at least one major political party to express what many people are concerned about:

No matter how much the war in Vietnam is protested in the Bundesrepublik these protests remain unsupported, because neither the government nor any of the major parties is ready to take up the protest of the youth and the uneasiness of social classes and effectively to give it political articulation. Therefore the protest suffers. Without an addressee, and left alone, it forgets its basis, and is subverted often enough into a pretext for a permanent "great happening" and functions then only as a release for a critical pressure. . . .

The government strains itself to be silent. Its consideration for the great ally appears more American than the Americans. The servile muteness of a falsely understood alliance-loyalty is the counterpart of the gestures of the morally intended, but politically powerless protests, which with too little pressure and with increasing anti-Americanism attempt poorly to define what is American.[8]

Noting that on January 5, 1967, the SPD decided to break the silence by backing U Thant's call for an end to the bombing of North Vietnam, Grass continues:

Then later, and hopefully not too late, the SPD national committee decided to give up the crippling passivity in order to take a stand: not against the United States, but for those political forces, which in the United States are attempting to bring peace; they too are America. . . .

Kurt Georg Kiesinger's lack of courage gags German foreign policy and is not serving the American ally in any respect.

. . . Not the increasing hate of everything American, not the squeezed mixture of sex and Vietnam coverage, which the magazine *Konkret* makes unbelievable, but the political-moral claim to our government should give form to the Vietnam protest. . . .

The United States needs the criticism of its allies, just as the Bundesrepublik needs the criticism of its allies. Germany was forced to experience the bombing of open cities in the Second World War. Dresden followed Coventry. This insight gives us the right to speak.[9]

The Bundesrepublik, in blunt terms, has yet to pass its test of manhood, not against the Communists, but against the United States. This, as I have said before, does not mean the Bundesrepublik must adopt a xenophobic foreign policy with isolation and self-sufficiency as its goal. Rather, it must avoid the nationalist verbiage of the NPD while demonstrating its ability to plot the goals and assess the needs and commitments of the republic as an independent nation.

8. Günter Grass, "The Vietnam War concerns us all," in *Die Zeit*," January 23, 1968, p. 2.
9. *Ibid.*

From the evidence presented in Chapter IV, it is clear that the attitudes and symbolism which made up the Volk ideology are still held by large minorities and even, in several instances, majorities of the voter population. In some respects these attitudes are less prevalent in the younger generation, under twenty-four years of age, and yet these differences were less striking than the basic similarity of the distributions of these attitudes over all age groups. The NPD survey evidence indicates that one long-run necessity for reducing the right-radical potential is the refutation of the underlying prejudices and social myths of the Volk ideology. Instead of conspiracy theories and scapegoat symbolism, the real social problems of a developing Western society must be recognized, and realistic attempts at solutions posited. The frustrations of the right-radical voter are real frustrations, but the answers given to these problems by the NPD are fantasies and therefore cannot reduce, but rather exacerbate, the feeling of anxiety about the ways in which society is changing. Only a clear explanation which both recognizes the sources and legitimacy of these anxieties, and attempts to give a reasoned response, can hope to reduce the influence of the Volk ideology. The attitudinal responses to strongly formulated questions about democratic institutions, minority rights, the Nazi past, and foreign influences indicate that an alarming number of people still perceive the world, and in particular their own society, in terms of specters and myths which dominated the Third Reich. It is clear that the concept of democracy in particular needs to be perceived as something more than simply *Spielregeln* (rules of the game), as Fritz Thielen called them, for there are, as the NPD has said, all sorts of democracies under this understanding of the word. Democracy must be shown to have substance, a view of the rights of the individual which is independent of these different sets of Spielregeln.

The 1966–67 recession in the Bundesrepublik and the accompanying governmental switch to the Great Coalition was a comparatively mild crisis; until the attitudinal basis for right-radical recruitment is significantly diminished, the potential of movements such as the NPD during periods of unrest and crisis will remain intact. In such a situation, one can hope only that no long lasting or severe crises occur. To base one's actions on such a hope would be short-sighted in the extreme. Thus in the long run only the basic change in the attitudinal structure can be relied upon to preserve the foundations of the democracy in times of strains, and to keep dissent and reform within the democratic framework. This basic change has not been accomplished since World War II; in fact the underlying attitudes of right-radicalism have been passed on to new generations, with only slight reductions in strength.

For the short run, however, the presence of such attitudes among a large number of the people must be recognized. Such attitudes will not change over night, nor would it be wise to attempt a crash campaign to attempt it. The short-run factors which affect right-radical political recruitment are a sense of crisis, and the lack of viable social opposition among the classic parties. In periods of widespread prosperity and economic growth there is no pressing motivation for the large numbers of people who hold basically antidemocratic opinions to leave their nominal party affiliations. Only among certain social groups—especially small businessmen, small farmers and, to some extent also, unskilled workers—will the continuing evolution of society create enough frustration, even in times of general prosperity, to support an extremist protest. Within these classes, which are in a position of increasing conflict with the modernization of the economy and the pluralization of life styles, the discontent will be salient enough to mobilize the underlying Volk ideology into political activity against the establishment. When, however, a crisis appears which spreads these anxieties to all segments of society, the potential for mobilization of antidemocratic attitudes to protest the system is escalated.

However, it may be that one of the classic parties, in all likelihood the SPD, may be able to afford a viable social opposition sufficient to retain protest votes within the system. The example of Schleswig-Holstein has shown that at the state level at least, the SPD can still attract people who feel outside the system and seek to protest it. Steffen's vigorous campaign in Schleswig-Holstein undoubtedly retained for the SPD enough of the image of a protest party to deny many votes to the NPD. But Joachim Steffen, the SPD in Schleswig-Holstein, and a few other SPD organizations are exceptions; it will be increasingly difficult for the SPD to play both the role of social opposition and copartner in the Great Coalition at the same time.[10]

10. Recent signs from the SPD national conference in Nürnberg in March of 1968 show that the SPD is indeed attempting to preserve its former role as a social opposition and that its new program represents a slight but meaningful shift to the left.

For reasons which I have already stated, the FDP is at present poorly equipped to assume the role of social opposition, although a small group of Free Democrats such as Dahrendorf, Hamm-Brücher, and Rubin are trying to restructure the FDP as a more left-oriented opposition party. Whether they will succeed is still in doubt.

As for the Christian Democrats, it may be that Franz-Josef Strauss will be able to play the role of social opposition on the right side of the political spectrum for Catholics without encouraging a general rise in the level of nationalist sloganism and a greater neglect of the reasoned, problem-solving approach to Bundesrepublik politics. Strauss' idea of taking over certain NPD themes, as discussed earlier, is perhaps the most risky course of action, for it envisages meeting the NPD on its own grounds, which are outside the framework of looking for reasonable solutions within the democratic framework of a modern Western society.

It is clear that the Bundesrepublik has emerged from the era of postwar politics with heavy reliance on the United States both for protection and for a sense of political direction. The example of Gaullist France has been instructive in this sense, and the NPD can be instructive also if seen in the proper perspective. The NPD on the right, as well as student unrest on the left, are warning signals that significant numbers of people and sectors of society are alienated from the present party system. Until some party which can work within the democratic framework addresses itself to real frustrations and anxieties, these people will be open to recruitment by extremist protest movements. Both on the left (as Günter Grass states) and on the right, such protest movements, finding no meaningful dialogue within the present political establishment, will turn from the real issues to more generalized and sloganized symbols. This process of alienating protest makes it all the more difficult to produce a reasonable reply to the reasonable bases for the original protest; alienation from the established political system, and recruitment into movements such as the NPD create additional barriers to future reincorporation or assimilation back into that system.

Hopefully, the democratic parties of the Bundesrepublik will heed these warning signals and make serious efforts to address themselves to the real social sources of the new wave of protest which often has been forced to caricature itself in order to be heard and feared. To reply only to the distortion of the original protest is not enough. The era of reconstruction and the economic miracle is past; the society of the Bundesrepublik is evolving in directions which go beyond the policies and postures of the postwar era. The established political superstructure of the republic must evolve to meet these new developments if it is not to drift into irrelevancy.

VII

Epilogue

Since I completed this study in the spring of 1968, several events have occurred which call for further explanation and analysis. This epilogue will examine in particular the reasons why the National Democrats—after hitting a high point of nearly 10 percent of the vote in the Baden-Württemberg election in April, 1968—fell to only 4.3 percent of the vote in the federal elections in September of 1969, and thus failed to gain any seats in the Bundestag.

First let me make it quite clear that it is premature and somewhat naive to state (as did the *New York Times* in its editorial on two days after the election) that "West German voters have delivered their verdict on the NPD, and may, indeed, have consigned it to the scrap heap, which has been the destination of earlier extreme right-wing parties." One election outcome cannot be taken at face value as a final verdict, and should not be projected into the future without careful analysis of the various factors contributing to the election results. The NPD's poor showing resulted from a constellation of factors which may not be present nor be so effective in future elections. Now is not the time to assume that the NPD will fade away. Deeply rooted social and political movments do not simply fade away unless the social sources from which they are generated first have been transformed. Now is the time for a progressive and reform-oriented government led by the SPD to introduce measures which over time will effectively deal with the tensions and frustrations which are the basis for rightist movements such as the NPD.

What factors defeated the NPD in its attempt to gain the necessary 5 percent of the votes for representation in the Bundestag? First among these was the return of economic prosperity to the Bundesrepublik, the development of a boom period at a time when many other Western European economies were experiencing difficulties. Unemployment had been wiped out once again and, by the end of 1968, new highs were being reached in numbers of foreign workers employed in a thriving economy starved for labor. Although the recession of 1966 and 1967 had been still fresh in the minds of many voters in early 1968, by the summer of 1969 and the campaign for the federal elections, the overwhelming majority of German citizens once again were confident of their economic future. As we have seen, adverse economic expectations have been the major catalyst in mobilizing potential right-radical voters. Only in the agricultural sector and in a few other isolated areas of the economy, such as the Saar coal-mining region, was the outlook for the future less than rosy. In these areas the National Democrats continued to have success in recruiting support for their cause.

For the most part, the return to prosperity benefited the Social Democrats more than the Christian Democrats or the Free Democrats. The bulk of working-class support for the NPD has returned to its traditional adherence to the Social Democrats, while traditionally conservative farmers still are being attracted from the CDU/CSU to the National Democrats, and the small businessman—likewise a traditional mainstay of the Christian Democrats—has been somewhat slower in migrating back to his original position, perhaps because of a greater ideological affinity to the NPD. In general, however, conservatives who voted for the NPD in times of economic crisis have tended also to return to the CDU/CSU during the present period of economic boom.

A second factor—perhaps equally important in the recent defeat of the right-radicals—has been the continuous and serious debate over the possibility of banning the NPD, either as a successor party to the NSDAP or as an undemocratic party. While this has always been mentioned by opponents of the NPD as one of the ways to deal with the problem of right-radicalism, it had not taken the form of serious policy debate within the highest circles of the federal government until the second half of 1968. Public-opinion polls show a sharp dropoff (about 50 percent) in support for the NPD from the third quarter of 1968, through 1969.

It is well known that the Great Coalition government was under pressure from the United States, as well as other nations, to do something about von Thadden's party. The Social Democrats pressed for bringing the NPD to court as a neofascist successor to Hitler's NSDAP but, for various reasons and not without dissent within their own ranks, the Christian Democrats refused to go along. For one thing, the Christian Democratic leadership of Kiesinger and Strauss hoped to be able to lure basically conservative or nationalist NPD voters to the CDU/CSU by taking over several NPD slogans or attitudes, thus seeming more sympathetic to voters who had been attracted to the right-radicals. Also, many CDU/CSU leaders at that time were convinced that the National Democrats, as in state elections since 1966, would drain more votes from the SPD in the upcoming federal elections than from their own party. Further, the existence of the NPD to represent the radical right could enable Kiesinger and Strauss to appear as representatives of a relatively more moderate and rational new German nationalism or conservatism. Only so long as the NPD existed could Strauss argue that to combat right-radicals, one of the major parties must itself move to the right to reincorporate NPD voters into the mainstream of German politics.

Christian Democratic and Social Democratic leaders struck a compromise which permitted the National Democrats to continue their activities without a court fight, but which also constantly reminded them (and the public) that the NPD stood forever on the brink of being banned. Under these conditions, many "respectable" citizens who were either supporters or potential supporters of the NPD were scared away by the threat of social (and perhaps economic) repercussions if they were to be linked with a party which might be banned at any moment. This condition of constant uncertainty was almost certainly responsible for much of the drop in NPD membership since the middle of 1968, and for increased difficulties in party finances which previously had been very sound.

A third tactic which hurt the NPD in 1969 was the *rechts überholen* plan of Franz Josef Strauss, leader of the CSU and Finance Minister of the Great Coalition, which emerged in the summer of 1969. Strauss had long advocated a more nationalist, tougher law-and-order appeal to the electorate; in the summer of 1969 it appeared that Kiesinger too had become convinced that this strategy would be politically profitable, particularly with respect to convincing former NPD supporters that they could hear the things they wanted to hear from the CDU/CSU as well as from the NPD. This strategy, labeled in the press as *rechts überholen*, or "pass [the NPD] on the right," tried to convince people that the CDU/CSU stood for many of the same goals as did the National Democrats, and that in addition the Christian Democrats were a more socially acceptable and politically effective alternative to von Thadden's NPD, which now lived under the sword of Damocles.

For example, the NPD advocates stricter military discipline and holds that the military services should have the role of straightening out any rebellious behavior among the nation's youth. The NPD, with significant support from Bundeswehr officers, has argued against the present citizen-soldier concept which tries to bring the traditionally authoritarian and autonomous military services closer to the civilian sphere of life and under civilian control.

In the spring of 1969 it came to public attention that a Bundeswehr general by the name of Grashey had been making disparaging speeches at the officer's academy about the citizen-soldier concept, which is the official government policy. Several SPD leaders and members of the press called upon the Defense Minister, Schröder, to censure General Grashey for his remarks, but Schröder and other Christian Democratic leaders rose to defend Grashey, and refused to take any action. Meanwhile, the NPD was already proclaiming Grashey as a national hero. Soon the Social Democrats decided to let the affair drop, fearing the loss of votes of military personnel in the coming election.

That summer Kiesinger seemed to raise the question of the military's social function again with a controversial speech in which he asserted that the military was the "school of the nation," implying that military service, as NPD propaganda claimed also, was supposed to indoctrinate the nation's young in the proper norms of behavior. When it was pointed out that this *Schule der Nation* concept of the military dated back to Imperial Germany under Kaiser Wilhelm, Kiesinger replied that of course he had not meant to imply that he wanted to return to the blind obedience to authority which had characterized the Kaiser's *Schule der Nation* concept. Yet it is quite clear that Kiesinger was appealing to voters who view the military as the purveyor of the values and attitudes which they would like to see instilled into today's young people.

Strauss soon followed with harsh denunciations of the student

left which rivaled those of the NPD. Strauss asserted that the followers of the leftist APO (*Ausserparlamentarische Opposition*, i.e. extraparliamentary opposition) had become "animalized," behaved like
animals, and therefore laws made to govern men were no longer sufficient to control them. While Strauss did not publicly spell out how
one does deal with rebellious animals, the conclusions to be drawn
from his remarks are consistent with NPD suggestions for handling
such political dissidents.

        In addition, Kiesinger and Strauss repeatedly went out of their
way to defend the great mass of National Democratic voters as good
Germans who were simply protesting against certain developments,
such as student militance, the crime rate, and the lack of national pride.
Both defended the party, particularly the voters of the NPD, against
charges of fascism or neofascism, although they admitted that there
were some fascist influences in the party leadership. Strauss offered
the suggestion that these voters, if they wanted to express their views,
should vote for the CDU/CSU, because the Christian Democrats had
taken these same positions as the NPD for years. It was apparent to
most observers that Kiesinger and Strauss at that time hoped to gain
an absolute majority in the next Bundestag, and felt that winning over
NPD voters might make the difference in putting them over the top.

        In addition to the above-mentioned factors, the election cam-
paign for the Sixth Bundestag also cut down on the NPD vote in several ways, aside from the CDU/CSU *rechts überholen* strategy. There
was the constant disruption of NPD rallies by students and by some
union organizations. The leftist APO had vowed to disrupt the normal
campaign activities of all parties, including the new German Communist Party, but by far their greatest effort was directed against the
National Democrats. Time after time NPD meetings were broken up;
for the most part the local police were not overeager to protect NPD
gatherings, at least not until the planned rally had actually been dis-
rupted. Early in the campaign—actually during the precampaign period
in July and August of 1969—some analysts feared that von Thadden
would only profit from such tactics, and that many citizens might vote
for the National Democrats as a backlash against the militant left.
Then the NPD decided to organize its own corps of guards (*Ordner*),
wearing helmets and armed with clubs, to protect their meetings from
interference. In several instances, however, this corps of shock troops
definitely got out of hand and went far beyond any provocation from

anti-NPD demonstrators. Several times the Ordner simply charged into the ranks of the demonstrators, severely beating a number of youths. Scenes on German television of NPD guards hitting and kicking young men and women surely evoked for many voters memories of the Nazi brown shirts battling with political opponents in the streets during the Weimar Republic. Thus while most citizens disapproved of the tactics of the anti-NPD demonstrators, the National Democrats became associated not with "security through law and order," which was the party's main slogan, but rather with the disorder and tumult which erupted at every NPD gathering. Adolf von Thadden, in an interview with *Spiegel* magazine two weeks after the election, said that he had considered canceling all major NPD rallies at which he was to appear, but had decided to go on with them rather than admit defeat. When asked whether he thought this decision was wise, von Thadden replied "It apparently had the result that voters said to themselves: 'If there were no NPD, there would be no riots.'"

In the same interview, von Thadden listed another reason for his party's poor showing, namely the closeness of the election. For the first time since the founding of the Bonn democracy, there was the real possibility, even likelihood, as the election approached, of an SPD-led coalition with the reconstituted liberal FDP. For those voters who feared most of all the coming to power of the Social Democrats with Brandt as Chancellor, a vote for the NPD may have increasingly seemed like a wasted vote, since the NPD's chances of getting into the Bundestag were uncertain. If one wanted to prevent the SPD/FDP coalition, the most effective way was to vote for the Christian Democrats.

While the above logic of the "wasted vote" may in fact have hurt the NPD's chances, I would point out that in this perhaps most important election in the history of the Bundesrepublik, the National Democrats did hold the balance of power. Had the NPD gotten seven-tenths of one percent more of the vote, an SPD/FDP coalition would have been a mathematical impossibility, even if the SPD and FDP had done better than they actually did. In that event, no government could have been formed without the CDU/CSU. Either a return to the Great Coalition, which had become an undesirable solution for the long run, or another Christian Democrat/Free Democrat coalition would have been required. This would have meant that one of the two liberal parties, who agreed on most issues among themselves but disagreed with the CDU/CSU, would have been forced to renounce its platform in order to find a majority coalition with the Christian Democrats. A clear-cut change in government and a clear mandate, either for reform or for continuance of the traditional Adenauer "No Experiments" policy, were possible only if the NPD failed to get the necessary 5 percent.

On September 28, 1969, the National Democratic Party of Germany received 1,422,106 votes, or 4.3 percent of the total vote, and thus no seats in the Sixth Bundestag. Based on analysis of election returns done by the Godesberg Institut für angewandte Sozialwissenschaft (INFAS), it appears that the NPD voter profile remains largely what it had been but on a reduced scale, except for apparently heavier-than-average losses in the industrial working class. The National Democrats did better in Protestant districts than in Catholic districts, did best in rural areas and districts with large numbers of self-employed and in regions still having economic difficulties. Thus, for example, the National Democrats made its strongest statewide showing in the Saar (where the long-suffering coal industry has not yet been consolidated and refinanced with government aid, as has been done in the Ruhr).

The thesis that economic crisis acts as a catalyst to mobilize latent right-radical attitudes seems particularly strengthened by comparison of the Saar and Ruhr coal mining regions. Two years earlier, the National Democrats were hard at work agitating among miners in the Ruhr area, with reports of considerable success. The coal industries had been on the decline for many years and miners, threatened with loss of job and untrained for any other work, were looking for an effective and strong voice of protest. The National Democrats seemed on the verge of making further breakthroughs into the normally SPD working-class vote. But in the intervening period before the federal elections of 1969 the Great Coalition government stepped in to consolidate, refinance, and modernize the coal industries in the Ruhr region. Thus the NPD averaged only 2.7 percent of the vote in districts with high (over 30 percent) proportions of coal miners in the Ruhr, whereas in the Saar region, where the government has yet to act, von Thadden's party got 6.7 percent of the vote in similar districts.

Still, the 4.3 percent nationwide vote for the National Democrats represented a gain over the 2.0 percent which they received in 1965, and in many areas this gain was registered at the expense of the Free Democrats, who were the biggest losers of the 1969 elections as far as vote totals are concerned. As the FDP has shifted to the left, becoming more of a twentieth-century than a nineteenth-century liberal party, the old right-wing voter following has abandoned it in favor of either the CDU/CSU or the NPD. Districts in which both CDU/CSU and NPD made significant gains were usually areas in which the FDP was being decimated by wholesale emigration of the right wing of the party.

In attempting to outline future possibilities for the National Democrats and for right-radicalism in the Bundesrepublik, I would repeat that the greatest danger lies in an optimistic assumption that the NPD has now been relegated to the past and presents no more problems for the political system. The fact is that, although the NPD has been stopped in an important election, the underlying attitudes in the electorate which form the long-run basis of right-radicalism have not been significantly changed since the NPD's victory in Baden-Württemberg; these attitudes await only another economic or social crisis to be catalyzed into votes for the National Democrats.

But why is it not sufficient to avoid any further major crisis situations in order to keep the NPD at a harmless level of popular support? After all, recessions, depressions, and other forms of social conflict are not fatalistic or random occurrences which are impossible to prevent. A wise government following sound economic and social policies should be able to ward off such situations.

There are two difficulties with this point of view. First, external events, pressures, and crises may effect the well-being of the German economy, and these external inputs are only marginally controllable by even the wisest government of the Bundesrepublik. Secondly, I would contend that economic and social policies designed to avoid crisis would be part and parcel of economic and social policies aimed at reforms which would diminish the attitudinal basis of right-radicalism.

At present there are several tendencies within German politics which are designed, in one way or another, to deal with the NPD. One is the continuation of the threat to ban the NPD. This tactic proved effective in the defeat of the National Democrats in the 1969 elections, and is likely to remain in force. It has the additional advantage of being a relatively inexpensive strategy, since it requires no great budgetary or manpower effort on the government's part. However, it is likely also that the effect of the threatened ban will diminish over time as it becomes clear that the party will not in fact ever be brought to court. As long as the NPD leadership, under Adolf von Thadden, is able to keep its state and local organizations under control and out of conflict with the judicial apparatus, right-radicals will learn to live with the threatened ban. The earlier right-extremist SRP had paved the way for its final demise as its leaders and local organizations, growing ever more radical and uncontrollable, found themselves brought to court on a variety of criminal charges. Although there are some signs that criminal proceedings may be brought against some NPD leaders associated with the training and command of the party corps of guards, the apparatus of the National Democrats, still composed largely of old DRP members, has proved obedient to the leadership of von Thadden, who is well aware of the need to stay clear of confrontation with the judicial system. Clearly von Thadden's major task at present is to avoid the fate of the SRP.

A second strategy affecting the future of the NPD is the continuation of Franz Josef Strauss' *rechts überholen* policy. With the Christian Democrats now in the opposition, Strauss may soon make a bid to succeed Kurt Georg Kiesinger as leader of the combined CDU/CSU on the premise that his strategy offers the best chance for the Christian Democrats to return to power. It is becoming apparent within the ranks of the Christian Democrats that the old Adenauer formula for victory is losing its effectiveness. It is also probable that the moderates and progressives within the CDU/CSU are too few in number to reconstruct the party on a platform of social reform able to compete with the Social Democrats on its own grounds. There remains the temptation to turn to Strauss' alternative of a modern nationalism, incorporating many of the ideas and goals of the NPD, in somewhat more rational and moderated form. Strauss can point to evidence that, contrary to past experience, NPD votes hurt the Christian Democrats more than the Social Democrats. He has already boasted that his CSU won the federal election in Bavaria—implying that if he had been leader of the CDU as well as the CSU, the Christian Democrats would have won the last election. Should Strauss be able to dump Kiesinger in the near future and steer the Christian Democrats down this path, the fortunes of the NPD might well completely collapse, though the future of right-radicalism itself would be enhanced. In essence, the ideology of the radical right would have captured the CDU/CSU, and would have gained in the process more powerful and effective spokesmen.

The new SPD/FDP coalition government under Chancellor Willy Brandt offers a third approach to dealing with the NPD. The Brandt-Scheel government was elected on the basis of a program of internal and foreign-policy reform which in part would help undermine the sources of discontent and frustration which are associated with right-radicalism.

High on the list of priorities in the domestic field for the new government is expansion, modernization, and partial democratization of the educational system. Some reforms, such as greater student and faculty participation in the running of the universities, were already started during the Great Coalition period, and would be continued under Brandt's leadership. Other changes, such as a great expansion of the institutions of higher education, would be aimed particularly at widening opportunities for attending a university. At present, the percentage of young people from working-class backgrounds who are able to attend a university is very low, approximately the same figure as in the Kaiser's Germany more than fifty years ago.

Along with reforms in the formal educational structure would go expansion and further development of job retraining programs (such as those initiated in coal-mining regions of the Ruhr) designed to ease the transition from declining occupational roles to more viable ones. Hopefully, similar programs could be developed for people in other sectors, such as small farmers or small businessmen, who also find their present economic positions untenable and might appreciate assistance in retraining without disadvantage to themselves.

Such reforms would help to decrease the right-radical potential among the social classes which find themselves most at odds with present economic and technological trends by facilitating the transition to new roles within the economy. A much-expanded educational system similarly would increase the actual and psychological mobility of the individual in a changing society, making it easier for him to understand, adjust to, and benefit from progressive innovation.

In the field of foreign policy, the Brandt government aims at a step-by-step easing of tensions with the states of Eastern Europe, including the regime in East Germany (DDR). This policy, an extension of the earlier Brandt Ostpolitik, includes an official repudiation of the 1938 Munich agreement which ceded the Sudetenland areas of Czechoslovakia to Hitler's Third Reich. Until now this agreement has not been disavowed as a legal treaty by the Bundesrepublik. Brandt hopes also to establish normal diplomatic relations with Poland, which would include some sort of recognition of the Oder-Neisse line as the western frontier of Poland.

The SPD/FDP coalition is certain to bury the already defunct Hallstein doctrine and to maintain normal diplomatic and trade relations with other states regardless of their recognition of the DDR. In this regard, the Brandt leadership may be expected to move towards an easing of hostility with the DDR, possibly through the signing of a nonaggression pact recognizing the DDR as a "second state of the German nation," making the distinction between the German people and formal governmental structures which govern the German people. While not accepting the DDR as a government based on popular consent or support, a nonaggression pact would recognize that final settlement of the reunification question could not be reached through use of force. These reforms in foreign policy would signify an end to Bonn's claim to represent and speak for all Germans, including those in the DDR. In return, Brandt hopes to settle the question of the status of West Berlin, first, through guarantees of access rights by the *Deutsche Demokratische Republik* and, second, by granting full voting rights to West Berlin within the political system of the Bundesrepublik. This would have the additional advantage for Brandt of increasing his majority in the Bundestag, since West Berlin's representatives, who presently cannot vote in the Bundestag, are predominantly Social Democrats.

At the same time Brandt would like to maintain friendly relations with the West, and would work more vigorously for entry into the Common Market not only of Britain but also of several other countries which have applied for membership.

With regard to the potential of right-radicalism, the Brandt-Scheel foreign policy, if successfully carried out, would go a long way within the Bundesrepublik towards final popular acceptance of the present boundaries of the nation and of the democratic system as established by the Basic Law as the legitimate political system of a fully sovereign nation. Over time this would diminish the kind of challenges to and questioning of the legitimacy and permanence of the present system which characterizes so much of the right-radical propaganda.

The future of the National Democratic Party of Germany rests on the results of these various strategies, together with the maintenance of a sound economy over the coming years. However, only the last strategy of social and foreign policy reform, I would argue, has the possibility of reaching to the roots of support for movements like the NPD, and thus of permanently decreasing the potential of right-radicalism.

Bibliography

PRIMARY SOURCES: PARTY DOCUMENTS AND SPEECHES

Anrich, Ernst. "Die deutsche Demokratie," Speech delivered at the NPD party conference of 1966 in Karlsruhe.

Kühne, Lothar. "Die Nation im Recht" in *Deutsche Nachrichten* (Special Issue, Number III/1965).

Lauer, Peter. "Die junge Generation heute und morgen." Speech delivered at the NPD party conference of 1966 in Karlsruhe.

NPD Parteivorstand. "Satzung der Nationaldemokratischen Partei Deutschlands" (1964).

———. "Manifest der Nationaldemokratischen Partei Deutschlands NPD" (1965).

———. "Entschliessungen des NPD-Parteitages 1965."

———. "Musterrede A,B,C,D,E,F,G,H." Standardized speeches for NPD speakers.

———. "Wehrpolitische Denkschrift des NPD-Parteivorstandes."

———. "Anmerkungen zum Manifest und zu den Grundsätzen der NPD: Volk und Staat" (1966).

NPD Landesvorstand Nordrhein-Westfalen. "Einheitliche NPD-Aussage." A set of standardized NPD replies to expected questions.

NPD congress in Franke, July 2, 1966. "Aus der Arbeitsunterlage zu Sozialpolitik, Arbeiter-und Gewerkschaftsfragen."

von Thadden, Adolf. "Mut zu neuen Wegen." Speech delivered at the NPD party conference of 1966 in Karlsruhe.

Thielen, Fritz. Text of press conference given in Bonn on March 31, 1966.

———. Letter from the chairman to all NPD members, dated May 2, 1967.

Secondary Sources

Allgemeine Zeitung (Frankfurt).

Bärwald, Helmut, and Herbert Scheffler. *Rechts-Links, Bemerkungen über den Rechtsradikalismus in Deutschland* (Bad Godesberg: Hohwacht-Verlag, 1968).

Bracher, Karl Dietrich. *Die Deutsche Diktatur* (Köln: Verlag Kiepenheuer & Witsch, 1969).

——. "Historische Komponenten des Rechtsradikalismus in Deutschland," in *Die neue Gesellschaft* (Number 4, 1967).

Bruggeman, Agnes. "Anhänger und Gegner der Nationaldemokratischen Partei Deutschlands (NPD): eine sozialpsychologische Untersuchung." Unpublished doctoral dissertation, University of Bonn, 1969.

Büsch, Otto, and Peter Furth. *Rechtsradikalismus in Nachkriegsdeutschland* (Berlin: Verlag Franz Vohlen, 1957).

Cole, Taylor. "Neo-Fascism in Western Germany and Italy," in *American Political Science Review* (XLIX, 1955).

Deutsche Nachrichten (Official NPD party newspaper).

Duve, Freimut, et al. *Die Restauration entlässt ihre Kinder oder Der Erfolg der Rechten in der Bundesrepublik* (Reinbek bei Hamburg: Rowohlt Taschenbuch, 1968).

Fetscher, Irving, et al. *Rechtsradikalismus* (Frankfurt/Main: Europäische Verlagsanstalt, 1967).

Frankfurter Rundschau.

Frederick, Hans. *NPD—Gefahr von Rechts?* (Munich: Verlag Politisches Archiv, 1967).

Götz, Wolfgang, and Joachim Sieden. . . . *Bis alles in Scherben fällt. Wohin führt der Rechtsradikalismus?* (Mainz: von Hase and Köhler, 1967).

Hartenstein, Wolfgang, and Günter Schubert. *Mitlaufen oder Mitbestimmen* (Frankfurt/Main: Europäische Verlagsanstalt, 1961).

Heberle, Rudolf. *Landbevölkerung und Nationalsozialismus* (Stuttgart: Verlag Enke, 1963).

Hirsch, Kurt. *Kommen die Nazis wieder? Gefahren für die Bundesrepublik* (Munich: Verlag Kurt Desch, 1967).

INFAS (Institut für angewandte Sozialwissenschaft). "Rechtsstimmen under der Lupe" (Bad Godesberg, 1966).

——. "Deutsche und Gastarbeiter" (Bad Godesberg, 1966).

——. "Anhänger der neuen Rechtspartei" (Bad Godesberg, 1967).

——. "Rechtswähler in Niedersachsen und Hessen," manuscript Bad Godesberg, 1967).

——. "Die Propaganda der NPD-Führung," manuscript (Bad Godesberg, 1967).

——. "Rechtswähler in den Hansestädten," manuscript (Bad Godesberg, 1967).

Jenke, Manfred. *Verschwörung von Rechts?* (Berlin: Colloquium Verlag, 1961).

——. *Die nationale Rechte; Parteien, Politiker, Publizisten* (Berlin: Colloquium Verlag, 1967).

Kahle, Sigrid. "Nynazism och högerradikalism" in *Ord och Bild*, (Number 4, 1967: Swedish).

Knütter, H. H. *Ideologien des Rechtsradikalismus im Nachkriegsdeutschland* (Bonn: Röhrscheid, 1961).

Kühnl, Reinhard. "Der Rechtsextremismus in der Budesrepublik" in *Politische Vierteljahresschrift* (Number 3, 1968).

——et al. *Die NPD-Struktur, Ideologie, und Funktion einer neofaschistischen Partei* (Frankfurt/Main: Suhrkamp Verlag, 1969).

Liepelt, Klaus. "Anhänger der neuen Rechtspartei," in *Politische Vierteljahresschrift*, (Number 2, 1967).

Lipset, S. M. "Faschismus—rechts, links, und in der Mitte," in his *Soziologie der Demokratie* (Neuwied: Herman Luchterhand, 1962).

Lücke, Paul. "Wiederholt sich Weimar?" in *Die neue Gesellschaft* (Number 4, 1967).

Maier, Hans. *NPD-Struktur und Ideologie einer 'nationalen Rechtspartei'* (München: Verlag R. Piper & Co., 1967).

Merkl, Peter H. *Germany Yesterday and Tomorrow* (New York: Oxford University Press, 1965).

Nemitz, K. "Das Regime der Mitläufer; soziologische Notizen zur Renazifizierung," in *Die neue Gesellschaft* (Number 3, 1955).

New York Times.

Newsweek.

Noelle, Elisabeth, and Peter Erich Neumann. *Jahrbuch der öffentlichen Meinung*, volumes 1947–1955; 1957; 1958–1964 (Allensbach am Bodensee: Allensbach Institut, 1955, 1957, and 1964).

Parsons, Talcot. *Essays in Sociological Theory*, especially "Towards a program for institutional change for Germany" (New York: Free Press, 1954).

Pross, Harry. "Hundert Jahre deutsche 'Rechte' " in *Die neue Gesellschaft* (Number 4, 1967).

Richards, Fred H. *Die NPD: Alternative oder Widerkehr?* (Munich: Günter Olzog Verlag, 1967).

Ritter, Waldemar, and Ernst Eichengrün. "Information für Demokraten-NPD," published by the Jungsozialisten in their series of brochures, 1967.

Rogge, Hans, and Eugen Weber, eds. *The European Right* (Berkeley and Los Angeles: University of California Press, 1965).

Rohter, Ira S. "The Righteous Rightists," in *Transaction*, (May, 1967).

Scheuch, Erwin K. "Die NPD in der Bundesrepublik," in *Die neue Gesellschaft* (Number 4, 1967).

———. "Theorie des Rechtsradikalismus in westlichen Industriegesellschaften," in *Hamburger Jahrbuch für Wirtschafts- und Gesellschaftspolitik*, (Tübingen, 1967).

——— and Hans D. Klingemann. "Beiträge zur politischen Soziologie. Materialien zum Phänomen des Rechtsradikalismus in der Bundesrepublik 1966," in manuscript (University of Cologne, 1967).

Smoydzin, Werner. *NPD-Geschichte und Umwelt einer Partei, Analyze und Kritik*, (Pfaffenhofen a.d. Ilm: Ilmgau Verlag, 1967).

Der Spiegel (Hamburg).

Streit, Wolfgang. "Der Neofaschismus," in *Die neue Gesellschaft* (1955).

Süddeutsche Zeitung (Munich).

Tauber, Kurt F. *Beyond Eagle and Swastika: German Nationalism since 1945* (Middletown, Conn.: Wesleyan University Press, 1967).

Winter, Franz-Florian. *Ich glaubte an die NPD*, (Mainz: von Hase and Koehler, 1968).

Die Welt (Hamburg).

Die Zeit (Hamburg).

Index